ADDICTION, BEHAVIORAL CHANGE AND SOCIAL IDENTITY

Changing health-related behavior is for many people a lonely and isolating experience. Individual willpower is often not enough, particularly in addressing addictive behavior, but research increasingly points to the potential of group identity to shape behavior change and support recovery.

This important collection explores the social and cognitive processes that enable people who join recovery groups to address their addictive issues. In an era of increasing concern at the long-term costs of chronic ill-health, the potential to leverage group identity to inspire resilience and recovery offers a timely and practical response.

The book examines the theoretical foundations to a social identity approach in addressing behavior change across a range of contexts, including alcohol addiction, obesity and crime, while also examining topics such as the use of online forums to foster recovery. It will be essential reading for students, researchers and policy makers across health psychology and social care, as well as anyone interested in behavioral change and addiction recovery.

Sarah A. Buckingham is a Freelance Researcher. Previously Sarah has worked as an integrative psychotherapist in the NHS and as a Froebel trained primary school teacher. She is also a practising artist.

David Best is Professor of Criminology and Head of Research in the Department of Law and Criminology at Sheffield Hallam University, UK and is Associate Professor at Monash University in Melbourne, Australia.

ADDICTION, BEHAVIORAL CHANGE AND SOCIAL IDENTITY

The path to resilience and recovery

Edited by
Sarah A. Buckingham and David Best

Routledge
Taylor & Francis Group
LONDON AND NEW YORK

First published 2017
by Routledge
4 Park Square, Milton Park, Abingdon, Oxon OX14 4RN

and by Routledge
605 Third Avenue, New York, NY 10017

Routledge is an imprint of the Taylor & Francis Group, an informa business

British Library Cataloguing in Publication Data
A catalogue record for this book is available from the British Library

Library of Congress Cataloging in Publication Data
Names: Buckingham, Sarah A., editor. | Best, David (Lecturer in addictions), editor.Title: Addiction, behavioural change and social identity: the path to resilience and recovery / edited by Sarah A. Buckingham and David Best.
Description: Abingdon, Oxon ; New York, NY : Routledge, 2017.
Identifiers: LCCN 2016024133| ISBN 9781138934078 (hardback : alk. paper) | ISBN 9781138934085 (pbk. : alk. paper) | ISBN 9781315678207 (e-book)
Subjects: LCSH: Compulsive behavior. | Behavior modification. | Addicts--Rehabilitation. | Recovering addicts. | Group identity.
Classification: LCC RC533 .A3185 2017 | DDC 362.29--dc23
LC record available at https://lccn.loc.gov/2016024133

ISBN: 978-1-138-93407-8 (hbk)
ISBN: 978-1-138-93408-5 (pbk)
ISBN: 978-1-315-67820-7 (ebk)

Typeset in Bembo, Stone Sans
by Florence Production Ltd, Stoodleigh, Devon

Dedicated to

Hannah, Joseph, Tony and all fellow travellers (SAB)

My wonderful son, Billy, who is my pride and joy, and to the great friends I have had who have helped me through a really tough couple of years (DB)

CONTENTS

FIGURES AND TABLES

Figures

Tables

CONTRIBUTORS

Ian P. Albery – London South Bank University, UK
Melinda Beckwith – Monash University, Australia
Brandon G. Bergman – Harvard Medical School, USA
David Best – Sheffield Hallam University, UK
Ana-Maria Bliuc – Western Sydney University, Australia
Sarah A. Buckingham – Freelance Researcher
Tegan Cruwys – University of Queensland, Australia
Edward Day – National Addiction Centre, Kings College, London, UK
Genevieve A. Dingle – University of Queensland, Australia
Claire Farrow – Aston University, UK
Daniel Frings – London South Bank University, UK
Katharine Greenaway – University of Queensland, Australia
S. Alexander Haslam – University of Queensland, Australia
Catherine Haslam – University of Queensland, Australia
Muhammad Iqbal – Monash University, Australia
Jolanda Jetten – University of Queensland, Australia
John F. Kelly – Harvard Medical School, USA
Sammyh Khan – Keele University, UK
Jock Mackenzie – University of Queensland, Australia
Jacqueline Malton – Counsellor, HMP, UK
Kirsty Miller – University of Dundee, UK
Fabio Sani – University of Dundee, UK
Mark Tarrant – University of Exeter, UK
Corrie L. Vilsaint – Harvard Medical School, USA
Juliet R. H. Wakefield – Nottingham Trent University, UK

1

INTRODUCING ADDICTION, BEHAVIOURAL CHANGE AND SOCIAL IDENTITY

Sarah A. Buckingham and David Best

Become who you want to be by joining with the in-crowd, whoever you define them to be . . .

Sarah A. Buckingham

The aim of this volume is to investigate how behavioural change (with a specific emphasis upon addiction behavioural change, e.g., recovery) may be actioned through the lens of the social identity approach (Tajfel & Turner, 1979; Turner, Hogg, Oakes, Reicher & Wetherill, 1987). Emergent voices have begun to utilise this approach to investigate the social and psychological processes that might be in operation when individuals seek health behaviour change through joining with similar others (see Best, 2014; Jetten, Haslam & Haslam, 2012; Kelly & White, 2011).

Main themes and objectives

This fresh perspective for positive health behaviour change in the field of addictive behaviours demonstrates how people gain resilience from joining others with similar goals through a process of subjective identification. As such, a distinct social identity that is positive in health outcomes (e.g., recovery identity) emerges as a distinct comparison to the prior social identity that has become corrosive and damaging (e.g., addiction identity). This volume considers such change as a long-term process, with individuals who have sought addiction behavioural change as the sample in most, but not all, of the examples cited. It also presents addiction recovery as a social movement where social change can take place creatively and has implications for giving individuals who seek behaviour change and for professional treatment providers, the chance to regain a sense of hope, by building bridges into new worlds that are sustainable.

The key areas of interest that social identity research has explored (such as prejudice, discrimination, social conflict and social change) are a close fit with the challenges of active addiction and the recovery process. The social identity approach is a theory of social change. It is an integrative theory that *does not* pathologise. It is a theory that addresses group status. This is especially pertinent with low status groups such as addiction and associated stigmatised identities, where minimal resources are allotted to treatment. This approach illuminates why this might be both a novel perspective for this chronic social problem and a socially creative resolution.

In summary, this text brings together a growing body of research interest and insight about how social group membership and the resultant social identity formation can play a critical role in helping people to overcome addictive behaviours and practices. In essence, what this book attempts to do is to reconcile two literatures – one in relation to what we know about addiction behavioural change and the other in relation to social identity, to produce a strong and convincing narrative about the role that social identity change plays in the recovery process. For that reason, this chapter sets out with an overview of the background and history to the social identity approach, followed by a brief summary of the recovery literature, and finally a section where we will attempt to reconcile the two and lay out our hopes and expectations for this edited collection.

Why groups matter

Social relationships impact on our health. They have potential to have detrimental (Rook, 1984) or positive influence upon the individual (Sani, 2012; Jetten et al., 2012), depending on the nature of the relationship. Mutual respect, trust and support are indicative of positive involvement as opposed to abusive, mistrustful and emotionally neglectful relationships which are likely to have a detrimental effect on a range of aspects of wellbeing. What gives social relationships their beneficial impact upon the individual, and what makes group membership so important? Baumeister and Leary (1995) highlight the difference between feelings of belongingness and mere social contact. It is the emotional significance and the intimate connection that are pivotal. Becoming involved with social groups can offer a sense of meaning to people, and motivate them to become responsible for other group members, giving a sense of wellbeing and purposefulness that stem from a feeling of belonging. Ultimately the innate human need to belong and be part of the collective can be a motivator for extending the self beyond the individual perspective (Baumeister & Leary, 1995) and contribute significantly to a meaningful existence.

Putnam (2000), in his work on social capital, stated that the chances of dying in the following year would be halved if an isolated individual became part of a group. Therefore, to feel part of and socially connected to other group members can have positive implications for both physical and mental health (Jetten et al., 2012). Social connectedness can be both emotionally and psychologically enhancing, by contributing to the self-construct and its consequent impact on perception and behaviour (Oakes, 1987; Turner, 1982). Group treatment programmes have often been perceived from an individualistic viewpoint, where the group is an aggregate of 'I's'. Floyd Allport famously stated that "there is no psychology of groups which is not essentially and entirely a psychology of individuals" (Allport, 1924. p. 3).

The group in this context is not an epiphenomenon (a consequence of an aggregate of individuals who happen to have come together) but a distinct psychological entity (Sani, 2012). For the purpose of this current work we perceive the group to be greater than the sum of the individual parts and to have uniquely emergent psychological properties. The positive qualities of group membership can be indicative of complex change with a depth of understanding, not possible by isolated individuals, and that can have profound impact on those who join and integrate with such groups. In contrast, membership of unhealthy and excluded groups can have a persistent and deleterious effect on members.

Introducing the social identity approach: A new perspective

The regeneration of European social psychology began in the early 1960s in Italy. The *European Journal of Social Psychology* was launched in 1971. Its birth symbolised the consolidation of European social psychology and consequent independence from American influence and the individualistic perspective (Hogg & Williams, 2000). Within this framework, Tajfel and Turner (1979) proposed 'an integrative, theory of intergroup conflict'. Traditionally based on large social groups the key areas for their research investigation were prejudice, discrimination, social conflict and social change.

Seemingly irrevocable trends in social psychology set by Allport (1924) were empirically challenged by the Bristol group. Tajfel and then Turner and colleagues developed the emergent theory we now know as the social identity approach incorporating social identity theory and subsequently self-categorisation theory, promoting the concept of the group as a psychological entity with emergent qualities but with the possibility of individual differences.

The emergent theory

In the original theory of social identity (Tajfel & Turner, 1979), the membership of social groups and the inter-relational qualities of alternative groups was of pivotal importance. Both social identity theory and self-categorisation theory (which followed), describe the cognitive, evaluative and emotional aspects of group membership as the predominant features present within smaller groups and in more global social categories. The social identity approach (Hogg and Abrams, 1995) introduced a change in perspective from the individual as part of a group to where significant group memberships are characterised as part of an individual who belongs to that group.

"Psychological group formation takes place to the degree that two or more people come to perceive and define themselves in terms of some shared in-group/out-group categorisation" (Turner et al., 1987, p. 51). They range in size from the social group (that takes place on a face-to-face basis), to large groups, to collective identities (i.e., cultural identities). The purpose for such membership may incorporate many variables but significant factors for attraction to join a group may incorporate common fate, shared threat, perception of similarities between fellow members and close proximity. For this discussion, we focus upon psychological group formation as a vehicle for change. 'Positive distinctiveness theory' as it was first named, was defined as: "the individual's knowledge that he belongs to certain social groups together with some emotional and value significance to him of this group membership" (Tajfel, 1972a, p. 292). It is not enough to be defined by others as belonging to social groups and being classified by others as belonging to such. It is an intrinsic part of this theory that individuals internalise qualities of their group into their self-concept and are subjectively attached to it. They perceive themselves and may be perceived by others (inside and outside of the group) as 'ingroup' members. As such, the individual behaves in certain ways and perceive themselves in differing lights dependent upon current environmental and social influence.

Social categorisation

Social identity theory describes how individuals' social perception is accrued through affiliation with significant others who share similar ingroup properties. Classification of self and others into social categories is dependent upon social consensus, social comparison, social competition, social learning and social control and emotional involvement. Social categorisation (into ingroup and outgroups) triggers inter-group discrimination and competiveness in the need to create a discrete social category we call the ingroup. This social category is made meaningful and real in comparison to an outgroup. It is through social categorisation and stereotyping that our perception of the world appears ordered and simplified, allowing individuals to navigate with clearly defined rules for behaviour through their daily lives. Hogg and Abram (1995, p. 17) described how lack of this effect would totally debilitate us: 'we would be overwhelmed and paralysed by overstimulation'.

Tajfel argued that through social categorisation and intergroup discrimination, individuals strive for a positive self-concept, the self becoming positively evaluated through inter-group differentiation and distinctiveness (Tajfel, 1972b), delivering meaning to the social situation, and a framework for making sense of the challenges of daily life. Social identities were now perceived as mechanistic – flexible constructs mediating between the individual and his environment as vehicles for social change (Tajfel, 1974).

Social mobility and social change

How do people achieve social change? Subjective belief systems are intrinsically linked to social consensus.[1] These personal belief systems are based upon how an individual perceives social group relations within their society and how others perceive them (Tajfel & Turner, 1979; Turner et al., 1987). By re-defining group boundaries and subjective belief systems from within, group members may, through their collective action, elevate their social status and consequently their individual levels of self-esteem and efficacy (St. Claire & Clucas, 2012). This may occur through introduction of novel group norms, where new self-categories may change the perception of both individual and group members. It is an adaptive process described by self-categorisation theory (Turner et al., 1987).

Self-categorisation theory

Self-categorisation theory (Turner et al., 1987) could be described as the cognitive and perceptual component underlying social identity theory. It describes an adaptive process. This theory attempts to portray the current psychological reality of the individual interacting within their social environment. Behaviour is shaped through psychological group formation where collective action and identification with similar others is influential through mutuality and co-operation. According to situational relevance and the perception of reality that is directed by the social context, an individual may become depersonalised (they do not operate from an individual perspective) and adopt a prototypical identity linked to accessible groups that are central and important to the person. Attraction to an ingroup ('us') against others who form the outgroup ('them') at any given moment, helps define the self in the best possible light (see Turner, 1987). The context of comparison between groups may be actual or symbolically represented (Oakes, 1987). The self is perceived as being as one with the ingroup (Smith & Henry, 1996) and therefore interchangeable with other ingroup members. Prototypes for groups are the most representative and typical cases of group identity and are context-dependent.

Self-categories are creative, perceptual constructs of the self, dependent upon emotional significance, past, present and future allegiances, current motivations, goals and expectations. The process of self-categorisation defines the self-concept at a given level of abstraction or inclusiveness. Therefore personal identity may come to the fore at a given time ('I' and 'me') or a collective identity may be more appropriate to define the self ('we' and 'us') always in environmental context (internal and external). Prior history of similarity (comparison) at a higher level of inclusiveness is essential for later comparison between self-categories. These are hierarchically organised at differing levels of abstraction and inclusiveness, for example, *Homo Sapiens, woman, Eve.* It is emphasised that self-categorisations are not self-images that are static but more a cinematic action picture with behaviour and environment intrinsically linked in motion. The individual as actor reacts or responds to others through time and space.

Overall, social identity theory provides us with a series of hypotheses about behaviour and behaviour change that have been widely applied across a series of health behaviours (e.g., Jetten et al., 2012) and increasingly to mental health (e.g., Cruwys et al., 2014) and homelessness (Walter et al., 2015). In the next section, we provide a brief overview of the concept of addiction, behavioural change and social identity and what the evidence is around recovery from addiction, before providing a brief overview of how the social identity model has been applied in understanding addiction behavioural change processes in a wider context.

Recovery

Although it remains a contested and controversial term, there have been several attempts at defining addiction recovery. The Betty Ford Institute Consensus Panel defines recovery from substance dependence as a "voluntarily maintained lifestyle characterised by sobriety, personal health and citizenship" (2007, p. 222). This position is consistent with the UK Drug Policy Commission statement on recovery as "voluntarily sustained control over substance use which maximises health and wellbeing and participation in the rights, roles and responsibilities of society" (2008, p. 6). However, this characterisation of recovery is only partial as it largely ignores the experiential and personal components of recovery, focusing instead on the visible and observable components of recovery. This distinction has been made clearly in the mental health field, by Slade (2010) who has differentiated between clinical recovery (symptom remission), functional recovery (getting a job and coping with daily life demands), personal recovery (improvements in wellbeing and life satisfaction) and social recovery (developing strong and supportive social networks).

From the subjective perspective, client-led perspectives on recovery, such as Valentine's (2011) statement "you are in recovery if you say you are" (p. 264), emphasise the importance of the subjective experience of change. This definition is consistent with the mental health recovery model advanced by Deegan (1988). She argues that recovery constitutes the lived experience of people as they accept and overcome the challenge of disability, "recovering a new sense of self and of purpose within and beyond the limits of the disability" (Deegan, 1988, p. 54).

As Llewellyn, Archibald, Clairmont and Crocker (2013), have argued in the context of restorative justice, there are strong grounds for regarding recovery as an intrinsically 'relational' model. The existing evidence supports claims that simply belonging to one or more social groups or networks is supportive of recovery (Best et al., 2010). In a retrospective analysis of recovery pathways, Best et al. (2008) found that while cumulative dissatisfaction with the lifestyle was associated with the initial decision to stop, it was moving away from the using network and their replacement with a non-using network that was associated with sustained recovery.

Additional support for this argument comes from a study of 141 cocaine-dependent individuals by Zywiak and colleagues (2009) who found that patients who had better treatment outcomes typically had larger social networks, more frequent contact with their social network, and an increase over time in the proportion of people in their social network who did not use any substances. Similarly, Litt, Kadden, Kabela-Cormier and Petry (2009) found, in a randomised trial of individuals completing residential detoxification for alcohol dependence, compared to standard aftercare, those who added at least one non-drinking member to their social network showed a 27 per cent increase at 12 months post-treatment in the likelihood of treatment success, and sustaining abstinence.

Finally, Longabaugh, Wirtz, Zywiak and O'Malley (2010) found that greater opposition to a person's drinking from within their social network predicted more days without alcohol use both during and after treatment, and fewer heavy drinking days post-treatment. In addition, less frequent drinking within the person's social network predicted more days without alcohol use during and after treatment. On this basis, the authors concluded that transition to sustained recovery was underpinned by a move from a social network supportive of problematic drinking to one supportive of recovery. Thus, there is a strong evidence base suggesting that there is a strong social component in recovery from alcohol and drug problems.

Social identity approaches to understanding recovery

There is a history in the addictions research field of linking recovery with identity, starting with qualitative research by Biernacki (1977). In the UK, McIntosh and McKeganey (2000) have argued, on the basis of 70 in-depth interviews with recovering drug users in Glasgow, Scotland, that recovery involves the restoration of a 'spoiled identity'. This approach has been challenged on the grounds that it is unnecessarily stigmatising to people with drug problems (the using identity does not have to be spoiled) and that it over-simplifies the multiple identities that many drug users have (such as the mothering role; Radcliffe, 2011). However, the current approach would suggest that it is a social, rather than an individual model, of addiction recovery that offers the greater explanatory potential. To date, this has been articulated in two conceptual models.

Frings and Albery (2014) have developed a Social Identity Model of Cessation Maintenance (SIMCM), which draws on previous research showing that group interventions that create a sense of shared identification are the basis for cure or, in the present context, recovery. SIMCM highlights the importance of social identity processes in recovery maintenance, but it applies this specifically to group therapy for addiction, seeing this as a scaffold from which to promote and strengthen a positive recovery-based identity.

One of the authors of the current chapter (DB) led a collaboration of recovery and social identity theorists in developing a broader and more ambitious Social Identity Model of Recovery (SIMOR) in which the transition from active addiction to recovery is conceptualised as being a process of social identity change in which exposure to attractive and engaging recovery groups leads to the emergence of a recovery identity and the rejection of the addict identity (Best et al., 2016). The SIMOR model outlines how this transition takes place as a gradual process with an 'early recovery' period in which the pull of both addict and recovery groups exist and where relapse is possible. In this model, it is only when the recovery identity (based on a sense of belonging to the recovery group) is highly attractive, salient and fits with the person's goals, that the likelihood of relapse is significantly reduced.

The SIMOR model is consistent with evidence from the alcohol outcomes literature (Moos, 2007) which has shown that alcohol recovery is associated with four processes – social learning (observing and copying those already in recovery); social control (adhering to the abstinence rules of recovery groups); coping skills (the accrual of key life skills) and behavioural economics (in which the benefits of recovery are perceived by the individual to be greater than those of substance use and the related lifestyle).

Social identity approaches to understanding addiction behavioural change

Within the social identity approach, membership to groups is successful through attraction and how subjective attachment is fundamental for group specific behaviour activation. The Associative Reflective Model of Social Identification (ARMS), (see Buckingham this volume), as a dual process model, acknowledges more broadly how emotive and value-laden benefits of group memberships may more efficiently direct social behaviour through internalisation of specific group norms. As such, addiction behavioural change may be linked with the recovery movement but does not preclude alternative behavioural change groups and their associated norms (see Farrow, Tarrant & Khan, this volume) to complement or as standalone options. No social identity fits all (Bienarcki, 1986) and as such, more accessible or attractive alternatives may emerge at the beginning of the behavioural change process or may develop as time goes on.

This volume celebrates both broader social identity behavioural change options for problematic addictive behaviours and, more specifically, focusses upon the recovery movement as a vehicle for effective behavioural change. Chapters from eminent and emerging figures within the applied social care settings, the addiction treatment field and the social identity arena have made contributions that demonstrate the flexibility of application of the social identity approach. As an overall introduction, Haslam, Haslam, Cruwys, Jetten, Dingle and Greenaway from the University of Queensland, Australia, outline key conceptual issues for consideration drawing upon the application of social identity and self-categorisation in health and social care. As such, these social processes are fundamental when application and implementation of behavioural change norms are presented through groups where the manipulation of social identities is considered to be always political.

Following on from this Kelly, Bergman and Vilsaint (US), focus upon Mutual Help Organisations (MHOs) such as Alcoholics Anonymous (AA). With a historical perspective providing a basis for the presentation of current research, they proceed to demonstrate the efficacy of mutual help and the significant predictors for behavioural change within these peer-led groups. Where linkage is provided between professional treatment providers to these MHOs the outcomes appear positive and productive. Most relevant is the availability and accessibility of such groups, crossing continents to deliver effective behavioural change resources for all, without charge.

Chapter 4 from Farrow, Tarrant and Shan (UK) investigates food as an addiction and draws upon research conducted within naturally occurring groups, weight loss support groups, virtual online support groups and professionally led groups to explore how their social norms impact weight management goals. More specifically a population awaiting bariatric surgery was investigated to examine how their social identity allegiance to their professionally led group effected their health outcomes and overall weight management both pre and post surgery (if applicable). A manual for professionals is introduced (Tarrant et al., 2015 in press) to aid in implementation of group specific components that encourage psychological properties of the treatment group to emerge.

Peer group norms are predictive of adolescent behaviour and may be the precursor to later problematic addictive behaviours. Alternatively, families and schools may offer behavioural options where these alternative social allegiances offset the often corrosive impact of peer pressure in relation to for example, drinking and illegal drug use. In Chapter 5, Miller, Sani and Wakefield (UK) explore these components and suggest that multiple social identity allegiances that promote healthy lifestyle choices may be effective in the prevention of future problems.

In Chapter 6, Malton demonstrates through qualitative research how Fiske's five core social motives (Fiske, 2004) with an emphasis upon belonging, may be significant motivators for the adoption and maintenance of a criminal identity and the need to feel part of an esteemed peer led group, albeit driven by anti-social norms. Behavioural change opportunities within the Criminal Justice System are highlighted and potential routes for recovery explored.

Indeed, the need to belong and the significance of this becomes more apparent in Chapter 7 where one of the current authors (SB) introduces the Associative Reflective Model of Social Identification (ARMS). This dual process model is designed to incorporate contemporary thought on the automaticity of social life alongside reflective processes and most importantly how health behaviour change may be more appropriately addressed through consideration of both conscious and nonconscious processes. This model was tested with a group of smokers who had all attempted to quit where some had been successful and some had not.

Expanding upon this Frings and Albery demonstrate, using the Social identity Model of Cessation Maintenance (SIMCM), the importance of considering explicit and implicit social cognitive processes in addiction recovery. Self-categorisation activation may be encouraged by greater cue accessibility and more complex social identity allegiance, with specific attention given to addiction recovery groups such as Alcoholics Anonymous. Continued allegiance would therefore be essential for such cessation maintenance or alternatively internalisation of treatment group norms may determine the efficacy of group treatment. Activation potential of addiction and recovery social identities may therefore be determined by explicit and implicit levels of identity, related self and collective efficacy, self-esteem and self-regulated attendance at recovery based groups.

Being able to connect to a wide range of addiction recovery support networks via online groups has potential to shape social identity formation and transformation. Bliuc, Best, Beckwith and Iqbal (Australia and UK) in Chapter 9 discuss differing approaches to data analysis of online forums and the use of contemporary software packages to track the development of the recovery identity and intra-group influences through monitoring of prototypicality of members and levels of engagement through formation of shared language. Thus, these naturalistic observations have potential to pin down what recovery actually means for individuals who utilise such resources.

Alternative solutions for tracking and promoting.social identity transition based on the Social Identity Model of Identity Change (SIMIC) emerge with Haslam, Dingle, Best, Mackenzie and Beckwith (Australia and UK) in Chapter 10 with the application of Social Identity Mapping (SIM) within a Therapeutic Community (TC) at two time points. Focusing upon addiction behavioural change and drawing upon the Social Identity Model of Recovery (SIMOR; Best et al., 2016) SIM enables exploration of wider social influences that may inhibit or encourage recovery identity formation. The key factor in this work is that multiple group memberships offer protection and greater potential for social identity transition when promoting health group norms that are compatible. Applying SIM in clinical settings offers great potential for insight and further social identity development.

Further clinical application of social identity processes with a particular emphasis upon heroin users and opiate substitution treatment (OST) are reviewed by Day (UK) in Chapter 11. The importance of naturalistic group of friends and family, professional clinical intervention for social identity management and assertive linkage to the recovery community are enabled through the use of the Social Network Diagram (SND). The implementation of this technique offers a simple visual tool that is easy to use and is also an efficient vehicle for building a therapeutic allegiance to effect change within a clinical setting.

It is clear that social identities matter in adopting lifestyle changes that offer greater health behavioural benefits and can offset dangerous and corrosive social identity allegiances that are no longer effective. We hope you enjoy this volume and gain insight and inspiration from the differing perspectives of this social identity application to addiction behavioural change. Before you read on, just ponder for a moment and consider your own social influences and how they have impacted your own health behaviour in the past and how they determine who you are as an individual in this current moment.

Note

1 Social or group consensus is the ingroup's current dominant attitude within the immediate social context. This is achieved through coordination of beliefs regarding ingroup/outgroup attitudes created *in situ* through dynamic influence of the psychological frame of reference and current goals; the current social norm.

References

Allport, F.H. (1924). *Social psychology*. New York: Houghton Mifflin.

Baumeister, R.F. & Leary, M.R. (1995). The need to belong: Desire for interpersonal attachments as a fundamental human motive. *Psychological Bulletin*, 117, 497–529.

Best, D. (2014). *Strength, support, setbacks and solutions: The developmental pathway to addiction recovery*. Brighton, UK: Pavilion.

Best, D., Beckwith, M., Haslam, C., Haslam, S.A., Jetten, J., Mawson, E., & Lubman, D.I. (2016). Overcoming alcohol and other drug addiction as a process of social identity transition: The Social Identity Model of Recovery (SIMOR). *Addiction Research and Theory*, 24, 111–123.

Best, D., Ghufran, S., Day, E., Ray, R., & Loaring, J. (2008). Breaking the habit: A retrospective analysis of desistance factors among formerly problematic heroin users. *Drug and Alcohol Review*, 27, 619–624.

Best, D., Rome, A., Hanning, K., White, W., Gossop, M., Taylor, A., & Perkins, A. (2010). *Research for recovery: A review of the drugs evidence base*. Crime and Justice Social Research, Scottish Government. Edinburgh, UK: Scottish Government.

Betty Ford Institute Consensus Panel (2007). What is recovery? A working definition from the Betty Ford Institute. *Journal of Substance Abuse Treatment*, 33, 221–228.

Biernacki, P. (1977). *Pathways from heroin addiction: Recovery without treatment*. Beverly Hills, CA: Sage.

Biernacki, P. (1986). *Pathways from heroin addiction: Recovery without treatment*. Philadelphia, PA: Temple University Press.

Cruwys, T., Dingle, G., Hornsey, M., Jetten, J., Oei, T., & Walter, T. (2014). Social isolation schema responds to positive social experiences: Longitudinal evidence from vulnerable populations. *British Journal of Clinical Psychology*, 53, 265–280.

Deegan, P.E. (1988). Recovery: The lived experience of rehabilitation. *Psychosocial Rehabilitation Journal*, 11, 11–19.

Fiske, S.T. (2004). *Social beings: A core motives approach to social psychology*. Indianapolis, IN: Wiley.

Frings, D. & Albery, I. (2014). The social identity model of cessation maintenance: Formulation and initial evidence. *Addictive Behaviors*, 44, 35–42.

Hogg, M.A. & Abrams, D. (1995). *Social identifications: A social psychology of intergroup relations and group processes*. London and New York: Routledge.

Hogg, M.A. & Williams, K.D. (2000). From I to we: Social identity and the collective self. *Group Dynamics: Theory, Research, and Practice*, 4, 81–97.

Jetten, J., Haslam, C., & Haslam. (2012). *The social cure*. Hove, UK & New York: Psychology Press.

Kelly, J.F. & White, W.L. (2011). *Addiction recovery management: Theory, research and practice*. New York, Dordrecht, Heidelberg, London: Humana Press.

Litt, M.D., Kadden, R.M., Kabela-Cormier, E., & Petry, N.M. (2009). Changing network support for drinking: Network Support Project 2-year follow-up. *Journal of Consulting and Clinical Psychology*, 77, 229–242.

Llewellyn, J., Archibald, B., Clairmont, D., & Crocker, D. (2013). Imagining success for a restorative approach to justice: Implications for measurement and evaluation. *Dalhousie Law Journal*, 36, 281–316.

Longabaugh, R., Wirtz, P.W., Zywiak, W.H., & O'Malley, S.S. (2010). Network support as a prognostic indicator of drinking outcomes: The COMBINE study. *Journal of Studies on Alcohol and Drugs*, 71, 837.

McIntosh, J. & McKeganey, N. (2000). Addicts' narratives of recovery from drug use: Constructing a non-addict identity. *Social Science & Medicine*, 50, 1501–1510.

Moos, R.H. (2007). Theory-based active ingredients of effective treatments for substance use disorders. *Drug and Alcohol Dependence*, 88, 109–121.

Oakes, P.J. (1987). The salience of social categories. In J. Turner et al., *Rediscovering the social group: A self-categorization theory* (pp. 117–141). Oxford. Blackwell.

Putnam, R.D. (2000). *Bowling alone: The collapse and revival of American community*. New York: Simon and Schuster.

Radcliffe, P. (2011). Motherhood, pregnancy and the negotiation of identity: The moral career of drug treatment. *Social Sciences and Medicine*, 72, 984–991.

Rook, K.S. (1984). The negative side of social interaction: Impact on psychological well-being. *Journal of Personality and Social Psychology*, 46, 1097–1108.

St. Claire, L. & Clucas, C. (2010). In sickness and in health. Influences of social categorizations on health-related outcomes. In T. Postmes, & N.R. Branscombe, (Eds.), *Rediscovering social identity* (p. 130). New York and Hove, UK: Psychology Press.

Sani, F. (2012). Group identification and health. In J. Jetten, C. Haslam, & A. Haslam (Eds.), *The social cure*. (pp. 21–38). Hove, UK & New York: Psychology Press.

Slade, M. (2010). Mental illness and well being: The central importance of positive psychology and recovery approaches. BMC Health Services, Research, 10, 26. Retrieved from: www.bmchealthservres.biomedcentral.com/articles/10.1186/1472-6963/-10-26.

Smith, E.R. & Henry, S. (1996). An in-group becomes part of the self: Response time evidence. *Personality and Social Psychology Bulletin*, 22, 635–642.

Tajfel, H. (1972a). Social categorization. In S. Moscovici (Ed.), *Introduction a la psychologie sociale* (Vol. 1). Paris: Larouse.

Tajfel, H. (1972b). Some developments in European social psychology. *European Journal of Social Psychology*, 2, 307–22.

Tajfel, H. (1974). Social identity and intergroup behaviour. *Social Science Information/Information sur les Sciences Socials*, 13 (2), 65–93. In T. Postmes & N.R. Branscombe (Eds.), (2010). *Rediscovering social identity* (pp. 77–96). New York and Hove, UK: Psychology Press.

Tajfel, H. & Turner, J.C. (1979). An integrative theory of intergroup conflict. In W.G. Austin & S. Worchel (Eds.). *The social psychology of intergroup relations* (pp. 33–48). Monterey, CA: Brooks/Cole.

Tarrant, M., Warmoth, K., Code, C., Dean, S., Goodwin, V. A., Stein, K., & Sugavanam, T. (2015 in press). Nurturing psychological connections in healthcare: Towards a guidance framework for developing group-based interventions, *British Medical Journal Open*.

Turner, J.C. (1982). Towards a cognitive redefinition of the social group. In H. Tajfel (Ed.), *Social identity and intergroup relations* (pp. 15–40). Cambridge: Cambridge University Press.

Turner, J.C. (1985). Social categorization and the self-concept: A social cognitive theory of group behaviour. In J. Lawler (Ed.), *Advances in group processes* (Vol 2). Greenwich, CT: JAI Press. In T. Postmes & N.R. Branscombe, (Eds.), (2010). *Rediscovering social identity* (pp. 243–272). New York and Hove, UK: Psychology Press.

Turner, J.C. (1987). Rediscovering the social group. In J.C. Turner, M.A. Hogg, P.J. Oakes, S.D. Reicher, & M.S. Wetherell, *Rediscovering the social group: A self-categorization theory*. Oxford: Basil Blackwell.

UK Drug Policy Commission. (2008). *The UK drug policy commission recovery consensus group: A vision of recovery*. London: UK Drug Policy Commission.

Valentine, P. (2011). Peer-based recovery support services within a recovery community organization: The CCAR experience. In J.F. Kelly & W.L. White (Eds.), *Addiction recovery management* (pp. 259–279). New York: Humana Press.

Walter, Z.C., Jetten, J., Dingle, G.A., Parsell, C., & Johnstone, M. (2015). Two pathways through adversity: Predicting well-being and housing outcomes among homeless service users. *British Journal of Social Psychology, 55*, 357–374.

Zywiak, W., Neighbors, C., Martin, R., Johnson, J., Eaton, C., & Rosenhow, D. (2009). The important people drug and alcohol interview: Psychometric properties, predictive validity and implications for treatment. *Journal of Sub*

2

APPLYING THE SOCIAL IDENTITY APPROACH IN CLINICAL AND HEALTH DOMAINS

Key principles and insights

S. Alexander Haslam, Catherine Haslam, Tegan Cruwys, Jolanda Jetten, Genevieve A. Dingle and Katharine Greenaway

Principles for applying the social identity approach in clinical and health domains

Over the course of the last five decades, social identity theorizing has emerged as a major framework for understanding group processes and the psychology of group life (e.g., see Reicher, Spears, & Haslam, 2010; Turner, 1999). At its core, work in this tradition serves to explain how social behaviour is structured not merely by people's sense of themselves as individuals (as 'I' and 'me') but also, and often more importantly, by their sense of themselves as members of social groups (as 'us' and 'we'). This observation reflects a core insight of the social identity approach – namely that humans' psychological make-up is largely a product of the fact that we live, and have evolved to live, in social groups. As a result, groups are not simply external features of the world that provide a backdrop for our behaviour. Rather, they structure our psychology through their capacity to be internalized as part of our sense of self. More particularly, they provide us with a sense of *social identity*: the "knowledge that [we] belong to certain social groups together with some emotional nd value significance to [us] of this group membership" (Tajfel, 1972, p. 292).

Speaking to the importance of this observation, there is now a massive literature that engages with the two theories that together comprise the social identity approach: *social identity theory* (SIT; Tajfel & Turner, 1979) and *self-categorization theory* (SCT; Turner, Hogg, Oakes, Reicher, & Wetherell, 1987). Work informed by SIT has examined the dynamics that shape group members' reactions to each other and the strategies that they pursue in order to achieve a positive, distinct and enduring sense of collective self (e.g., Ellemers, 1993; Ellemers & Haslam, 2012). Work inspired by SCT has attended more broadly to the underpinnings and sequelae of group formation and coordinated action. In particular, it has been concerned with understanding the social categorization processes that lead people to believe they share (or do not share) group membership, and with the ways in which this then affects their understanding of the world and their interactions within it. Indeed, a pivotal observation here is that it is social identity that makes it possible to engage in any form of group behaviour at all (Turner, 1982). The reason for this is that it provides the basis for people (a) to perceive themselves to be psychologically connected and aligned (Turner, Oakes, Haslam, & McGarty, 1994), and (b) to engage in mutual social influence (Turner, 1991).

Most of the foundational work with these two theories has been theoretical in nature, in so far as it has focused on testing the key tenets of SIT and SCT and clarifying the importance of social identity for various forms of social behaviour. Nevertheless, the proponents of the approach – Henri Tajfel and John Turner – both had a clear sense of the applied relevance of their social psychological theorizing. This reflected their acute sensitivity to the practical impact that social identities and social identifications have in the world at large (e.g., in World War II and its aftermath). Indeed, in some sense Tajfel and Turner's whole approach to social psychology was motivated by a concern not just to understand the underpinnings of group life but to also clarify the implications of this for the welfare and well-being of members of specific social groups (e.g., powerless minorities).

Nevertheless, it is only relatively recently that the applied relevance of social identity and self-categorization theories has become a defining interest for both academics and practitioners. The work that has developed in response to this interest has had three distinct foci – one related to intergroup relations (e.g., Dixon, Levine, Reicher, & Durrheim, 2012; Hewstone & Brown, 1986), one related to organizational issues (e.g., Haslam, 2001/2004; Haslam, Postmes, & Ellemers, 2003; Haslam, Reicher, & Platow, 2011; Hogg, & Terry, 2001), and one related to matters of health (Haslam, Jetten, Postmes, & Haslam, 2009; Jetten, Haslam & Haslam, 2012). In the latter area, the key idea that has been explored is that groups, and the social identities that underpin them, are central to processes of health and well-being.

Since it is central to the concerns of this volume, the logic that underpins this idea is worth briefly elaborating. It relates to the claim that group life is what makes us human and that, as a result, groups and group activity are a key source of personal meaning, purpose and worth (Greenaway, Cruwys, Haslam, & Jetten, in press). Among other things, this means that physical and psychological isolation are as inimical to our well-being as things like hunger and thirst (Cacioppo & Hawkley, 2003; House, 2001). And in this regard, the fundamental significance of social identity is that, without it, group life is compromised – among other things, because there is no basis for trust, cooperation, and shared endeavour (Turner et al., 1987). In a very real sense, then, social identities are a bedrock of physical and psychological welfare (Jetten, Haslam, Haslam, Dingle, & Jones, 2014).

Yet for all the applied relevance of such ideas, the progenitors of social identity theorizing never laid out ground rules for applying these theories in the field. Consequently, until very recently, insights from the approach had never been translated into codified, manualised programmes for practitioners to be taught and to deliver. What, then, might these look like? And what are the key principles upon which they might be built? These are the key questions that the present chapter attempts to answer (after Haslam, 2014).

There are a range of interrelated key reasons why this task is important. The first is that, almost as soon as social identity theorizing was first fleshed out, it became apparent that this had practical relevance, albeit this was not initially realised in relation to health. Accordingly, attempting to clarify the extent and nature of its relevance for the area of health would seem to make a lot of sense. The second is that interest in applications to health has increased dramatically in recent years and so there is clearly demand for such analysis. Early work addressed issues such as symptom appraisal, stigma and prejudice, and coping, but more recent work has seen applications to topics as diverse as clinical assessment, depression, successful aging, trauma resilience, and drug and alcohol rehabilitation (for reviews see Haslam, et al., 2009; Jetten et al., 2012). As other chapters in this volume attest (see also Haslam, Jetten, Cruwys, Dingle, & Haslam, in prep), an array of other health-related topics are now becoming a focus for application, and so the need to cater to this demand is only increasing.

A third reason for wanting to do this relates to the oft-repeated dictum that "there is nothing so practical as a good theory" (Lewin, 1952, p. 169). So, if we accept that SIT and SCT are good theories, it then follows that these theories must also be very practical. But if that is so, one might well ask why it is that they are not found at the heart of clinical and health psychology courses, health professional training programs, or standardized health interventions? And if they should be, how might this translation occur? Moreover, fourth, we need to address these questions for the simple reason that these are the ones asked most frequently by the increasing number of health practitioners who have been exposed to the social identity approach – and who are persuaded by what it has to say – but remain unclear about how exactly to bring it to bear upon their day-to-day professional activity.

To address these various needs this chapter attempts to spell out five key principles that pertain to the application of the social identity approach in a range of health and social welfare domains and to clarify some of the concrete ways in which these can be translated into practice. A core message that emerges from this analysis is that just as it is impossible for clinical and health interventions to not involve political choices, so too it is impossible for them to avoid issues of social identity management. If any more were needed, this, then, is a final reason for wanting to clarify what these issues are and for trying to come to terms with their professional and practical implications.

Applied principles of the social identity approach

Principle 1: Groups and social identities matter

The importance of this principle can be traced back to the core idea, alluded to above, that social identity is the basis for distinct forms of social behaviour (Tajfel,

1978) and, indeed, is what makes group behaviour possible (Turner, 1982). In line with this point, the original studies that formed the basis for SIT – Tajfel and colleagues' minimal group experiments (Tajfel, Flament, Billig, & Bundy, 1971) – provided compelling evidence that when individuals come to define themselves in terms of a given group membership they strive to advance that group in ways that make it positive, distinct, and enduring. Moreover, it is clear that these motivations have important consequences. For example, when they define themselves in terms of a given group membership, individuals will often make profound personal sacrifices (to the point of giving up their life) to advance the interests of that group.

A large body of research has supported such claims by showing that people's behaviour is often determined more by the circumstances, needs and aspirations of their ingroup than by their idiosyncratic personal concerns (for reviews see Akerlof & Kranton, 2010; Ellemers, De Gilder, & Haslam, 2004; Tyler & Blader, 2003). The fundamental point here is that in a wide range of social contexts – including those in which many clinical interventions are delivered (e.g., see Cruwys, Haslam, Dingle, & Jetten, 2014a; Cruwys, Haslam, Fox, & McMahon, 2015a) – social identities serve to structure (and restructure) people's perception and behavior: their values, norms and goals; their orientations, relationships and interactions; what they think, what they do, and what they plan to do. In this way, the active ingredient of clinical interventions is often as much the group context in which they are delivered as the specific content of the intervention (Frings & Albery, 2015; Haslam et al., 2014; Gleibs, Haslam, Haslam & Jones, 2011). This point is routinely overlooked in clinical practice, but it is one that practitioners are ill-advised to neglect.

Self-categorization theory has contributed to researchers' appreciation of such dynamics primarily through its specification of the way in which social identities are defined and made salient as a function of social context (Oakes, Haslam, & Turner, 1994; Turner, 1985). The theory has further applied relevance and explanatory power as a result of Turner's (1991) observation that social identity is also a basis for *social influence*. This means that people are able to exert positive influence over others to the extent that they are seen to embody a social identity that they and those others share. This point has been shown to have broad relevance to applied domains, with large bodies of work confirming that various forms of communication (e.g., health warnings, environmental campaigns, political advertising) tend to have intended effects only to the extent that recipients perceive themselves to share social identity with the source from which they emanate (for an illustrative review see Tarrant, Hagger, & Farrow, 2011). So for example, the degree to which people engage with, and follow, various types of instructions depends critically upon whether they identify with the source of those instructions (Greenaway, Wright, Reynolds, Willingham, & Haslam, 2015; Reicher, Haslam, & Smith, 2012). Apart from anything else, this explains why influence attempts often fail (or worse, backfire) if they are perceived to originate from an outgroup – especially one with whom one's ingroup is in some form of conflict or competition. Critically too, it also explains why the therapeutic alliance is so important for successful intervention (Haslam et al., forthcoming) and why peer groups and expert practitioners often play a critical role in effective treatment (Best et al., 2014).

Work that has explored these dynamics of influence already hints at one important reason why social identity matters for health. After all, because much of our health-related behaviour is shaped by the information we receive from others (e.g., about what is good for us and what is not, what we should do and what we should not) then clearly it is important to understand when and why this information is (or is not) taken at face value. Relatedly, self-categorization theory also suggests that whether or not we give useful social support to others (and receive it ourselves) should vary as a function of the identity-based relationship between those who give support (e.g., carers, health professionals, leaders) and those who receive it. Again, this is a prediction that has received considerable support – not least, from studies of people in health and care settings (for a review see Haslam, Reicher, & Levine, 2012).

Even more fundamentally, recognition that social identity is a critical substrate of physical and psychological integrity (Haslam et al., 2009; Jetten et al., 2012) has been the stimulus for a large number of observational, experimental, and intervention studies that have been conducted over the course of the last decade and, as we intimated above, it has led to a surge of interest in the social identity approach among clinical and health psychologists. Among other things, the work this has led to has shown that social identities play a critical role in helping people to deal with challenging life transitions such as recovering from injury or illness (e.g., stroke, Haslam et al., 2008; or head trauma, Jones et al., 2011; Jones et al., 2012), entering a care home (Knight, Haslam, & Haslam, 2010; Ysseldyk, Haslam, & Haslam, 2013), and living through large-scale social conflict (Muldoon, Schmid, & Downes, 2009) or disaster (Drury, 2012).

By the same token, when people's capacity for social identification is compromised (e.g., because a valued social identity is lost) then this is likely to have adverse consequences for their mental and physical health. This point is brought home especially powerfully in studies that provide compelling evidence of strong links between social identity and depression (e.g., Cruwys et al., 2014b; Cruwys, South, Greenaway, & Haslam, 2015; Sani, Herrera, Wakefield, Boroch, & Gulyas, 2012; Wakefield, Bickley, & Sani, 2013; for a review see Cruwys, Haslam, Dingle, Haslam, & Jetten, 2014a). Indeed, a key message of all this research is that social identity matters not just because it serves to structure social cognition (Turner et al., 1994) but because it also enables and brings meaning to social life (Greenaway et al., in press).

Principle 2: Self-categorizations matter

Having observed that social identities matter because they underpin a range of positive health and clinical outcomes, one might be tempted to conclude that a more basic lesson to draw from previous work is that one should do whatever one can to promote social identities wherever possible. We will have more to say about the dangers of this conclusion later, but at this point it is important to note that even if this were a reasonable goal, the promotion of social identities by external agencies will often fail because social identification is a subjective psychological process in which the perspective and *self*-categorizations of would-be group members is all-important (Reicher & Haslam, 2006).

More specifically, self-categorization theory explains that social identities are only likely to be a basis for perception and behaviour to the extent that they (a) have *a priori* meaning and also (b) capture meaningful patterns of intra-group similarity and intergroup difference in the situation at hand (Oakes et al., 1994). The more general point here, then, is that a person's self-categorizations (as opposed to their nominal group memberships) always need to be taken into account – for it is these that provide the basis for psychological group membership and its consequences (Reicher & Haslam, 2006; van Dick, Wagner, Stellmacher, & Christ, 2005). The empirical basis for such an assertion can again be found within early experimental research. In particular, work by Ellemers and her colleagues showed that when individuals assigned themselves to minimal groups they identified more strongly with those groups and were more likely to behave in ways that were informed by their group membership than was the case when they were assigned to groups by an experimenter (e.g., see Ellemers, Kortekaas, & Ouwerkerk, 1999).

The significance of this point for applied intervention was initially revealed in research that sought to shed critical light on the pervasive practice of using focus groups to engage with, and elicit opinions from, members of a given community. The problem, however, is that while a given demographic characteristic (e.g., being a woman, being homeless, suffering from dementia) *may* be a basis for a given individual's self-categorization – and hence for their group behaviour – it also may not be (Walter, Jetten, Dingle, & Parsell, in press). As a result, both psychologically and practically, the groups that practitioners create (and engage with) are often peculiarly *un*focused in so far as they offer only a very limited opportunity for psychological engagement on the part of their members (Eggins, O'Brien, Reynolds, Haslam, & Crocker, 2008).

More generally too, within the intergroup power dynamic that is characteristic of many applied contexts, this lack of psychological focus – reflecting a failure to attend to the perspective of group members themselves (including their willingness to take on *new* social identities in the course of an intervention) – can be a potent source of perceived *illegitimacy* that undermines both the credibility of authorities and the respect they are accorded that leads easily to dysfunctional forms of *mis*engagement (e.g., those that promote resistance or backlash; Creed & Scully, 2000; Drury, Stott, & Farsides, 2003).

At one level the proof of this point comes from a large number of studies that manipulate self-categorization and show that this has powerful implications for individuals' social orientation and behaviour (e.g., Haslam, Morton et al., 2012; Levine, Prosser, Evans, & Reicher, 2005; Levine & Reicher, 1996). In the organizational field research has also shown that when employees are given the opportunity to specify the groups with which they identify, the ones they report are often quite different from those that managers use as a basis for their own managerial practices (e.g., restructuring that attempts to rationalize work flow according to role or function; Eggins et al., 2008; O'Brien et al., 2004). Moreover, research indicates that even if these two things are identical, there is an important practical difference between being told (e.g., by a researcher, a manager, or a clinician) that you are a member of a particular group, and making this assertion yourself. For example, Eggins and colleagues showed that participants who were asked to identify the groups that were relevant to a given conflict and then to indicate which one they belonged to were more likely (a) to identify with this group, (b) to find the conflict management process useful, and (c) to commit to the outcomes of this process than were those who were assigned to exactly the same groups by an experimenter (Eggins et al., 2008).

Along related lines, in an experimental intervention study in which people were randomly assigned to different conditions in order to examine the impact of group reminiscence on the health and well-being of older adults in care, Haslam and her colleagues found that positive effects were not observed across the board but were restricted to those individuals for whom the groups were a meaningful basis for self-categorization from the outset (Haslam, Haslam, Ysseldyk, et al., 2014). Whether the therapeutic power of group memberships is unlocked thus depends critically on group members' *social identification* with relevant groups – since this determines whether their minds are open to what it is that the groups have to offer (for evidence in relation to the efficacy of Alcoholics Anonymous groups, see Kelly, this volume).

The foregoing analysis suggests that the best way to harness the power of group life – or what we have more ambitiously referred to as "the social cure" (Jetten et al., 2012) – is not to randomly assign people to groups or to make assumptions about the groups one is dealing with, but to build group interventions around (diverse) social identities that have some prior meaning and fit for participants (Haslam, Jetten, & Haslam, 2012). After more than a decade of research this is a prediction that now enjoys a broad base of support – with relevant evidence having been garnered from quantitative and qualitative studies of hospital staff (O'Brien et al., 2004), military medics (Peters, Haslam, Ryan, & Fonseca, 2012), the Copenhagen climate change conference (Batalha & Reynolds, 2012), school teachers and students (Reynolds, Subasic, Lee, & Tindall, 2014), and even a simulated expedition to Mars (Persaud et al., 2003).

Related to this point, our current research points to the considerable value of *Social Identity Mapping* as a procedure that can be used to inform both clinical diagnosis and intervention (e.g., Best et al., 2014; Cruwys et al., 2016; Jetten, Haslam, Iyer, & Haslam, 2010). The core goal of this is to find out what social identities matter to people and how much, and to clarify their inter-relationship (see Haslam, Best, Dingle, Mackenzie, & Beckwith, this volume, for more detail). Importantly too, this insight can then be used as a platform for interventions – as it is in GROUPS 4 HEALTH (G4H; Haslam, Cruwys, Haslam & Dingle, 2015a, 2015b; Haslam, Cruwys, Haslam, Dingle, & Chang, 2016) – which seek to promote positive health outcomes by building and maintaining valued social identities.

Principle 3: The power of groups is unlocked by working with social identities (not across or against them)

As key tenets of the social identity approach, the previous two points could be illustrated with reference to very broad literature. However, once one starts to *work* with groups, the social identity literature becomes more scant. Indeed, this is one reason why (at least in the past) health and clinical practitioners who work with groups have tended to overlook the approach or to assume that it has little to offer them. Tellingly, then, "How to" books about groups rarely incorporate wisdom from social identity research and most fail to index social identity as a relevant construct (e.g., see Alle-Corliss & Alle-Corliss, 2009; Johnson & Johnson, 2012; Tyson, 1998). As a result, it is common for those who work with groups to imagine, or at least act as if, there is little to be gained by engaging with groups in their own members' terms. The consequences of this assumption can be seen in research to which we have already alluded. For example, if practitioners who are engaging with disadvantaged groups pay no heed to the identities that matter for their members, then their efforts to bring about change (e.g., in cognitions, in lifestyle) are likely to meet with indifference – and possibly opposition – from those whose identities are impacted by that change (Mols, Haslam, Steffens, & Jetten, 2014; Walter, Jetten, Parsell, & Dingle, 2015).

The importance of working with valued social identities is confirmed by our own research in a range of health settings. In care homes, for example, we have found that when space is managed in ways that align with, and help to build, residents' sense of shared identity, this has substantial positive consequences not only for their comfort but also for their productive use of that space (Haslam, Haslam, Knight et al., 2014; Knight et al., 2010). Building on such observations, a growing number of intervention studies have also shown that activities that help to build (or reinforce) individuals' sense that they share social identity with other people have a range of positive consequences for physical, mental and cognitive health (Cruwys, Dingle et al., 2013; Dingle, Brander, Ballantyne, & Baker, 2013; Gleibs, Haslam, Haslam, & Jones, 2011; Gleibs, Haslam, Jones et al., 2011; Haslam, Cruwys et al., 2016; Haslam, Haslam, Knight/Ysseldyk et al., 2014).

As we have already intimated, these studies also provide evidence that the health-enhancing role of social identities is independent of, and typically much larger than, the specific features of a particular therapy that are usually seen to be responsible for positive outcomes. Thus in a water club, a reminiscence group, a choir, or a design team, the principal curative agent is not the water, the reminiscence, the singing, or the design (important as these things may be), but the group in which these things are shared and that endows its members with a sense of identity-based solidarity and connection. Critically, this serves to make the activity in question meaningful so that members are able to extract maximum value from participating in it. Moreover, because the various outcomes that are measured in these studies are all key health indicators (e.g., the experience of social isolation, tests for dementia, number of GP visits) it is hard to argue with the conclusion that in this domain there are immense benefits to practices that seek to work with, and promote, the social identities of those that one has responsibility to manage and care for. Indeed, it was the fact that it is hard to imagine anything that could be more beneficial and entail fewer deleterious side-effects that led us to develop GROUPS 4 HEALTH (Haslam, Cruwys, Haslam, & Dingle, 2015a, 2015b; Haslam et al., 2016).

As a number of studies have now shown, a key benefit of programmes that work with groups in this way is that the process of giving voice to subjectively important group identities and treating them respectfully increases the legitimacy of – and trust in – both the programmes themselves and those who deliver them (Peters, Haslam, Ryan, & Steffens, 2014; Tyler & Blader, 2003). As a result, this also leads to markedly better outcomes. This is especially true in the case of powerless and disenfranchised groups (e.g., of the form commonly found in addiction programmes; Dean & Rud, 1984) whose members are typically marginalized by regimes of control and whose energies are therefore often directed *against* the system within which they are being managed (Helliwell, 2011; O'Brien et al., 2004). Critically too, engaging with groups *in their own members' terms* (e.g., in the form revealed by social identity mapping; Cruwys et al., 2016) gives those responsible for programme management and delivery access to the *identity knowledge* they need in order to be able to harness the power of groups in optimal ways. Because it can be abused and disregarded (and often is), possession of this knowledge is a guarantee of neither success nor progress. Nevertheless, without it, the force of the group will not be with you, and – like the Jedi Ranger Lanoree en route to Nox (Lebbon, 2014, p. 110) – one is flying blind into a potential storm.

Principle 4: Social identities need to be made to matter

The work that supports Principle 3 accords with a large literature which speaks to the importance of procedural justice – treating people fairly and respectfully – as an underpinning of well-being and constructive forms of engagement (e.g., Tyler & Blader, 2003). Yet evidence from the range of studies that we have already discussed suggests that if one is serious about wanting to reap the benefits of social identities – especially as a vehicle for change – then this is something that one needs to do more than just talk about. For example, in our intervention studies in care homes, it is not simply the respectful engagement with social identities that makes a positive difference to residents but also the fact that these groups become a vehicle for *material change* to residents' lives and to their environment. On the one hand this is seen in the various forms of productive interaction that social identity promotes (e.g., such that residents talk and listen to each other more, and are less likely to be socially isolated). On the other hand, it is reflected in people's ability to work together to create a world whose fabric better reflects their own tastes and aspirations (Haslam et al., 2010; Knight et al., 2010). The key point here is that such interventions provide a basis for group members to set about creating a space in which their desired identities can be lived out (Haslam, Reicher, & Platow, 2011; Steffens et al., 2014).

Although this recommendation will often be uncontroversial, it is important to acknowledge that there are an array of contexts in which the process of bringing social identities out into the open and "making them matter" might be seen to entail huge risk. This is the case, for example, where one is dealing with vulnerable populations or with problematic identities built around abuse and harm. Shouldn't we "Just say no" to these groups and everything they do and stand for? More specifically, as qualified professionals, should we not be striving to suppress unwanted group memberships, and working instead to *impose* preferred social identities ourselves from the top down?

It is certainly the case that in an array of applied settings, concerns and reservations of this form are frequently articulated – especially at the outset. For example, in care homes, we have observed that it is common for (well-meaning) managers to question the capacity for vulnerable older adults to have meaningful input into decisions about their own management (Haslam, Haslam, Knight et al., 2014). Likewise, in therapeutic community contexts, the existence of toxic social identities can be seen to be what needs to be rectified rather than what needs to be celebrated (Buckingham, Frings, & Albery, 2013; Dingle, Stark, Cruwys, & Best, 2015b). As a result, in such contexts it is often the professional prerogative – in which the clinician is understood to know, and to have the right to say, what is best for their clients – that holds sway.

Against this, though, we would argue that, whatever their form, there is a need to recognize and engage with people's important social identities rather than to sweep them under the carpet. Not least, this is because strategies of social identity denial or suppression will tend to avoid acknowledging, and therefore coming to terms with, the very issues that have led people to seek help in the first instance. At the same time too they fail to capitalize on the potential for group memberships to be a basis for cognitive engagement, creativity and change (Branscombe, Fernández, Gómez, & Cronin, 2011; Buckingham et al., 2013; Haslam, 2001; Haslam, Adarves-Yorno, Postmes, & Jans, 2013; Tajfel & Turner, 1979). In the field of addiction, this point is brought home clearly by the work of Dingle, Cruwys and Frings (2015a) which observes that the road into abuse is often bereft of meaningful social identities, while the road out is typically paved by opportunities for the (re)discovery of positive group-based connections.

These claims are supported by evidence from diverse strands of research. In dealing with substance abuse, for example, there is evidence that the efficacy of programmes such as Alcoholics Anonymous arises partly from their ability to recognize problematic social identities (e.g., "us alcoholics") and then use this as a platform for constructive change (Best et al., 2016; Buckingham et al., 2013). Likewise, research with young adults suffering from eating disorders suggests that group programmes which embrace the problematic identities at the heart of relevant conditions (e.g., "us anorexics") are effective in part because the group is ultimately the most effective vehicle for delivering and sustaining effective change (e.g., in eating-related norms; Cruwys, Haslam et al., 2015a). Research with individuals suffering from psychosis (Crabtree, Haslam, Postmes, & Haslam, 2010), physical disability (Branscombe et al., 2011) or multiple sclerosis (Tabuteau-Harrison, Mewse, & Haslam, 2016) also suggests that the process of embracing stigmatized social identities allows group members to start to challenge the basis of that stigma and thereby to counteract some of the negative social consequences of their condition.

The key point here, then, is that in an array of clinical and applied contexts, as well as being a large part of the problem, social identities are also a large part of the solution. Accordingly, if one fails to engage with them directly, there is a very real danger not only that one will fail to come to grips with the underlying social reality-based challenges that people face and that demand attention, but also that one will fail to embrace the most effective pathways to progress.

Principle 5: Psychological intervention always involves social identity management and hence is always political

It is tempting to draw this chapter to a close at this point since, although it is not exhaustive, the foregoing review is already quite extensive. However, in returning to reflect upon the challenges that we identified at the outset, it needs to be recognized that the obstacles that confront practitioners who seek to use social identity principles in their applied work do not relate only to a lack of available tools. It therefore follows that improving these tools, though important, will not necessarily open up clinical and health practitioners to all that the social identity approach has to offer.

A key reason for this is that preference for this, or any other, approach to health and health management has *political* as much as practical underpinnings (Haslam, 2004). This point has already been alluded to in noting that those who commission and deliver applied services are sometimes skeptical about what a social identity approach might offer because it does not mesh with their preference either to impose identities from the top, to treat people as if they were all individuals, or to otherwise conceal group-level realities. Accordingly, in claiming that the principles we identified above contribute to evidence-based best practice, we would not want to suggest that adhering to them will allow researchers to avoid thorny issues of politics. On the contrary, they will often bring them to the fore. In particular, this is because many of the principles we have identified involve engaging with, and exposing, the inherently political nature of various applied settings (e.g., entailing identity-based power differences between groups; Crabtree et al., 2010; Knight et al., 2010; O'Brien et al., 2004). Yet, having done this, they are a basis for programmes (e.g., G4H) that involve working with groups to develop appropriate and sustainable solutions to the various issues they confront.

Of course, this itself raises the question of what makes a particular strategy 'appropriate', and who is in a position to authorize particular solutions as having this quality. One inescapable reality here is that managers and clinicians are unlikely to engage with approaches and solutions that appear to be at odds with the interests of the groups they represent. This speaks to the more general point that in the applied arena the various (and sometimes conflicting) social identities of practitioner groups are often every bit as important in shaping emergent realities (not least in terms of the interventions and treatments that they offer) as those of their clients. It has been observed, for example, that the design of clinical interventions is often dictated as much, if not more, by the needs of therapists as by those of their clientele (Berwick, 2009).

Having said this, in spelling out the principles above, our goal is certainly not to work against practitioners' identity-based interests. Nevertheless, we would argue that one of the particular challenges faced by practitioners who want to implement social identity-based approaches is to reappropriate the prevailing agendas of specific health professions (e.g., clinical psychology) so that these are dictated by more than just the perceived expertise of high-status groups. This involves recognizing – on the basis of the copious empirical literature that now supports this point – that in clinical and other applied contexts there are always multiple collective interests at play and that, if one is interested in securing optimal outcomes, it is important to recognize and respect all of these.

The essential point to note here is that attempting to reach optimal outcomes in applied domains always involves a process of *social identity management* – on the part of both professionals and their clients (e.g., see Branscombe et al., 2011; Illic et al., 2014; Jones et al., 2012). In our various empirical projects we have therefore tried to show how this might be done successfully so as to improve the health and well-being of both individuals and collectives (e.g., Haslam, Cruwys et al., 2016; Haslam, van Knippenberg, Platow, & Ellemers, 2003; Jetten et al., 2012). At the same time, though, it is also important to make the point that if practitioners or policy makers choose *not* to go down the paths we have discussed, this does not allow them to escape the politics of identity management.

To this, the skeptic might retort that much of the appeal of dominant interventions such as cognitive behaviour therapy (Beck, 2011) is that they are activities informed by value-neutral science that is attuned primarily to the needs of the individual. Yet the sensibilities that accompany familiarity with the social identity approach (after Tajfel & Turner, 1979) suggest that there is no such thing as identity-neutral science (e.g., see Morton, Haslam, Postmes, & Ryan, 2006) or identity-neutral practice. Because they involve decisions to mobilize the power inherent in certain social identities and, at the same time, to demobilize, ignore or otherwise weaken others, *all* psychological interventions are political. Indeed, social psychological research alerts us to the fact that calls to treat everyone as individuals are themselves generally voiced most loudly by members of high-status groups who are motivated to protect their interests through efforts to maintain the status quo (Tajfel & Turner, 1979; Verkuyten & Martinovic, 2006).

Accordingly, to respond to a given clinical problem (e.g., lack of motivation, stress, anhedonia, addiction) as if this were only a problem of individual psycho(patho)logy – rather than something that derives, at least in part, from the conditions of group life – needs to be understood as the instantiation of a very particular set of identity-based values and beliefs. Moreover, the choices underlying such responses are far from routinely unproblematic (e.g., see Haslam & Reicher, 2006; St. Claire & Clucas, 2012). Ultimately, then, we see that all practitioners have decisions to make about the political priorities that inform the processes of identity management they enact. Indeed, one important contribution of the present analysis should be to bring this fact into the open, so that those practitioners can have evidence-based discussion with those who commission and use their services about the nature and consequences of these choices.

Conclusion

More than four decades after the first social identity research was published, there is now a colossal literature that speaks to the importance of internalized group memberships for people's sense of self, for their psychology more generally, and for their behaviour. Yet it is only relatively recently that social identity researchers have turned their attention to practical questions of ingroup identity that are of profound relevance to applied fields.

In this new venture, the theory has held up well and the transition from laboratory to field has been relatively smooth. There are at least three reasons for this. First, the theoretical knowledge that has been acquired through 'pure' research is not only considerable, but, critically, it is also integrated and systematic (in ways recommended by Ellemers, 2013). Second, this coherence has in turn made the theory very portable – so that insights gained in one domain can easily be used to shed light on another. And, third, from the outset, researchers in the social identity tradition have always been interested in 'the world out there' as much as the mind 'in here', so they are (or should be) no strangers to complex environments (Reicher et al., 2010).

That said, there are some very particular challenges associated with making the move into applied domains. Most arise from the fact that whereas in the laboratory one can study psychology in the raw without necessarily needing to reflect on the political implications of one's choices and actions, in the applied arena these issues are generally more fraught. For example, it is a relatively easy matter to conduct a study to show that by building social identifications one can increase a person's sense of social control (Greenaway, Haslam et al., 2015) or their self-esteem (Jetten et al., 2014). However, one's willingness to recommend this as practice in the field is necessarily tempered by the nature and objectives of the social identities one builds. After all, the Nazi movement may have proved to be a very effective way of promoting the health and well-being of many Germans, but this came at huge expense to other groups. Put another way, applications of social identity theorizing typically bring issues of *identity content* to the fore, so that one is mindful of the fact that the practical consequences of social identification are not necessarily desirable (e.g., see Livingstone & Haslam, 2008; Muldoon et al., 2009; Reicher & Haslam, 2006).

It is for this reason that the principles outlined above are intended to be value-neutral (i.e., of the form "social identities matter" rather than "social identities are good"). Yet, as Principle 5 indicates (and although the machinery of conventional psychological practice typically camouflages this), a key point about applied research is that it puts researchers on the spot by requiring them to make choices about the social identities they want to promote. As we have suggested, sometimes these choices are problematic (as in the case where identities centre on forms of abuse; Dingle, Stark et al., 2015b). Sometimes, though, they are not. Few people would argue with the importance of enhancing the quality of life of care home residents, depression sufferers, or the socially isolated, or with the goal of developing leadership to promote efficient and effective clinical intervention. Importantly, these are all areas in which social identity researchers can point to the positive and considerable impact that they have had not just on theoretical knowledge but on people's lives.

Clearly there is much more to be done on this front. Not least, the task of integrating the messages of social identity and self-categorization theories into applied spheres (e.g., so that they become an essential part of clinical and health training) has only just begun. For example, we are only just starting to assist practitioners by developing diagnostic tools (e.g., Best et al., in press; Cruwys, Steffens et al., 2016; Haslam et al., this volume) and by formalizing various intervention and training protocols (e.g., Haslam, Cruwys et al., 2015a, 2015b; 2016). Nevertheless, as the chapters that follow attest, researchers and practitioners are now turning themselves enthusiastically to these core tasks, and with great effect. Moreover, their efforts in this regard extend Lewin's dictum in showing not only that good theory is profoundly practical but also that the practical domain is the furnace of good theory – a place where it is not just applied and tested, but also tempered and steeled. In this endeavour, then, the social identity approach has found not only new converts but also new challenges, and we will all be the richer for rising to meet them.

Acknowledgements

This chapter is based closely on an earlier review by Haslam (2014). However, it updates the content of this – in particular, by focusing on a range of recent developments that are relevant specifically to the application of social identity principles in clinical and health contexts. We are grateful to John Dixon, John Drury, Ilka Gleibs, Kim Peters, Steve Reicher, Kate Reynolds, Nik Steffens, Clifford Stott, and Mark Tarrant for their input into work reported in this chapter – work which was also supported by funding from the Australian Research Council and the Canadian Institute for Advanced Research.

References

Akerlof, G. A., & Kranton, R. E. (2010). *Identity economics: How our identities shape our work, wages, and well-being.* Princeton, NJ: Princeton University Press.

Alle-Corliss, L. & Alle-Corliss, R. (2009). *Group work: A practical guide to developing groups in agency settings.* Chichester, UK: Wiley.

Batalha, L. & Reynolds, K. J. (2012). ASPIRing to mitigate climate change: Superordinate identity in global climate negotiations. *Political Psychology, 33*, 743–760.

Beck, J. S. (2011). *Cognitive behavior therapy: Basics and beyond* (2nd ed.). New York: Guilford Press.

Berwick, D. M. (2009). What 'patient-centered' should mean: Confessions of an extremist. *Health Affairs, 28*, w555–w565.

Best, D., Beckwith, M., Haslam, C., Haslam, S. A., Jetten, J., Mawson, E., & Lubman, D. I. (2016). Overcoming alcohol and other drug addiction as a process of social identity transition: The Social Identity Model of Recovery (SIMOR). *Addiction Research and Theory, 24*, 111–123.

Best, D., Lubman, D., Savic, M., Wilson, A., Dingle, G., Haslam, S. A., Haslam, C., & Jetten, J. (2014). Social and transitional identity: Exploring social networks and their significance in a therapeutic community setting. *Therapeutic Communities, 35*, 10–20.

Branscombe, N. R., Fernández, S., Gómez, Á., & Cronin, T. (2011). Moving toward or away from a group identity: Different strategies for coping with pervasive discrimination. In J. Jetten, C. Haslam, & S. A. Haslam (Eds.) *The social cure: Identity, health and well-being* (pp. 115–131). Hove, UK: Psychology Press.

Buckingham, S. A., Frings, D., & Albery, I. P. (2013). Group membership and social identity in addiction recovery. *Psychology of Addictive Behaviors, 27*, 1132–1140.

Cacioppo, J. T., & Hawkley, L. C. (2003). Social isolation and health, with an emphasis on underlying mechanisms. *Perspectives in Biology and Medicine, 46*, S39–S52.

Crabtree, J. W., Haslam, S. A., Postmes, T., & Haslam, C. (2010). Mental health support groups, stigma and self-esteem: Positive and negative implications of group identification. *Journal of Social Issues, 66*, 553–569.

Creed, W. D. & Scully, M. A. (2000). Songs of ourselves: Employees' deployment of social identity. *Journal of Management Inquiry, 9*, 391–412.

Cruwys, T., Dingle, G., Haslam, S. A., Haslam, C., Jetten, J., & Morton, T. (2013). Social group memberships protect against future depression, alleviate depression symptoms, and prevent depression relapse. *Social Science and Medicine, 98*, 179–186.

Cruwys, T., Haslam, S. A., Dingle, G. A., Haslam, C., & Jetten, J. (2014a). Depression and social identity: An integrative review. *Personality and Social Psychology Review, 8*, 215–238.

Cruwys, T., Haslam, S. A., Dingle, G. A., Jetten, J., Hornsey, M. J., Chonga, E. M. D., & Oeia, T. P. S. (2014b). Feeling connected again: Interventions that increase social identification reduce depression symptoms in community and clinical settings. *Journal of Affective Disorders, 159*, 139–146.

Cruwys, T., Haslam, S. A., Fox, N., & McMahon, H. (2015a). 'That's not what we do': Evidence that normative change is a mechanism of action in group interventions. *Behaviour Research and Therapy, 65*, 11–17.

Cruwys, T., South, E., Greenaway, K., & Haslam, S. A. (2015b). Social identity reduces depression by fostering positive attributions. *Social Psychological and Personality Science, 6*(1), 65–74.

Cruwys, T., Steffens, N., Haslam, S. A., Haslam, C., Jetten, J., & Dingle, G. (2016). *Social Identity Mapping (SIM): A procedure for visual representation and assessment of subjective group memberships*. Unpublished manuscript: The University of Queensland.

Dean, J. C. & Rud, F. (1984). The drug addict and the stigma of addiction. *Substance Use & Misuse, 19*, 859–869.

Dingle, G. A., Brander, C., Ballantyne, J., & Baker, F. A. (2013). 'To be heard': The social and mental health benefits of choir singing for disadvantaged adults. *Psychology of Music, 41*, 405–421.

Dingle, G. A., Cruwys, T., & Frings, D. (2015a). Social identities as pathways into and out of addiction. *Frontiers in Psychology, 6*, 1795.

Dingle, G. A., Stark, C., Cruwys, T., & Best, D. (2015b). Breaking good: Breaking ties with social groups may be good for recovery from substance misuse. *British Journal of Social Psychology*, *54*, 236–254.

Dixon, J., Levine, M., Reicher, S., & Durrheim, K. (2012). Beyond prejudice: Are negative evaluations the problem and is getting us to like one another more the solution? *Behavioral and Brain Sciences*, *35*, 411–466.

Drury, J. (2012). Collective resilience in mass emergencies and disasters. In J. Jetten, C. Haslam, & S. A. Haslam (Eds.), *The social cure: Identity, health, and well-being* (pp. 195–215). London and New York: Psychology Press.

Eggins, R. A., O'Brien, A. T., Reynolds, K. J., Haslam, S. A., & Crocker, A. S. (2008). Refocusing the focus group: AIRing as a basis for effective workplace planning. *British Journal of Management*, *19*, 277–292.

Ellemers, N. (1993). The influence of socio-structural variables on identity management strategies. *European Review of Social Psychology*, *4*, 27–57.

Ellemers, N. (2013). Connecting the dots: Mobilizing theory to reveal the big picture in social psychology (and why we should do this). *European Journal of Social Psychology*, *43*, 1–8.

Ellemers, N. & Haslam, S. A. (2012). Social identity theory. In P. van Lange, A. Kruglanski, & T. Higgins (Eds.), *Handbook of theories of social psychology* (pp. 379–398). London: Sage.

Ellemers, N., De Gilder, D., & Haslam, S. A. (2004). Motivating individuals and groups at work: A social identity perspective on leadership and group performance. *Academy of Management Review*, *29*, 459–478.

Ellemers, N., Kortekaas, P., & Ouwerkerk, J. (1999). Self-categorization, commitment to the group and group self-esteem as related but distinct aspects of social identity. *European Journal of Social Psychology*, *29*, 371–389.

Frings, D. & Albery, I. (2015) The social identity model of cessation maintenance: Formulation and initial evidence. *Addictive Behaviors*, *44*, 35–42.

Gleibs, I., Haslam, C., Haslam, S.A., & Jones, J. (2011). Water clubs in residential care: Is it the water or the club that enhances health and well-being? *Psychology and Health*, *26*, 1361–1377.

Gleibs, I., Haslam, C., Jones, J., Haslam, S.A., McNeil, J., & Connolly, H. (2011). No country for old men? The role of a Gentlemen's Club in promoting social engagement and psychological well-being in residential care. *Aging and Mental Health*, *15*, 465–466.

Greenaway, K., Cruwys, T., Haslam, S. A., & Jetten, J. (in press). Social identities promote well-being because they satisfy global psychological needs. *European Journal of Social Psychology*.

Greenaway, K., Haslam, S. A., Branscombe, N. R., Cruwys, T., Ysseldyk, R., & Heldreth, C. (2015). From 'we' to 'me': Group identification enhances perceived personal control with consequences for health and well-being. *Journal of Personality and Social Psychology*, *109*, 53–74.

Greenaway, K., Wright, R., Reynolds, K. J., Willingham, J., & Haslam, S. A. (2015). Shared identity is key to effective communication. *Personality and Social Psychology Bulletin*, *41*, 171–182.

Haslam, C., Cruwys, T., Haslam, S. A., & Dingle, G. (2015a). *GROUPS 4 HEALTH Manual.* Queensland: The University of Queensland.

Haslam, C., Cruwys, T., Haslam, S. A., & Dingle, G. (2015b). *GROUPS 4 HEALTH Workbook.* Queensland: The University of Queensland.

Haslam, C., Cruwys, T., Haslam, S. A., Dingle, G., & Chang, M. X.-L. (2016). GROUPS 4 HEALTH: Evidence that a social-identity intervention that builds and strengthens social group membership improves mental health. *Journal of Affective Disorders*, *194*, 188–195.

Haslam, C., Haslam, S.A., Jetten, J., Bevins, A., Ravenscroft, S., & Tonks, J. (2010). The social treatment: Benefits of group reminiscence and group activity for the cognitive performance and well-being of older adults in residential care. *Psychology and Aging, 25*, 157–167.

Haslam, C., Haslam, S. A., Knight, C., Gleibs, I., Ysseldyk, R., & McCloskey, L.-G. (2014). We can work it out: Group decision-making builds social identity and enhances the cognitive performance of care home residents. *British Journal of Psychology, 105*, 17–34.

Haslam, C., Haslam, S. A., Ysseldyk, R., McCloskey, L.-G., Pfisterer, K., & Brown, S. (2014). Collective cognition in aging: Social identification moderates cognitive health and well-being following story- and song-based reminiscence. *Aging and Mental Health, 18*, 425–434.

Haslam, C., Holme, A., Haslam, S. A., Iyer, A., Jetten, J., & Williams W. H. (2008). Maintaining group membership: Identity continuity and well-being after stroke. *Neuropsychological Rehabilitation, 18*, 671–691.

Haslam, C., Jetten, J., Cruwys, T., Dingle, G., & Haslam, S. A. (in prep). *Advancing the social cure: Social identity and the new psychology of health*. London: Psychology Press.

Haslam, C. Jetten, J., & Haslam, S. A., (2012). Advancing the social cure: Implications for theory, practice and policy. In J. Jetten, C. Haslam, & S. A. Haslam (Eds.), *The social cure: Identity, health, and well-being* (pp. 319–343). Hove, UK: Psychology Press.

Haslam, C., Jetten, J., Cruwys, C., Dingle, G., & Haslam, S. A. (forthcoming). *The new psychology of health: Unlocking the social cure*. London: Psychology Press.

Haslam, C., Morton, T. A., Haslam, S. A., Varnes, L., Graham, R., & Gamaz, L. (2012). 'When the age is in, the wit is out': Age-related self-categorization and deficit expectations reduce performance on clinical tests used in dementia assessment. *Psychology and Aging, 27*, 778–784.

Haslam, S. A. (2004). Psychology in organizations: The social identity approach (2nd ed.). London: Sage.

Haslam, S. A. (2014). Making good theory practical: Five lessons for an Applied Social Identity Approach to challenges of organizational, health, and clinical psychology. *British Journal of Social Psychology, 53*, 1–20.

Haslam, S. A., Postmes, T., & Ellemers, N. (2003). More than a metaphor: Organizational identity makes organizational life possible. *British Journal of Management, 14*, 357–369.

Haslam, S. A., Adarves-Yorno, I., Postmes, T., & Jans, L. (2013). The collective origins of valued originality: A social identity approach to creativity. *Personality and Social Psychology Review, 17*, 384–401.

Haslam, S. A., Jetten, J., Postmes, T., & Haslam, C. (2009). Social identity, health and well-being: An emerging agenda for applied psychology. *Applied Psychology: An International Review, 58*, 1–23.

Haslam, S. A. & Reicher, S. D. (2006). Stressing the group: Social identity and the unfolding dynamics of responses to stress. *Journal of Applied Psychology, 91*, 1037–1052.

Haslam, S. A., Reicher, S. D., & Levine, M. (2012). When other people are heaven, when other people are hell: How social identity determines the nature and impact of social support. In J. Jetten, C. Haslam, & S. A. Haslam (Eds.), *The social cure: Identity, health, and well-being* (pp. 157–174). London & New York: Psychology Press.

Haslam, S. A., Reicher, S. D., & Platow, M. J. (2011). *The new psychology of leadership: Identity, influence and power*. New York and Hove, UK: Psychology Press.

Haslam, S. A., van Knippenberg, D., Platow, M., & Ellemers, N. (Eds.) (2003b). *Social identity at work: Developing theory for organizational practice*. New York and Hove, UK: Psychology Press.

Helliwell, J. F. (2011). Institutions as enablers of wellbeing: The Singapore prison case study. *International Journal of Wellbeing, 1*, 255–265.

Hogg M. A. & Terry, D. J. (Eds.) (2001). *Social identity processes in organizational contexts.* Philadelphia, PA: Psychology Press.

House, J. S. (2001). Social isolation kills, but how and why? *Psychosomatic Medicine, 63*, 273–274.

Ilic, M., Reinecke, J., Bohner, G., Röttgers, H. O., Beblo, T., Driessen, M., Frommberger, U., & Corrigan, P. W. (2014). Managing a stigmatized identity: Evidence from a longitudinal analysis about people with mental illness. *Journal of Applied Social Psychology, 44*, 464–480.

Iyer, A., Jetten, J., Tsivrikos, D., Postmes, T., & Haslam, S. A. (2009). The more (and the more compatible) the merrier: Multiple group memberships and identity compatibility as predictors of adjustment after life transitions. *British Journal of Social Psychology, 48*, 707–733.

Jetten, J., Haslam, C., & Haslam, S.A. (Eds.) (2012). *The social cure: Social identity, health and well-being.* Hove, UK: Psychology Press.

Jetten, J., Haslam, C., Haslam, S. A., Dingle, G., & Jones, J. J. (2014). How groups affect our health and well-being: The path from theory to policy. *Social Issues and Policy Review, 8*, 103–130.

Jetten, J., Haslam, S. A., Iyer, A., & Haslam, C. (2010). Turning to others in times of change: Social identity and coping with stress. In S. Stürmer & M. Snyder (Eds.), *The psychology of pro-social behavior: Group processes, intergroup relations, and helping* (pp. 139–156). Oxford: Blackwell.

Johnson, D. W. & Johnson, F. P. (2012). *Joining together: Group theory and group skills* (11th ed.). Engelwood Cliffs, NJ: Prentice-Hall.

Jones, J. M., Haslam, S. A., Jetten, J. Williams, W. H., Morris, R., & Saroyan, S. (2011). What doesn't kill you can make you stronger (and more satisfied with life): The impact of identity on well-being after acquired brain injury. *Psychology and Health, 26*, 353–369.

Jones, J. M., Williams, W. H., Jetten, J., Haslam, S. A., Harris, A., & Gleibs, I. H. (2012). The role of psychological symptoms and social group memberships in the development of post-traumatic stress after traumatic injury. *British Journal of Health Psychology, 17*, 798–811.

Knight, C., Haslam, S.A., & Haslam, C. (2010). In home or at home? Evidence that collective decision making enhances older adults' social identification, well-being and use of communal space when moving to a new care facility. *Aging and Society, 30*, 1393–1418.

Lebbon, T. (2014). *Star wars: Dawn of the Jedi: Into the void.* New York: Random House.

Levine, R. M., Prosser, A., Evans, D., & Reicher, S. D. (2005). Identity and emergency intervention: How social group membership and inclusiveness of group boundaries shapes helping behavior. *Personality and Social Psychology Bulletin, 31*, 443–453.

Levine, R. M. & Reicher, S. D. (1996). Making sense of symptoms: Self-categorization and the meaning of illness and injury. *British Journal of Social Psychology, 35*, 245–256.

Lewin, K. (1952). *Field theory in social science: Selected theoretical papers by Kurt Lewin* (D. Cartwright, Ed.). London: Tavistock.

Livingstone, A. & Haslam, S. A. (2008). The importance of social identity content in a setting of chronic social conflict: The case of intergroup relations in Northern Ireland. *British Journal of Social Psychology, 47*, 1–21.

Mols, F., Haslam, S. A., Steffens, N., & Jetten, J. (2015). Why a Nudge is not enough: A social identity critique of governance by stealth. *European Journal of Political Research, 54*, 81–98.

Morton, T. A., Haslam, S. A., Postmes, T., & Ryan, M. K. (2006). We value what values us: The appeal of identity-affirming science. *Political Psychology, 27*, 823–838.

Muldoon, O. T., Schmid, K., & Downes, C. (2009). Political violence and psychological well-being: The role of social identity. *Applied Psychology: An International Review, 58*, 129–145.

Oakes, P. J., Haslam, S. A., & Turner, J. C. (1994). *Stereotyping and social reality*. Oxford: Blackwell.

O'Brien, A. T., Haslam S. A., Jetten, J., Humphrey, L., O'Sullivan, L., Postmes, T., Eggins, R. A., & Reynolds, K. J. (2004). Cynicism and disengagement among devalued employee groups: The need to ASPIRe. *Career Development International, 9*, 28–44.

Persaud, R., Robles, S. R., Clarke, J. D., Dawson, S., Mann, G. A., Waldie, J., Piechocinski, S., & Roesch, J. (2003). Expedition One: A Mars Analog Research Station 30-day mission. *American Astronautical Society Science and Technology Series, 107*, 53–87.

Peters, K. O., Haslam, S. A., Ryan, M. K., & Fonseca, M. (2012). Working with subgroup identities to build organizational identification and support for organizational strategy: A test of the ASPIRe model. *Group and Organization Management, 38*, 128–144.

Peters, K. O., Haslam, S. A., Ryan, M., & Steffens, N. (2014). To lead, ASPIRe: Managing diversity and building social capital by empowering subgroups and embedding organic organizational identity. In S. Otten, K. van der Zee, & M. Brewer (Eds.), *Towards inclusive organizations: Determinants of successful diversity management at work* (pp. 87–107). Hove, UK: Psychology Press.

Reicher, S. D., & Haslam, S. A. (2006). Rethinking the psychology of tyranny: The BBC Prison Study. *British Journal of Social Psychology, 45*, 1–40.

Reicher, S. D., Haslam, S. A., & Smith, J. R. (2012). Working towards the experimenter: Reconceptualizing obedience within the Milgram paradigm as identification-based followership. *Perspectives on Psychological Science*, 7, 315–324.

Reicher, S. D., Spears, R., & Haslam, S. A. (2010). The social identity approach in social psychology. In M. S. Wetherell & C. T. Mohanty (Eds.), *Sage Identities Handbook* (pp. 45–62). London: Sage.

Reynolds, K. J., Subasic, E., Lee, E., & Tindall, K. (2014). Does education really transform us? The impact of school-based social processes on the person. In K. J. Reynolds & N. R. Branscombe (Eds.). *The psychology of change: Life contexts, experiences, and identities*. Hove, UK: Psychology Press.

Sani, F., Herrera, M., Wakefield, J. R., Boroch, O., & Gulyas, C. (2012). Comparing social contact and group identification as predictors of mental health. *British Journal of Social Psychology, 51*, 781–790.

St Claire, L. & Clucas, C., (2012). In sickness and in health: Influences of social categorizations on health-related outcomes. In Jetten, J., Haslam, C., & Haslam, S. A. (Eds.), *The social cure: Identity, health, and well-being* (pp. 75–95). London and New York: Psychology Press.

Steffens, N., Haslam, S. A., Reicher, S. D., Platow, M. J., Fransen, K., Yang, J., Ryan, M. K., Jetten, J., Peters, K. O., & Boen, F. (2014). Leadership as social identity management: Introducing the Identity Leadership Inventory (ILI) to assess and validate a four-dimensional model. *Leadership Quarterly, 25*, 1001–1024.

Tabuteau-Harrison, S., Mewse, A., & Haslam, C. (2016). Adjusting to living with multiple sclerosis: The role of social groups. *Neuropsychological Rehabilitation, 26*, 36–59.

Tajfel, H. (1972). Experiments in a vacuum. In J. Israel & H. T. Triandis (Eds.), *The context of social psychology: A critical assessment* (pp. 69–119). London: Academic Press.

Tajfel, H. (1978). Interindividual behaviour and intergroup behaviour. In H. Tajfel (Ed.), *Differentiation between social groups: Studies in the social psychology of intergroup relations* (pp. 27–60). London: Academic Press.

Tajfel, H., Flament, C., Billig, M. G., & Bundy, R. F. (1971). Social categorization and intergroup behaviour. *European Journal of Social Psychology, 1*, 149–177.

Tajfel, H., & Turner, J. C. (1979). An integrative theory of intergroup conflict. In W.G. Austin & S. Worchel (Eds.), *The social psychology of intergroup relations* (pp. 33–47). Monterey, CA: Brooks/Cole.

Tarrant, M., Hagger, M., & Farrow, C.V. (2011). Promoting positive orientation towards health through social identity. In J. Jetten, C. Haslam & S. A. Haslam (Eds.), *The social cure: Identity, health and well-being* (pp. 39–54). Hove, UK: Psychology Press.

Turner, J. C. (1982). Towards a cognitive redefinition of the social group. In H. Tajfel (Ed.), *Social identity and intergroup relations* (pp. 15–40). Cambridge: Cambridge University Press.

Turner, J. C. (1985). Social categorization and the self-concept: A social cognitive theory of group behaviour. In E. J. Lawler (Ed.), *Advances in group processes* (vol. 2, pp. 77–122) Greenwich, CT: JAI Press.

Turner, J. C. (1991). *Social influence*. Milton Keynes, UK: Open University Press.

Turner, J. C. (1999). Some current issues in research on social identity and self-categorization theories. In N. Ellemers, R. Spears, & B. Doosje (Eds.), *Social identity: Context, commitment, content* (pp. 6–34). Oxford: Blackwell.

Turner, J. C., Hogg, M. A., Oakes, P. J., Reicher, S. D., & Wetherell, M. S. (1987). *Rediscovering the social group: A self-categorization theory*. Oxford: Blackwell.

Turner, J. C., Oakes, P. J., Haslam, S. A., & McGarty, C. A. (1994). Self and collective: Cognition and social context. *Personality and Social Psychology Bulletin, 20*, 454–463.

Tyler, T. R. & Blader, S. (2003). The group engagement model: Procedural justice, social identity, and cooperative behavior. *Personality and Social Psychology Review, 7*, 349–361.

Tyson, T. (1998). *Working with groups*. Melbourne: Macmillan Education.

van Dick, R., Wagner, U., Stellmacher, J., & Christ, O. (2005). Category salience and organizational identification. *Journal of Occupational and Organizational Psychology, 78*, 273–285.

Verkuyten, M. & Martinovic, B. (2006). Understanding multicultural attitudes: The role of group status, identification, friendships, and justifying ideologies. *International Journal of Intercultural Relations, 30*, 1–18.

Wakefield, J. R., Bickley, S., & Sani, F. (2013). The effects of identification with a support group on the mental health of people with multiple sclerosis. *Journal of Psychosomatic Research, 74*, 420–426.

Walter, Z. C., Jetten, J., Dingle, G. A., & Parsell, C. (in press). The impact of self-categorizing as 'homeless' on well-being and service use. *Analyses of Social Issues and Public Policy.*

Walter, Z. C., Jetten, J., Parsell, C. & Dingle, G. A. (2015). The impact of self-categorizing as 'homeless' on well-being and service use. *Analyses of Social Issues and Public Policy, 15*, 333–356.

Ysseldyk, R., Haslam, S. A., & Haslam, C. (2013). Abide with me: Religious group identification amongst older adults promotes health and well-being by maintaining multiple group memberships. *Aging and Mental Health, 17*, 869–879.

3

ADDICTION RECOVERY, MUTUAL-HELP ORGANIZATIONS AND SOCIAL IDENTITY

John F. Kelly, Brandon G. Bergman and Corrie L. Vilsaint

Mutual-help organizations and social identity

Recovery-focused mutual-help organizations (MHOs) are non-professional, peer-led entities that have emerged to help individuals with addiction problems achieve and sustain long-term remission. At their core, these groups are inherently social and often self-labelled as "fellowships", having the potential to catalyze or facilitate shifts in individuals' social identity away from being someone involved in active addiction toward being a person "in recovery". Consequently, MHOs are highly relevant to any discussion of the shifts in social identity that may occur as someone begins the process of addiction recovery.

MHOs that focus on assisting individuals maintain abstinence and achieve recovery from addictive behaviors have existed for over 160 years in the United States (White, 2014). Many of today's most influential MHOs, such as Alcoholics Anonymous (AA), owe their philosophies and practices to earlier recovery-focused movements. In 1840, for instance, a society known as the Washingtonians, which focused on maintaining abstinence from alcohol through mutual fellowship and social support, began in Baltimore, Maryland, and eventually reached a membership of 600,000 nationally (White, 2014). Emphasizing (a) public confession, (b) public commitment, (c) visits from established members, (d) economic assistance, (e) continued sharing of personal experiences, (f) acts of service toward other alcoholics, and (g) sober entertainment, it foreshadowed later social recovery MHOs. Several decades later, during the 1920s and 1930s, a religious organization known as the Oxford Group became a refuge for alcoholics (Kurtz, 1979/1991). This group was based on first century Christian principles and, although it was not explicitly a program of addiction recovery, its group meeting structure and program of personal change contributed substantially to the program and fellowship model of AA.

In the modern era, 12-step MHOs, such as AA and Narcotics Anonymous (NA), promote a particular philosophy of recovery characterized by an emphasis on total abstinence, service to others, personal and spiritual growth, and reciprocal ("mutual") helping (Humphreys, 2004; Kelly & Yeterian, 2013). Other MHOs, such as SMART Recovery and LifeRing, have a secular emphasis but contain many of the same social therapeutic dynamics as 12-step MHOs (Kelly, Magill, & Stout, 2009). During the past 40 years, much has been learned about the clinical and public health utility of MHOs, particularly AA, while during the past 25 years, these MHOs and clinical interventions designed to facilitate their use have been subjected to rigorous scientific scrutiny (Kelly & Yeterian, 2013; Laudet, Timko, & Hill, 2014; McCrady & Miller, 1993).

As is the case now, socially-oriented MHOs like AA and NA, and 12-step based professional treatments designed to facilitate their use, were influential and widespread in the United States prior to 1990, yet little was known from a scientific standpoint about their efficacy or effectiveness. Concerned about this state of affairs, the US Institute of Medicine (IOM) of the National Academy of Sciences called for more research on AA's impact and how it might work to aid recovery (Institute of Medicine, 1990). The call for more research from this prestigious scientific entity in the US, for the first time legitimized serious scientific investigation into this influential peer-led community recovery resource. Following a conference convened by Drs. William Miller and Barbara McCrady in Albuquerque, New Mexico, a monograph was published by Rutgers University Press that summarized what was known at the time on AA (McCrady & Miller, 1993). This volume also set forth the agenda for the next 25 years of research. Funding to conduct scientific research in these areas followed from the US National Institutes of Health (NIH) and the Department of Veterans Affairs.

Outcomes of these initiatives have been the accumulation of a body of scientific research that has supported the clinical and public health utility of 12-step MHOs and clinical interventions to facilitate their use, as well as elucidation of the mechanisms through which 12-step treatments and MHOs, like AA, confer benefits. As noted in more detail below, many of the mechanisms through which MHOs have been found to work include changing the nature and structure of individuals' social networks (Groh, Jason, & Keys, 2008) as well as other social-cognitive and spiritual constructs, such as social identity (Buckingham, Frings, & Albery, 2013; Kelly et al, 2009).

This chapter begins by briefly reviewing the evidence for the clinical and public health utility of MHOs in preventing relapse and enhancing remission rates for substance use disorders (SUDs) as well as associated reductions in health care costs that participation in MHOs can provide. This is followed by a review of the theoretical and empirical research that has focused on how exactly MHOs, like AA, confer benefits that support long-term recovery, including an examination of social identity theory (SIT) and social categorization theory (SCT) and why a focus in the areas might yield important additional information about the workings of MHOs.

Efficacy and effectiveness research on 12-step mutual-help organizations and treatments designed to facilitate their use

From a clinical and public health standpoint, in theory, there could be many potential positives of having a large social network of recovery-focused MHO members in one's community (Moos, 2007, 2008). SUD is endemic with approximately 22 million individuals meeting criteria in any given year in the US (Substance Abuse and Mental Health Services Administration, 2013, 2014, 2015). Worldwide, alcohol kills 3.3 million individuals and illicit drug use claims another 350,000 lives each year (World Health Organization, 2014). For a substantial proportion of the individuals affected by SUD, the clinical course tends to be chronic and susceptible to relapse over many years even after people have achieved full sustained remission (i.e., one year symptom free [Dennis, Scott, & Funk, 2003; Dennis, Scott, Funk, & Foss, 2005; McLellan, Lewis, O'Brien, & Kleber, 2000]). These disorders also exact an enormous public health toll in terms of premature mortality, disease, and disability, and cost the US alone approximately $700 billion per year in lost productivity, criminal justice, and health care expenditure (Intelligence, 2011; Rehm, Taylor, & Room, 2006). Consequently, some form of recovery management or recovery monitoring, such as engagement with a MHO, could be useful to help sustain people with SUD in remission over the long term.

MHOs are easily accessible and widely available in most communities in the US and in many other countries (Mäkela, 1996) and can be attended anonymously without signing any paperwork or getting prior third-party insurance approval to engage with the service (Jonas et al., 2014). MHOs also provide exposure to, and frequent social interactions with, peers, who possess the lived experience of active SUD and successful long-term recovery from serious addiction problems. There are literally millions of years of sober experience to draw upon in recovery-focused MHOs providing a rich reservoir of recovery knowledge borne out of personal hard-earned experience. These elements can facilitate strong identification with similar others who have had the same experiences. MHOs, such as AA and NA, often also provide round-the-clock support, notably at times of high relapse risk, when professional services often are not available, such as weekends, evenings, and holidays (Kelly & McCrady, 2012). Significant and noteworthy also is that MHOs are typically provided free of charge (except for voluntary contributions) (Humphreys, 2004) and can be attended as frequently as people want, and for as long as they need. Consequently, given the grave, chronic, and undulating nature of the relapse risks associated with addiction recovery, MHOs like AA and NA could provide a valuable community-based system that can be adaptively self-regulated according to perceived need over the long-term (Kelly et al., 2009).

In theory, then, MHOs may provide useful and cost-effective recovery support systems for a high volume and high burden disease such as alcohol and other drug addiction. Fortunately, research supports these potential benefits as findings from literally hundreds of studies have shown 12-step MHOs and professional treatments designed to stimulate participation in community-based 12-step MHOs, confer meaningful clinical and public health benefits as well as reduce health care costs by lowering the reliance on more expensive professional services (Humphreys & Moos, 2001; Humphreys & Moos, 2007). While other influential MHOs are also available, such as SMART Recovery, LifeRing, Women for Sobriety, Celebrate Recovery, and others, little research has been conducted on these (Horvath & Yeterian, 2013; Kelly & Yeterian, 2013). More research is needed on alternative MHOs, as there are many pathways to recovery, and not all individuals who suffer from SUD are willing or able to engage with 12-step MHOs (Brown et al., 2014). Increasingly there are online versions of these MHOs, but little is known about the extent to which individuals may use these resources, and whether they may be used as a substitute for or augmentation to face-to-face meetings.

On the other hand, there is a scientific literature outlining the effects of participation in 12-step MHOs and its relation to SUD, psychiatric, and quality of life, outcomes. This body of literature has been summarized in systematic reviews (Ferri, Amato, & Davoli, 2006; Kelly, 2003) as well as meta-analyses (Emrick, Tonigan, Montgomery, & Little, 1993; Kownacki & Shadish, 1999; Tonigan, Toscova, & Miller, 1996). In sum, these reviews have concluded that participation in peer-led MHOs, like AA and NA, and engagement with professional 12-step treatments (i.e., clinical treatments that systematically educate SUD patients about 12-step MHOs and pro-actively link patients with them), confers a modest beneficial effect that is on par in magnitude with other interventions (Emrick et al., 1993; Ferri et al., 2006). More recent naturalistic longitudinal studies using sophisticated statistical methods (such as time-lagged Hierarchical Linear Models [e.g., (Kelly, Stout, & Slaymaker, 2013)], Propensity Score Matching [e.g., Ye & Kaskutas, 2009]) and instrumental variables analysis (Humphreys et al., 2014; Zhong et al., 2015), to reduce the selection bias associated with 12-step MHO participation (e.g., addiction severity and abstinence motivation is associated with attendance), support a causal relationship between 12-step MHO participation and observed recovery benefit and have also yielded positive effects for 12-step participation on SUD outcomes.

In addition, studies have been conducted that have developed and investigated specific manualized interventions to test whether SUD treatments that systematically encourage participation in 12-step MHOs, often referred to as "Twelve-Step Facilitation [TSF]" interventions, can produce as good or better outcomes when compared to treatments that do not link patients to community recovery support organizations like AA. The term TSF was first used in a large multisite randomized controlled trial for alcohol use disorder known as Project MATCH in the 1990's and the approach was manualized to provide a replicable intervention procedure that addiction professionals could deliver (Nowinski, Baker, & Carroll, 1992; Project Match Research Group, 1993). TSF can be delivered individually or in-groups, and aims to facilitate 12-step MHO attendance and involvement. In addition to its use as a stand-alone treatment (Alterman, Koppenhaver, Mulholland, Ladden, & Baime, 2004; Crits-Christoph et al., 1999; Litt, Kadden,

Kabela-Cormier, & Petry, 2009; Project MATCH Research Group, 1997), TSF has been studied in several other formats, including as an integrated part of an existing treatment (Walitzer, Dermen, & Barrick, 2009), a distinct component of a multi-treatment package (Kaskutas, Subbaraman, Withrodt, & Zemore, 2009) and a modular appendage to concurrent treatment (e.g., adding a TSMHO linkage session or two to regular treatment; Kahler et al., 2004; Timko & DeBenedetti, 2007). As well as being utilized among addiction specialty providers, TSF has also been used in non-specialty primary care settings (Kelly & McCrady, 2008; Pettinati et al., 2005). Thus, clinicians wishing to utilize TSF have a variety of empirically-supported methods at their disposal, which provide several options for using TSF with varying degrees of intensity (Kelly & Yeterian, 2013).

In Project MATCH, for example, TSF was shown to be at least as effective at reducing the quantity and frequency of alcohol use post-treatment and at 1- and 3-year follow-ups as the more empirically-supported cognitive-behavioral therapy (CBT) and motivational enhancement therapy (MET) to which it was compared. Moreover, TSF was superior to CBT and MET at increasing rates of continuous abstinence, as 24 per cent of the outpatients in the TSF condition were continuously abstinent throughout the year after treatment, compared to 15 per cent and 14 per cent in CBT and MET, respectively (Project MATCH Research Group, 1997). Clinically, this is highly significant since this indicates that, compared to CBT, 60 per cent more cases (i.e., 24–15 per cent = 9 per cent and 9 per cent of 15 per cent = 60 per cent) receiving TSF were in fully sustained remission in the year following treatment. Abstinence rates at 3 years continued to favor TSF, with 36 per cent reporting continuous abstinence during the 90 days prior to follow-up, compared to 24 per cent in CBT and 27 per cent in MET (Cooney et al., 2003). Again, this means that relative to CBT, 50 per cent more cases (36–24 per cent = 12 per cent and 12 per cent of 24 per cent = 50 per cent) receiving TSF were completely abstinent at 3 years post-treatment. Independently from Project MATCH, a study of adults leaving residential SUD treatment compared two aftercare conditions: relapse prevention (RP), which was based on cognitive-behavioral techniques, and TSF, which was based on the Project MATCH TSF manual (Alterman et al., 2004). While both the RP and TSF conditions had an equally positive impact on substance use outcomes across the sample as a whole, the TSF condition produced better results for certain patient subgroups, including women, those using multiple substances, and those high in psychological distress. Specifically, women and individuals with a multiple substance misuse profile reported better alcohol outcomes with TSF aftercare than their cohorts exposed to RP aftercare. Individuals with high psychological distress at treatment entry were able to maintain longer periods of post-treatment abstinence with TSF aftercare compared to their cohorts exposed to RP (Brown et al., 2002).

Similar large-scale multisite studies have been conducted with cocaine (Crits-Christoph et al., 1999) and stimulant (including but not limited to cocaine) dependent (Donovan et al., 2013) patients. In Crits-Christoph et al. (1999), almost 500 patients received 12-step-based group drug counseling and were randomly assigned to receive one of three additional individually-delivered treatments: 12-step focused counseling, cognitive-behavioral therapy, or psychodynamic therapy ("supportive-expressive therapy"). Results at 9 months and 12 months following treatment initiation found that patients assigned to the individual 12-step counseling condition had better outcomes on the main outcome measures, with significantly lower levels of addiction severity and significantly fewer days of cocaine use in the past 30 days. The Donovan et al. (2013) study was conducted across multiple intensive outpatient treatment sites as part of the National Institute of Drug Abuse's Clinical Trials Network (NIDA CTN). Results showed that, among 471 patients randomized to receive either a focused and specific 12-step group treatment (called "STAGE-12") or treatment as usual (TAU), which also referred patients to 12-step MHOs, STAGE-12 patients had higher rates of 12-step meeting attendance and were engaged in more 12-step activities throughout both the active treatment phase and the entire 6-month follow-up period. This group also had significantly higher odds of abstinence during treatment but the advantage over TAU diminished over time following treatment.

Again with a focus on changing social structures to support remission and recovery, a randomized controlled trial with alcohol dependent outpatients (Litt et al., 2009) attempted to increase social network support (NS) for abstinence by delivering a treatment that systematically encouraged patients to make use of the social network of AA (using the TSF manual from Project MATCH). Results indicated that those in the 12-step NS condition had 20 per cent more abstinent days and greater AA attendance and involvement at two-year follow-up than a case management condition. Furthermore, AA participation and the number of abstinent friends was found to mediate (i.e., explain) this treatment benefit (Litt et al., 2009). As noted below in more detail, the nature of this intervention fits well with the major themes of the social identity and social categorization approaches to behavior change.

TSF can also be integrated into existing treatments. One study examined the incremental effects of incorporating TSF into an empirically supported cognitive-behavioral intervention (Social Skills Training [SST]; Walitzer et al., 2009). This study compared treatment as usual (TAU; i.e., CBT-based SST alone) to two approaches that combined both SST and TSF. One of these approaches was more directive, while the other was more client-centered and based on the principles of Motivational Interviewing (MI). Findings revealed that those in the directive TSF condition attended more AA meetings, became more involved in the AA program, and had about 10 to 20 more per cent days abstinent (PDA), on average, across the 12-month follow-up than those receiving CBT alone or the client-centered TSF (Walitzer et al., 2009). Also, in formal mediational analyses conducted to investigate why the TSF treatment did better, the advantage for directive TSF was explained by greater AA participation in the post-treatment period.

TSF may also be used as a distinct component of an existing treatment. A TSF intervention called "Making AA Easier" (MAAEZ; (Kaskutas et al., 2009)) was designed to help prepare patients to attend 12-step meetings by addressing negative attitudes or concerns about attendance and providing education about different aspects of 12-step programs. Results showed that individuals receiving outpatient, partial hospital ("day" treatment), short-term residential, and long-term residential treatment receiving the MAAEZ intervention were more likely to report past 30 day alcohol and drug abstinence at the 12-month follow-up than those only receiving treatment-as-usual. Also, two further studies tested TSF in a less intensive manner. In a sample of adults entering outpatient treatment, Timko and DeBenedetti (2007) compared standard referral to 12-step MHOs (i.e., therapists provided information on meetings and encouragement to attend) with intensive referral (e.g., therapists provided information on meetings with personal recommendations from previous clients, reviewed 12-step philosophy, and arranged a meeting between client and current 12-step member). Over the 12-month follow-up period, rates of attendance at 12-step meetings did not differ by condition, but those who received the intensive referral had better outcomes and were more likely than those who received the standard referral to be *actively involved* in 12-step groups (i.e., have a sponsor, have a spiritual awakening). Thus, the peer-to-peer engagement stimulated by the intensive referral may have created closer identification with TSMHO members leading to a stronger and more rapid shift to adopting a new identity as "recovering person".

Importantly, while TSF is not a direct test of the efficacy of 12-step MHOs like AA or NA, per se, in studies where the mechanisms of TSF advantages were formally tested through mediational analyses, results showed that these advantages were *explained by* increased rates of participation in 12-step MHOs (e.g., Litt et al., 2009; Longabaugh, Wirtz, Zweben, & Stout, 1998; Walitzer et al., 2009). In other words, consistent with the underlying theory of TSF, these treatments lead to better outcomes because they engage patients clinically with indigenous community recovery support resources like AA and NA. As explained in more detail below, these positive changes in substance use may be explained by shifts in how people view themselves as they change from a person actively using substances to a person in recovery.

As noted previously, MHOs operate free of charge apart from voluntary contributions. Given the high cost of professionally delivered health care services for chronic diseases such as addiction, studies have also tested whether treatments that engage patients in community MHOs can reduce the reliance on more expensive professional SUD services without negatively affecting health outcomes. Humphreys and Moos investigated a total of ten residential SUD treatment programs from various areas of the United States using a quasi-experimental study design. Five of these intensive treatment programs had a very strong cognitive-behavioral (CB) theoretical orientation, and five had a very strong 12-step orientation. Following discharge, in keeping with the different emphases of the programs, patients treated in CB programs tended to use AA and NA less and professional services much more than patients treated in 12-step residential programs, who used AA and NA much more and professional services much less. This difference in professional health care service use resulted in costs being approximately $8,000 per patient higher for those treated in CB programs compared to 12-step programs across two-year follow-up. When multiplied by all of the patients treated in this study (about 1,750), this signifies a potential cost savings across all ten programs if they were to all systematically encourage 12-step MHO participation of between $10–15 million. Importantly, at the beginning of the study, the demographic and clinical characteristics of the two sets of patients were not found to differ. At the one- and two-year follow-up, the patient groups also did not differ significantly on most clinical outcomes, except that, compared to CB treated patients, about one third more patients treated in 12-step residential programs were completely abstinent from substances. Thus, compared to treatments that do not facilitate involvement in community MHOs like AA and NA, treatments that do might expect to have better outcomes in terms of continuous abstinence at significantly reduced health care costs.

In sum, the evidence in support of socially oriented 12-step MHOs is strong. Rigorous clinical treatment studies have shown that 12-step MHO participation can be increased through the implementation of systematic intervention procedures and that these treatments produce significantly better outcomes and are highly cost-effective. In addition, mediational analyses have demonstrated that the reason why these professionally delivered treatments outperform other interventions is because they engage patients with the indigenous community social support structures provided by groups like AA. An obvious subsequent question stemming from this work, is how exactly does the socially supportive structure provided by these MHOs translate into lowered alcohol or drug use rates, and higher rates of continuous abstinence, remission, and recovery. The next section addresses this question by examining the theoretical and empirical mechanisms through which the social support provided by MHOs leads to these better recovery outcomes with a special emphasis on the potential role of social identity and social categorization theories.

Mechanisms of behaviour change within recovery mutual-help organizations and the role of social identity and social categorization

Various MHOs like AA, SMART Recovery, and LifeRing, have very different assumptions about the causes and maintaining conditions of addiction and relapse. However, there are therapeutic elements that are common to all MHOs. By definition, all MHOs involve helping others and can be said to involve the "helper principle" (Riessman, 1965), or the idea that those who help others also help themselves by reinforcing their own desire to change, increasing their self-esteem through the perception of helpfulness to others, and enhancing their self-efficacy and sense of autonomy (Kelly & Yeterian, 2013). This is a central tenet of 12-step groups, which is encapsulated in the 12th step of AA (". . . we tried to carry this message to alcoholics . . .") (Alcoholics Anonymous, 2001). Also, positive associations between helping and emotional well-being have been found in general population samples (e.g., lower depression and higher self-esteem; Piliavin, 2003) and to a lesser degree between helping (i.e., being a sponsor) and positive recovery outcomes (Zemore & Pagano, 2008). However, the degree of specific emphasis on helping others as an essential curative process varies substantially across different organizations. MHOs also possess other common therapeutic factors that are rarely explicitly mentioned, but that underlie professional group therapies more generally. As described by Yalom and Leszcz (2005), therapeutic qualities of treatment groups include altruism (i.e., helping others), universality (i.e., a sense of belonging and identification), imitative behavior (i.e., observing and "trying on" various behaviors and ways of coping), instillation of hope (i.e., feeling more hopeful about the possibility of change), imparting information (i.e., giving and getting tips and learning skills), and catharsis (i.e., openly expressing thoughts and emotions). Qualities of the group dynamics may vary across different MHOs, such as cohesion and expressiveness. Although research is scarce in terms of investigating the extent to which such elements contribute to behavior change in MHOs, preliminary systematic qualitative research studies with treated adolescents and young adults attending 12-step groups assessed what they valued most about attending 12-step meetings. These studies found that the most common responses were consistent with constructs in-group therapy dynamics, such as universality (i.e., a sense of belonging and identification), and instillation of hope (Kelly, Myers, & Rodolico, 2008; Labbe, Slaymaker, & Kelly, 2014). The social identity model perspective would suggest that this sense of belonging and identification would result in greater commitment to the group and greater salience of its values and norms and, in turn, result in less risk of relapse and return to the old maladaptive social networks and the linked using identity.

In keeping with many social theories of behavior change, social support network changes also appear to mediate the relationship between 12-step group involvement and substance use outcomes. Changing social networks away from ones that model and reinforce alcohol or drug use toward ones that model and reinforce recovery can reduce exposure to conditioned alcohol or drug cues that can elicit craving and increase the probability of relapse as well as reduce associated stress – both common precursors to relapse. For instance, Humphreys, Mankowski, Moos, and Finney (1999) found that 12-month network support for abstinence partially mediated the relationship between 12-step involvement after inpatient treatment and 12-month substance use outcomes. Similarly, Kaskutas, Bond, and Humphreys (2002) found that having a larger social network and greater network support explained the relationship between AA involvement and substance use outcomes and that reducing pro-drinking influences and increasing AA-related support for abstinence were particularly important. However, causal conclusions from these two studies are limited, as they examined variables during the same time period, as opposed to sequentially, which is important when determining cause and effect relations (Bradford Hill, 1965). A subsequent follow-up of the Kaskutas et al. (2002) sample found that among variables related to social networks (i.e., the per cent of drinkers in the network and network support for abstinence), only AA-specific network support mediated the association between alcohol abstinence and past-year 12-step MHO involvement three years following treatment (Bond,

Kaskutas, & Weisner, 2003). Similarly, Kelly, Stout, Magill, and Tonigan (2011) found that, among the 1,726 Project MATCH participants, AA attendance facilitated adaptive changes in the social networks of individuals with alcohol problems by substantially reducing exposure to and involvement with pro-drinking social ties, but also by increasing exposure to and involvement with pro-abstinent social ties. These changes in social network structure mediated the relationship between greater AA attendance and better subsequent drinking outcomes. Further research is needed to examine how such broader changes in social network support for abstinence relate to other change processes (e.g., motivation for abstinence) measured at the individual level, as well as shifts in social identity.

Relative to these social and group therapy theory processes that explain how individuals benefit from AA, identifying as a 12-step MHO member is a prominent social norm that is not as well understood. For example, first-person plural pronouns are used throughout AA's (e.g., "*We* admitted *we* were powerless over alcohol – that *our* lives had become unmanageable"; italics added, (Alcoholics Anonymous, 2001)) and NA's primary literature sources (e.g., "Who is an addict? *We* know! The following is *our* experience" (Narcotics Anonymous, 2008)). These pronouns tacitly imply the existence of a social group of AA and/or NA members to which these individuals belong and with which they identify. Despite the salience of membership and identification in 12-step parlance, whether enhancing identity as a 12-step MHO member or as a person in recovery more generally promotes recovery and remission has received relatively little attention in the scientific literature, although this idea does have some support (Dingle et al., 2015). Next, we review social identity and related self-categorization theories of behavior change, outline research on identity in 12-step MHOs, and offer potential directions for future studies.

Social identity and self-categorization theories of behaviour change

Social identity theory (SIT) posits that human beings seek a positive identity, and the groups to which people feel they identify with and belong to ("ingroup") have positive attributes and other groups to which the person does not belong ("outgroup") have less desirable attributes. This identification, in turn, predicts decision-making and behavior (Amaro, Spear, Vallejo, Conron, & Black, 2014). The SIT model illustrates three decision processes involved in evaluating oneself or other people as in-group or out-group members. First, during social categorization, people are assigned to a category (e.g., "girl"; "American"; "democrat" etc.) with the primary goal of understanding and identifying the group category. Next, through a process of social identification a person may adopt the values and identity of the group in which he/she has categorized him/herself. Last, a social comparison is made between the group with which the person has identified and other groups. Self-categorization theory (SCT) is an extension of SIT (Bowen et al., 2014; Turner, 1985), and operationalizes social cognitive processes to show how uniform behavior can result from self-categorizing and internalization of group concepts. Identity change takes place when an individual is faced with reconciling potential differences between him/herself and the ingroup versus outgroup. SCT outlines a social cognitive process whereby individuals are motivated a) to reduce the distress that accompanies an uncertain self-perception, and b) to enhance one's self-perception (Brewer et al., 2009; Britton et al., 2010). When a person's self-evaluation leads to categorization which highlights differences between a newly favored in-group and an older out-group, and underscores similarities within groups, identification with the in-group is likely to facilitate self-enhancement (Bowen et al., 2014; Brown, 2000; Turner, 1985). Although SIT and related SCT have helped to explain group phenomena with potentially negative social consequences, such as stereotyping and group polarization (Brown, 2000), it may also help explain salutary behavior change, including developing an identity as a 12-step member or person in recovery from addiction.

The role of social identity approaches in 12-step mutual-help organizations

References to 12-step MHOs as social groups to which individuals belong are evident in many of their social norms. At meetings the vast majority of individuals identify as individuals with severe problems (e.g., "I'm Bill and I'm an alcoholic"; "I'm Jimmy and I'm an addict"). While one function of this self-identification may be as an ongoing reminder that one has a chronic illness susceptible to relapse despite current remission, another function may be to create a sense of unity, belonging, and overarching group cohesion and identity. According to a social identity approach (i.e., the combination of concepts from both SIT/SCT), the groups to which recovering individuals formerly belonged during active addiction (i.e., the old "in-group") facilitated and perpetuated substance use and other unhealthy and risky behaviors. This is due to the fact that, during active addiction, individuals may have associated positive traits with members of the substance-using in-group (e.g., they were perceived as trustworthy, fun, happy, heroic, talented, gifted etc.). Over time, however, the addicted individual begins to accumulate increasing substance-related negative consequences so that continued use of alcohol or other drugs becomes less and less tolerable and more punitive than pleasurable. This can change their perspective of individuals who use substances. This same person then becomes motivated to stop the use of substances and, to the extent that this goal is found to be unachievable without outside support and help, becomes more open to new social role models and social groups that can offer hope of change and recovery. As the formerly addicted individual is exposed to successful "in-group" role models of recovery, this same individual becomes implicitly more open to trying this new "identity" and letting go of the old identity. The former "in-group" of addicted people may be increasingly viewed as having negative qualities (e.g., risky, selfish, isolated, unsuccessful). As individuals are exposed to recovery-focused MHO meetings the individual is faced with uncertainty around their self-categorized social identity and group membership; continuing to belong to the former "ingroup" of individuals who are still actively misusing substances may increase threat and diminish their positive self-concept, although they are likely to perceive recovering individuals as an "outgroup", at least initially. As they observe and interact with individuals at MHOs and perceive these potential "in-group" members to have positive attributes (e.g., are trustworthy, fun, happy) and membership to be associated with positive outcomes including contented sobriety and happiness, SIT/SCT suggests they will develop an in-group identity in order to reduce this uncertainty, and to enhance their own self-concept. Research suggests too, that some individuals may become "high" identifiers if they possess high levels of uncertainty in their self-concept and also have lower self-esteem (Hogg, 2004). In turn, this burgeoning social identity as a person in recovery may provide a basis for new meaning and purpose in life (Chen, Berger, Gandhi, Weintraub, & Lejuez, 2013).

Research on social identity approaches in 12-step MHOs

Research on the relationship between social identity and 12-step MHOs is relatively scant, though existing studies suggest greater attention to the construct might enhance our explanatory models of recovery. First, of the three most often used measures of participation in Alcoholics Anonymous (Humphreys, Kaskutas, & Weisner, 1998; Morgenstern, Kahler, Frey, & Labouvie, 1996; Tonigan, Connors, & Miller, 1996), two include an item that assesses perceived membership as a 12-step MHO member. Also, a comprehensive multi-dimensional measure of mutual-help activity that we have developed (the Multidimensional Mutual-Help Activity Scale, Kelly et al., 2013) also includes an item that assesses perceived membership. It is noteworthy that in the Humphreys et al. (1998) scale, AA membership had a strong loading in principal components analysis of the overall AA affiliation scale in both treatment seeking and community samples (p. 8).

Furthermore, considering oneself a 12-step member has been shown to be a strong predictor of positive outcomes. Employing a sample of 1506 individuals that participated in Project MATCH, Cloud, Ziegler, and Blondell (2004) used multiple and step-wise regression to determine which items of the nine-item AA Involvement scale (excluding whether one had a "sober birthday") comprised the most parsimonious subset of AA activities that predict simultaneous 90-day abstinence at one-year follow-up (association between AA activities nine–12 months and abstinence rates nine–12 months post-treatment). They found that meeting attendance, number of steps completed, and considered oneself an AA member, as a set, accounted for almost all variance in abstinence rates explained by the entire scale. When only the three-item scale was analyzed, identifying as an AA member was the strongest predictor of abstinence, accounting for roughly 9 per cent of the variance in abstinence. One significant question from a SIT/SCT standpoint is when and how does someone begin to change and start the process of identifying oneself as a "member of AA" or a "member of NA", and what are the recovery implications of this identification? It may be that it is a gradual shift that is mediated by "looking for the similarities and not the differences" so often recommended in 12-step MHOs.

The role of 12-step MHO identification also appears to extend to young people with SUD. Using time-lagged 12-step MHO variables and abstinence (e.g., the association between 12-step MHO activities at one time point and abstinence at a later time point (Kelly et al., 2013)) showed not only that 12-step MHO active involvement using an eight-item involvement scale (Kelly et al., 2011) was a significant predictor of abstinence across the entire post-treatment year among more than 300 residential treatment-seeking 18–24 year olds, but importantly, that considering oneself a 12-step member and verbally participating during meetings were the strongest individual 12-step involvement predictors of abstinence. It is important to note that these data do not suggest that an attitudinal shift, like identifying as a 12-step MHO member, is substantively more important to recovery, per se, than engaging in an active recovery-related behavior (e.g., socializing with recovering members outside meetings). Identifying as a member, however, may stimulate the development of subsequent recovery activities that predict positive outcomes, or conversely may constitute a social-cognitive shift that is a consequence of participation in several activities including, but not limited to, having a 12-step MHO sponsor, socializing with other members, and working the steps. In other words, self-categorization as a member of a 12-step MHO, may be a cause or a consequence (or, more likely, both) in the process of adaptive recovery-related change.

In addition to these studies that analyze 12-step membership dichotomously (yes/no), Buckingham et al. (2013) examined associations between identity as a person in recovery in a cross-sectional survey among 61 AA and NA members in the United Kingdom, with between one month and 30 years of continuous abstinence from alcohol and other drugs. The investigators found that one's preference for an identity as a person in recovery versus an addict identity was significantly associated with abstinence self-efficacy, which, in turn, was associated with more months of abstinence. They also found that the extent to which participants attached positive traits with their life as an AA/NA member relative to their life during active addiction was associated with fewer relapses during the past month, one year, and two years (using retrospective reports) and with fewer problematic appetitive behaviors (e.g., alcohol consumption, gambling, risky sexual behavior). While the cross-sectional nature of the data limit conclusions that can be drawn from these analyses, and findings need to be replicated in a longitudinal study, this study highlights recovery identity as a potentially key construct that could develop over time in 12-step MHO members and predict salutary outcomes. The key component of this study was the measure of differentiation (distance between ingroup and outgroup) that was linked with more positive health outcomes. At any given moment in the day this differentiation may shift. It is dependent upon the social frame of reference present at any given time. Therefore, shifting social allegiances and groups aids in this process.

Summary and future research directions

The helpful role of supportive social structures provided by ubiquitous recovery-focused MHOs has strong theoretical and empirical support. The process of addictive behavior change and recovery is a dynamic and evolving one and MHOs might be thought of as social "scaffolding" that helps to move individuals progressively toward beneficial therapeutic inter-dependence, deeper self-knowledge and keener self-awareness, the acquisition of recovery-specific skills, and an enhanced sense of meaning and purpose. With greater exposure and immersion, individuals may adopt the prototypical behavior of the group (i.e., normative group behavior including descriptive and prescriptive norms). Exposure to MHOs and the scaffolding they provide may facilitate a re-categorization of individuals' social identity and self-concept, which may shift either from one of an actively addicted individual to one of a healing and recovering individual. The extent to which this shift is a marker, reflection, or consequence of other processes, or is a principal driver of behavior change itself – or perhaps both – is unclear. Nevertheless, theory and existing data suggest recovery-related social identities appear to be important variables to investigate in the context of future 12-step MHO studies. For example, the limited research conducted in this area reveals that identification and self-categorization as a 12-step member is perhaps the strongest predictor of future abstinence out of any of the 12-step involvement indices. The reasons both how and why someone might begin to identify themselves as an MHO member, or as a recovering person more globally, and the immediate and long-term consequences of such a shift are open to speculation and further investigation. The social identity perspective captured by the concepts inherent within SIT and SCT provide a framework for investigating these phenomena and offer valuable conceptual knowledge that may enhance our theories of addictive behavior and recovery-related change.

References

Alcoholics Anonymous. (2001). *Alcoholics Anonymous: The story of how many thousands of men and women have recovered from alcoholism* (4th ed.). New York: Alcoholics Anonymous World Services.

Alterman, A. I., Koppenhaver, J. M., Mulholland, E., Ladden, L. J., & Baime, M. J. (2004). Pilot trial of effectiveness of mindfulness meditation for substance abuse patients. *Journal of Substance Use, 9*, 259–268.

Amaro, H., Spear, S., Vallejo, Z., Conron, K., & Black, D. S. (2014). Feasibility, acceptability, and preliminary outcomes of a mindfulness-based relapse prevention intervention for culturally-diverse, low-income women in substance use disorder treatment. *Substance Use and Misuse, 49*, 547–559.

Bond, J., Kaskutas, L. A., & Weisner, C. (2003). The persistent influence of social networks and alcoholics anonymous on abstinence. *Journal of Studies on Alcohol, 64*, 579–588. Retrieved from www.ncbi.nlm.nih.gov/entrez/query.fcgi?cmd=Retrieve&db=PubMed&dopt=Citation&list_uids=12921201.

Bowen, S., Witkiewitz, K., Clifasefi, S. L., Grow, J., Chawla, N., Hsu, S. H., . . . Larimer, M. E. (2014). Relative efficacy of mindfulness-based relapse prevention, standard relapse prevention, and treatment as usual for substance use disorders: A randomized clinical trial. *Journal of the American Medical Association: Psychiatry, 71*, 547–556.

Bradford Hill, A. (1965). The environment and disease: Association or causation. *Proceedings of the Royal Society of Medicine, 58*, 295–300.

Brewer, J. A., Sinha, R., Chen, J. A., Michalsen, R. N., Babuscio, T. A., Nich, C., . . . Rounsaville, B. J. (2009). Mindfulness training and stress reactivity in substance abuse: results from a randomized, controlled stage I pilot study. *Substance Abuse, 30*, 306–317.

Britton, W. B., Bootzin, R. R., Cousins, J. C., Hasler, B. P., Peck, T., & Shapiro, S. L. (2010). The contribution of mindfulness practice to a multicomponent behavioral sleep intervention following substance abuse treatment in adolescents: a treatment-development study. *Substance Abuse, 31*, 86–97.

Brown, R. A. (2000). Social identity theory: Past achievements, current problems and future challenges. *European Journal of Social Psychology, 30*, 745–778.

Brown, R. A., Abrantes, A. M., Minami, H., Read, J. P., Marcus, B. H., Jakicic, J. M., . . . & Stuart, G. L. (2014). A preliminary, randomized trial of aerobic exercise for alcohol dependence. *Journal of Substance Abuse Treatment, 47*, 1–9.

Buckingham, S. A., Frings, D., & Albery, I. P. (2013). Group membership and social identity in addiction recovery. *Psychology of Addictive Behaviors, 27*, 1132–1140.

Chen, K. W., Berger, C. C., Gandhi, D., Weintraub, E., & Lejuez, C. W. (2013). Adding integrative meditation with ear acupressure to outpatient treatment of cocaine addiction: A randomized controlled pilot study. *Journal of Alternative and Complementary Medicine, 19*, 204–210.

Cloud, R. N., Ziegler, C. H., & Blondell, R. D. (2004). What is Alcoholics Anonymous Affiliation? *Substance Use and Misuse, 39*, 1117–1136.

Crits-Christoph, P., Siqueland, L., Blaine, J., Frank, A., Luborsky, L., Onken, L. S., . . . Beck, A. T. (1999). Psychosocial treatments for cocaine dependence: National Institute on Drug Abuse Collaborative Cocaine Treatment Study. *Archives of General Psychiatry, 56*, 493–502.

Dennis, M. L., Scott, C. K., & Funk, R. (2003). An experimental evaluation of recovery management checkups (RMC) for people with chronic substance use disorders. *Evaluation and Program Planning, 26*, 339–352.

Dennis, M. L., Scott, C. K., Funk, R., & Foss, M. A. (2005). The duration and correlates of addiction and treatment careers. *Journal of Substance Abuse Treatment, 28 Suppl 1*, S51–S62.

Dingle, G. A., Stark, C., Cruwys, T., & Best, D. (2015). Breaking good: Breaking ties with social groups may be good for recovery from substance misuse. *British Journal of Social Psychology, 54*, 236–254

Donovan, D. M., Daley, D. C., Brigham, G. S., Hodgkins, C. C., Perl, H. I., Garrett, S. B., . . . Zammarelli, L. (2013). Stimulant abuser groups to engage in 12-step: A multisite trial in the National Institute on Drug Abuse Clinical Trials Network. *Journal of Substance Abuse Treatment, 44*, 103–114.

Emrick, C. D., Tonigan, J. S., Montgomery, H., & Little, L. (1993). Alcoholics Anonymous: What is currently known? In B. S. McCrady & W. R. Miller (Eds.), *Research on Alcoholics Anonymous: Opportunities and alternatives* (pp. 41–76). Piscataway, NJ: Rutgers Center of Alcohol Studies.

Ferri, M., Amato, L., & Davoli, M. (2006). *Alcoholics Anonymous and other 12-step programmes for alcohol dependence*. Cochrane Database of Systematic Reviews.

Groh, D. R., Jason, L. A., & Keys, C. B. (2008). Social network variables in alcoholics anonymous: A literature review. *Clinical Psychology Review, 28*, 430–450.

Hogg, M. A. (2004) Uncertainty and extremism: Identification with high entitativity groups under conditions of uncertainty. In V. Yzerbyt, C. M. Judd, & O. Corneille (Eds.), *The psychology of group perception: Perceived variability, entitativity, and essentialism*. New York: Psychology Press.

Horvath, A. T. & Yeterian, J. D. (under review). SMART Recovery: Self-empowering, science-based recovery support. *Journal of Groups in Addiction and Recovery*.

Humphreys, K. (2004). *Circles of recovery: Self-help organizations for addictions*. Cambridge: Cambridge University Press.

Humphreys, K., Blodgett, J. C., & Wagner, T. H. (2014). Estimating the efficacy of Alcoholics Anonymous without self-selection bias: an instrumental variables re-analysis of randomised clinical trials. *Alcoholism, Clinical & Experimental Research, 38*, 2688–2694.

Humphreys, K., Kaskutas, L. A., & Weisner, C. (1998). The Alcoholics Anonymous Affiliation Scale: Development, reliability, and norms for diverse treated and untreated populations. *Alcoholism: Clinical and Experimental Research, 22*, 974–978.

Humphreys, K., Mankowski, E. S., Moos, R. H., & Finney, J. W. (1999). Do enhanced friendship networks and active coping mediate the effect of self-help groups on substance abuse? *Annals of Behavioral Medicine, 21*, 54–60.

Humphreys, K., & Moos, R. H. (2001). Can encouraging substance abuse patients to participate in self-help groups reduce demand for health care? A quasi-experimental study. *Alcoholism: Clinical and Experimental Research, 25*, 711–716. Retrieved from www.ncbi.nlm.nih.gov/entrez/query.fcgi?cmd=Retrieve&db=PubMed&dopt=Citation&list_uids=11371720.

Humphreys, K. & Moos, R. H. (2007). Encouraging posttreatment self-help group involvement to reduce demand for continuing care services: Two-year clinical and utilization outcomes. *Alcoholism: Clinical and Experimental Research, 31*, 64–68.

Institute of Medicine. (1990). *Broadening the base of treatment for alcohol problems*. Washington, DC: The National Academies Press.

Intelligence, U. S. D. O. (2011). *The economic impact of illicit drug use on American society.*

Jonas, D. E., Amick, H. R., Feltner, C., Bobashev, G., Thomas, K., Wines, R., . . . & Garbutt, J. C. (2014). *Pharmacotherapy for Adults With Alcohol-Use Disorders in Outpatient Settings.* Rockville, MD: publisher.

Kahler, C. W., Read, J. P., Ramsey, S. E., Stuart, G. L., McCrady, B. S., & Brown, R. A. (2004). Motivational enhancement for 12-step involvement among patients undergoing alcohol detoxification. *Journal of Consulting and Clinical Psychology, 72*, 736–741.

Kaskutas, L. A., Bond, J., & Humphreys, K. (2002). Social networks as mediators of the effect of Alcoholics Anonymous. *Addiction, 97*, 891–900.

Kaskutas, L. A., Subbaraman, M. S., Withrodt, J., & Zemore, S. E. (2009). Effectiveness of Making Alcoholics Anonymous Easier: A group format 12-step facilitation approach. *Journal of Substance Abuse Treatment, 37*, 228–239.

Kelly, J. F. (2003). Mutual-help for substance use disorders: History, effectiveness, knowledge gaps & research opportunities. *Clinical Psychology Review, 23*, 639–663.

Kelly, J. F., & McCrady, B. S. (2008). Twelve-step facilitation in non-specialty settings. In M. Galanter & L. A. Kaskutas (Eds.), *Recent Developments in Alcoholism (vol. 18): Research on Alcoholics Anonymous and Spirituality in Addiction Recovery* (pp. 321–346). Totowa, NJ: Springer.

Kelly, J. F., Myers, M. G., & Rodolico, J. (2008). What do adolescents exposed to Alcoholics Anonymous think about 12-step groups? *Substance Abuse, 29*, 53–62.

Kelly, J. F., Magill, M., Stout, R. L. (2009) How do people recover from alcohol dependence? A sytstematic review of the mechanisms of behavior change through Alcoholics Anonymous confers benefits. *Addiction Research and Theory, 17*, 236–259.

Kelly, J. F., Stout, R. L., Magill, M., & Tonigan, J. S. (2011). The role of Alcoholics Anonymous in mobilizing adaptive social network changes: A prospective lagged mediational analysis. *Drug and Alcohol Dependence, 114*, 119–126.

Kelly, J. F., Stout, R. L., & Slaymaker, V. (2013). Emerging adults' treatment outcomes in relation to 12-step mutual-help attendance and involvement. *Drug and Alcohol Dependence, 129*, 151–157.

Kelly, J. F., & Yeterian, J. D. (2013). Mutual-help groups for alcohol and other substance use disorders. In B. S. McCrady & E. E. Epstein (Eds.), *Addictions: A comprehensive guidebook* (2nd ed.). New York: Oxford University Press.

Kownacki, R. J., & Shadish, W. R. (1999). Does Alcoholics Anonymous work? The results from a meta-analysis of controlled experiments. *Substance Use and Misuse, 34*, 1897–1916.

Kurtz, E. (1979/1991). *Not-God: A history of Alcoholics Anonymous*. Center City, MN: Hazelden.

Labbe, A. K., Slaymaker, V., & Kelly, J. F. (2014). Toward enhancing 12-step facilitation among young people: A systematic qualitative investigation of young adults' 12-step experiences. *Substance Abuse*, *35*, 399–407.

Laudet, A., Timko, C., & Hill, T. (2014). Comparing life experiences in active addiction and recovery between veterans and non-veterans: A national study. *Journal of Addictive Diseases*, *33*, 148–162.

Litt, M. D., Kadden, R. M., Kabela-Cormier, E., & Petry, N. M. (2009). Changing network support for drinking: network support project 2-year follow-up. *Journal of Consulting and Clinical Psychology*, *77*, 229–242.

Longabaugh, R., Wirtz, P. W., Zweben, A., & Stout, R. L. (1998). Network support for drinking, Alcoholics Anonymous and long-term matching effects. *Addiction*, *93*, 1313–1333. Retrieved from www.ncbi.nlm.nih.gov/entrez/query.fcgi?cmd=Retrieve&db=PubMed&dopt=Citation&list_uids=9926538.

Mäkela, K. (1996). *Alcoholics Anonymous as a mutual-help movement: A study in eight societies*. Madison, WI: University of Wisconsin Press.

McCrady, B. S. & Miller, W. R. (1993). *Research on Alcoholics Anonymous: Opportunities and Alternatives*. New Brunswick, NJ: Rutgers Center of Alcohol Studies.

McLellan, A. T., Lewis, D. C., O'Brien, C. P., & Kleber, H. D. (2000). Drug dependence, a chronic medical illness: Implications for treatment, insurance, and outcomes evaluation. *Journal of the American Medical Association*, *284*, 1689–1695.

Moos, R. H. (2007). Theory-based active ingredients of effective treatments for substance use disorders. *Drug and Alcohol Dependence*, *88*, 109–121.

Moos, R. H. (2008). Active ingredients of substance use-focused self-help groups. *Addiction*, *103*, 387–396.

Morgenstern, J., Kahler, C. W., Frey, R. M., & Labouvie, E. (1996). Modeling therapeutic response to 12-step treatment: Optimal responders, nonresponders, and partial responders. *Journal of Substance Abuse*, *8*, 45–59.

Narcotics Anonymous. (2008). *Narcotics Anonymous* (6th ed.). Chatsworth, CA: Narcotics Anonymous World Services.

Nowinski, J., Baker, S., & Carroll, K. (1992). *Twelve Step Facilitation Therapy Manual: A Clinical Research Guide for Therapists Treating Individuals with Alcohol Abuse and Dependence*. Washington, WA: Government Printing Office: NIAAA Project MATCH Monograph, Vol. 1, DHHS Publication No. (ADM) 92–1893.

Pettinati, H. M., Weiss, R. D., Dundon, W., Miller, W. R., Donovan, D., Ernst, D. B., & Rounsaville, B. J. (2005). A structured approach to medical management: a psychosocial intervention to support pharmacotherapy in the treatment of alcohol dependence. *Journal of Studies on Alcohol. Supplement*, *15*, 170–178; discussion 168–179. Retrieved from www.ncbi.nlm.nih.gov/entrez/query.fcgi?cmd=Retrieve&db=PubMed&dopt=Citation&list_uids=16223068.

Piliavin, J. A. (2003). Doing well by doing good: Benefits for the benefactor. In C. L. M. Keyes & J. Haidt (Eds.), *Flourishing: Positive psychology and the life well-lived* (pp. 227–247). Washington, DC: American Psychological Association.

Project Match Research Group. (1993). Project MATCH: Rationale and methods for a multisite clinical trial matching patients to alcoholism treatment. *Alcoholism: Clinical and Experimental Research*, *17*, 1130–1145.

Project MATCH Research Group. (1997). Matching alcoholism treatments to client heterogeneity: Project MATCH posttreatment drinking outcomes. *Journal of Studies on Alcohol*, 1–23.

Rehm, J., Taylor, B., & Room, R. (2006). Global burden of disease from alcohol, illicit drugs and tobacco. *Drug and Alcohol Review, 25*, 503–513.

Riessman, F. (1965). The 'helper therapy' principle. *Social Work, 10*, 27–32.

Substance Abuse and Mental Health Services Administration. (2013). *Results from the 2012 National Survey on Drug Use and Health: Summary of National Findings*. NSDUH Series H-46, HHS Publication No. (SMA) 13-4795. Rockville, MD: Substance Abuse and Mental Health Services Administration.

Substance Abuse and Mental Health Services Administration. (2014). *Results from the 2013 National Survey on Drug Use and Health: Summary of National Findings*. NSDUH Series H-48, HHS Publication No. (SMA) 14-4863. Rockville, MD: Substance Abuse and Mental Health Services Administration.

Substance Abuse and Mental Health Services Administration. (2015). *Behavioral Health Trends in the United States: Results from the 2014 National Survey on Drug Use and Health*. NSDUH Series H-50, HHS Publication No. (SMA) 15-4927. Rockville, MD: Substance Abuse and Mental Health Services Administration.

Timko, C., & DeBenedetti, A. (2007). A randomized controlled trial of intensive referral to 12-step self-help groups: One-year outcomes. *Drug and Alcohol Dependence, 90*, 270–279.

Tonigan, J. S., Connors, G. J., & Miller, W. R. (1996). Alcoholics Anonymous Involvement (AAI) Scale: Reliability and norms. *Psychology of Addictive Behaviors, 10*, 75–80.

Tonigan, J. S., Toscova, R., & Miller, W. R. (1996). Meta-analysis of the literature on Alcoholics Anonymous: sample and study characteristics moderate findings. *Journal of Studies on Alcohol and Drugs, 57*, 65–72. Retrieved from www.ncbi.nlm.nih.gov/entrez/query.fcgi?cmd=Retrieve&db=PubMed&dopt=Citation&list_uids=8747503.

Turner, J. C. (1985). Social categorization and the self-concept: A social cognitive theory of group behavior. In E. J. Lawler (Ed.), *Advances in group processes: Theory and research* (pp. 77–122). Greenwich, CT: JAI Press.

Walitzer, K. S., Dermen, K. H., & Barrick, C. (2009). Facilitating involvement in Alcoholics Anonymous during out-patient treatment: A randomized clinical trial. *Addiction, 104*, 391–401.

White, W. L. (2014). *Slaying the dragon: The history of addiction treatment and recovery in America* (2nd ed.). Bloomington, IL: Chestnut Health Systems/Lighthouse Institute.

World Health Organization. (2014). Global status report on alcohol and health - 2014 edn. Retrieved from http://apps.who.int/iris/bitstream/10665/112736/1/9789240692763_eng.pdf.

Yalom, I. D., & Leszcz, M. (2005). *The theory and practice of group psychotherapy* (5th ed.). New York: Basic Books.

Ye, Y., & Kaskutas, L. A. (2009). Using propensity scores to adjust for selection bias when assessing the effectiveness of Alcoholics Anonymous in observational studies. *Drug and Alcohol Dependence, 104*, 56–64.

Zemore, S. E., & Pagano, M. E. (2008). Kickbacks from helping others: Health and recovery. In M. Galanter & L. A. Kaskutas (Eds.), *Research on Alcoholics Anonymous and spirituality in addiction recovery. Recent developments in alcoholism* (pp. 141–166). New York: Springer Science + Business Media.

Zhong, N., Yuan, Y., Chen, H., Jiang, H., Du, J., Sun, H., . . . & Zhao, M. (2015). Effects of a randomized comprehensive psychosocial intervention based on cognitive behavioral Therapy Theory and Motivational Interviewing Techniques for Community rehabilitation of patients with opioid use disorders in Shanghai, China. *Journal of Addiction Medicine*.

4

USING SOCIAL IDENTITY TO PROMOTE HEALTH

The impact of group memberships on health in the context of obesity

Claire Farrow, Mark Tarrant and Sammyh Khan

In 2006 the celebrity TV chef Jamie Oliver launched a campaign in the UK to raise awareness about the impact of poor-quality school meals on children's health and the association with paediatric obesity. While improvements in the quality of school meals were welcomed by many families across the UK, some parties reacted negatively to this perceived infringement on their children's rights, with a group of mothers reportedly setting up a temporary service to provide fast food for their children through the school gates (BBC News, 2006). What motivates groups of people to conform to health messages and advice, while others react and resist these efforts to improve public health?

In reflecting on this question, the current chapter brings together research about the impact of social identity on health through groups, particularly in the context of eating behaviours and obesity. We begin by exploring research from the social cure literature which has linked social identity to health and ill-health behaviours (Jetten, Haslam, & Haslam, 2012), and explore how people's connections to social groups can determine existing health behaviours and underpin (and sometimes undermine) efforts and interventions to improve health. We then draw on research which has conceptualised obesity as an addiction to food, and explore how social identity can be used to facilitate efforts to lose weight when people are overweight or obese. Here we use evidence from different types of groups to evaluate the impact of social identity on eating behaviour; we review evidence from naturally occurring groups of family and friends; the impact of social identity for weight loss in support groups or virtual online groups; and the support offered by groups where people have been referred by a physician to manage or lose weight. We present findings concerning the impact of group support for patients enrolled onto a National Health Service (NHS) weight management programme and evaluate not only whether groups can positively impact on weight loss, but also the intricacies through which social identity can facilitate and encourage health in relation to eating and weight.

Social identity and health

Clearly, a range of individual and psychosocial factors impact on individual behavioural decision-making, but there is now substantial evidence that behaviour is also fundamentally shaped by people's group-level experiences. Studies within the framework of social identity and self-categorisation theories (Tajfel & Turner, 1986; Turner, Hogg, Oakes, Reicher, & Wetherell, 1987) have demonstrated that how we perceive ourselves and others in terms of salient social group memberships has a powerful impact on attitudes, cognitions and behaviours. When a group membership is salient, people have been shown to interpret information through the lens of that group, seeking to conform to the perceived attitudes and expected behavioural norms of the group which are perceived to be relevant for them at a given time. Whether the groups we belong to are seen as health promoting, or as normatively engaged in risky or addictive health behaviours, is central to decisions that we make about our own behaviours, with (often downstream) consequences for health outcomes (Tarrant, Hagger, & Farrow, 2012).

When it comes to addiction specifically, there is now a large body of evidence demonstrating that connections to and within social groups are important determinants of people's cognitions about what are healthy and acceptable behaviours, as well as their motivation and engagement with those behaviours. Oyserman, Fryberg, and Yoder (2007) have argued that people engage in health or ill-health behaviours that are congruent with their social-identity norms. Accordingly, health-promoting behaviours such as not smoking, eating healthily and exercising regularly can be seen not so much as individual choices but rather habits shaped and reinforced by social identity. Importantly social identities are complex and fluid and health related social norms may change as people move between different social groups or the salience of one particular group is highlighted (Tarrant & Butler, 2011). This may explain why so many individuals may engage in healthy behaviours when one social identity is salient (e.g., exercising with a fitness group) and unhealthy behaviours when another identity is salient (e.g., drinking to excess when socialising with friends) (Tarrant, Hagger, & Farrow, 2012). Indeed, Terry and Hogg (1996) found that people with a strong sense of identification with a group are particularly influenced by the perceived norms of that group (for example in the context of exercise behaviour); for people less identified with a group, personal factors such as perceived behavioural control were a more important determinant of behavioural decisions. Relatedly, group norms have been shown to be the strongest single predictor of cognitions and intentions about alcohol consumption (Previte, Fry, Drennan, & Hasan, 2015), and in terms of eating behaviour there is now a strong body of evidence that perceptions of social norms act as a guide to determine food choices and consumption (Higgs, 2015).

The above body of research is focused on understanding and explaining observed patterns of behaviours and the path to particular health outcomes like obesity. But a growing body of research is beginning to draw on the social identity perspective to consider what can be done to change health outcomes, both in terms of treating existing conditions (e.g., weight management) and preventing them (i.e., early intervention to reduce the risk of particular health outcomes). This research has explored how healthy cognitions and behaviours can be encouraged by making salient healthy social identities, or even manipulating the perceived health norms of identities (identity content). A central idea here is that in the same way that social identities can undermine health (see Buckingham this volume), so too can they offer a 'social cure' to improve health in a variety of ways, including mental health, physical health, resilience and adjustment (Jetten et al., 2012). For example, Tarrant and Butler (2011) highlighted the potential health benefits of encouraging people to self-categorise with groups where health is seen as normative. Using a student population, the authors found that participants reported health-inhibiting cognitions when their identity *as a student* was salient (a group often associated with unhealthy behaviours such as binge drinking) compared to when an alternative but equally relevant social identity was salient (e.g., nationality). In relation to diet, Robinson, Benwell, and Higgs (2013) have demonstrated that the consumption of cookies increases or decreases depending on whether participants were led to believe that the (group) social norm advocated eating a large or small number of cookies. Robinson, Fleming, and Higgs (2014) also found that in people who consume low amounts of fruits and vegetables, manipulating information that it is socially normative to consume fruits and vegetables is more effective at improving selection and intake of fruits and vegetables than is the provision of a health message. This suggests that public health campaigns which focus on promoting health messages *en masse* could potentially be more effective if they highlight healthy social norms or even promoted healthy norms rather than simply disseminating existing health information. Indeed, paediatric obesity interventions in schools which have been developed to draw on improving healthy norms and facilitating supportive structures with feedback from home to school groups, have been shown to be associated with more healthy child food intake, improved activity behaviours and a reduced prevalence of childhood overweight (Lloyd & Wyatt, 2015).

Even when it comes to addictive behaviours where there is strong evidence for personal dependency and physical reliance on substances such as drugs, alcohol and tobacco, groups are regularly used to treat addictions, and group norms can powerfully influence whether people recover from, or become more dependent on, addictive substances. In the case of nicotine dependence, it has been suggested that up to 38 per cent of adult smokers are intermittent or social smokers, who smoke primarily, even solely, because of social influences (Shiffman, Dunbar, Ferguson, Tindle, & Scholl, 2015). In the case of alcohol, there is evidence that many young people overestimate how normative it is to drink to excess and that these misperceptions may increase or reinforce binge drinking (Perkins, 2002). Where people are addicted to drugs such as nicotine and alcohol, the avoidance of social groups where it is normative to take drugs is known to help aid recovery (Hitchman, Fong, Zanna, Thrasher, & Laux, 2014), while the effectiveness of supportive group therapy is thought to be central to determining the ability to overcome such addictions (Frings & Albery, 2015).

Obesity as addiction

Several reviews have described how perceived social norms can be used to improve healthy eating behaviours and encourage more healthy food choices (Higgs, 2015; Robinson, 2015). The focus of this chapter is on the specific impact that social norms can have on improving health for individuals who are already obese. The use of the term 'food addiction' has been widely debated in recent years (Davis & Carter, 2009; Gearhardt et al., 2011). There is a long history of research which has explored the concept of addiction to food (e.g., Randolph, 1956), and there is evidence that certain forms of eating demonstrate behavioural and neurological similarities to other addictions, and that such responses are usually associated with foods that are high calorie, highly palatable, and usually bad for health (Meule & Gearhardt, 2014). There has undoubtedly been an increase in the availability of these high calorie foods and drinks (Wang, Bleich, & Gortmaker, 2008; Anderson & Butcher, 2006), and alongside this the prevalence of obesity has risen dramatically, with more than one third of adults in the United States (Ogden, Carroll, Kit, & Flegal, 2014) and nearly one quarter of adults in the UK now obese (Health & Social Care Information Centre, 2014).

Despite its increasing 'normality', obesity continues to be a highly stigmatised condition associated with negative stereotypes and discrimination (Puhl & Brownell, 2001). Stereotypes that obese people are lazy, unintelligent, greedy and weak-willed are widespread and research suggests that this stigma has actually increased in recent years (Andreyeva, Puhl, & Brownell, 2008; Latner & Stunkard, 2003). Most likely because of this stigma and exposure to discrimination, many people who are obese have a negative sense of self and demonstrate explicit and implicit anti-fat bias themselves (Wang, Brownell, & Wadden, 2004). In the context of obesity, social identity can be very complex, with obese people often holding negative attitudes towards obesity while simultaneously seeking to lose weight, or even being prescribed to lose weight (e.g., by general practitioners, and/or through attendance at weight loss support groups). Here group level factors such as the sense of support derived from weight loss groups may impact on the success of weight loss attempts.

Eating is very much a social activity; most eating purposely takes part in the presence of others and is deeply embedded within culture (Polivy & Pliner, 2015). There is a large body of literature concerned with the impact that social models can have on food intake (see Cruwys, Bevelander, & Hermans, 2014). Social modelling of food intake can be strong and stable and people tend to adapt their food intake to complement that of those around them, converging upon a norm reflecting context-specific acceptable consumption (Cruwys et al., 2014). However, in many contexts the norm is to overeat, or to eat when already satiated because of the presence of food, or simply because others are eating. It is therefore not surprising that in the context of adapting eating behaviour, or attempting to lose weight, the impact of others in social networks can be profound. Research in this area has typically focussed on three main types of groups that can be drawn on to influence weight. These include naturally occurring groups comprised of family and friends or groups of strangers who similarly want to lose weight, for example through community support groups, virtual online support forums, or clinically prescribed treatment groups. There are multiple other contexts where groups are likely utilised to moderate weight (e.g., sports groups). Here our focus is on the impact of naturally occurring groups and weight loss groups.

The impact of naturally occurring groups of family and friends

Achieving sustained reductions in weight can be exceptionally difficult and it is perhaps therefore not surprising that the support offered by immediate family and friends can have a significant impact on long-term improvements in healthy eating and weight loss. Research by Wing and Jeffery (1999) has demonstrated that recruiting participants to weight loss programmes with three friends is more effective than is recruiting participants alone. People recruited to these programmes with their friends are more likely to complete weight loss programmes than those recruited alone (98 per cent completion vs 79 per cent), they lose significantly more weight than those recruited alone (8.8kg vs 6.7kg after four months), and are also more likely to maintain their weight loss after 10 months (Wing & Jeffery, 1999). Moreover, the authors found that perceived social support from others in the groups was significantly related to weight loss (Wing & Jeffery, 1999), suggesting that it is not just the presence of friends that is important but the perceived support that they offer. As Haslam, Reicher, and Levine (2012) discuss, social support is structured and shaped by the identities that inform the support, with support that comes from an ingroup source being the most likely to be effective at achieving its intended goal (see also, Farrow & Tarrant, 2009).

Despite these encouraging findings, other studies have found no benefit on weight loss of friends attending weight loss groups together (Marquez & Wing, 2013), and no benefit of spouse attendance at weight loss groups (Black & Lantz, 1984; Jeffery et al., 1984). In other studies social support interventions utilising couple support have been shown to impact positively on weight loss after two to three months, but not thereafter (Black, Gleser, & Kooyers, 1990; Perri, McAllister, Gange, Jordan, McAdoo, & Nezu, 1988). In treating obese patients with type II diabetes, Wing, Marcus, Epstein, and Jawad (1991) found no significant difference in total weight loss post-treatment or at one-year follow-up for those treated alone or those treated with their spouses, although there were gender differences with women losing more weight when treated with their spouses and men achieving greater weight loss when treated alone. Although the reasons for this are debateable, Wing et al. discuss evidence suggesting that a man's weight often determines the food that is available within the household and therefore involving him in the weight loss programme may empower women to make changes to food planning and preparation; conversely husbands attending programmes with their partners may be more likely to delegate control over food planning to their wives and thereby become less involved and motivated if attending as a couple. Other studies indicate that partners may actually hinder weight loss by sabotaging attempts to lose weight or commenting critically about weight loss (e.g., you look 'too thin'), with participants commenting that they have felt guilty if they lost more weight than other dieting partners (Thomas, Hyde, Karunaratne, Kausman, & Komesaroff, 2008). These findings suggest that it is not just simply the presence and support of other ingroup members that can help to motive weight loss but, perhaps critically, whether or not those individuals share the values with the person trying to lose weight. Whether other ingroup members prioritise health or see behaviour change as self-relevant and identity affirming may be critical in determining the impact of their support.

Other close family members such as parents can have a positive impact on weight loss if involved in weight loss programmes for overweight children (Epstein, Valoski, Wing, & McCurley, 1990; Lloyd & Wyatt, 2015), although in adolescents the evidence for parental effects is mixed (McLean, Griffin, Toney, & Hardeman, 2003). This difference may reflect changes in independence that arise as children reach adolescence and the multiple influences that develop upon their food intake and other social activities, with peer groups and friendship groups becoming increasingly influential on eating behaviour during adolescence (Houldcroft, Haycraft, & Farrow, 2015). In the case of younger children, families can often be very involved in meal planning, preparation and access to exercise; therefore the motivation and support of family and friends can be key to ensuring success. Overall it seems that the group support offered by naturally occurring groups of family and friends *can* aid weight loss for overweight or obese individuals but this effect may often be transient and may depend very much on the kin's level of motivation, their own weight concerns, eating habits and the identity relevance of their weight to their self-concept.

The impact of weight loss support groups

Social group meetings for weight loss management

As Reider and Ruderman (2007) explain, eating and physical activity are both social behaviours, and sustained weight loss requires long-term behavioural changes which may require support that extends beyond personal resources. Observational and experimental studies have demonstrated that social support can be effective for reducing weight, and Reider and Ruderman (2007) conceptualise this support in terms of emotional support, instrumental support, informational support and appraisal. These forms of support can be provided in groups. Social support has long been seen as integral to the success of weight loss programmes and community-based models of weight loss support which utilise formally organised group contact can be effective, with weight losses sustained over follow up periods at six and 18 months (Latner, Ciao, Wendicke, Murakami, & Durson, 2013). These groups typically provide information about healthy eating, exercise, tips for making dietary changes and focus on shared encouragement and celebration of successful weight loss. Similarly to other mutual aid groups for addressing addictions such as

Alcoholics Anonymous (Rice & Tonigan, 2012), these formally organised groups will often focus on building group cohesion through sharing tips for achieving health targets and celebrating success when group members reach goals (in this case for weight loss). Indeed, King and Frederiksen (1984) found that in relation to jogging, social support interventions which focus on developing a group identity, fostering intragroup co-operation, inter-group competition, team building and social support within the group have been effective at nearly doubling the number of jogging episodes that individuals engage with in relation to a control condition.

A large number of commercial group programmes exist which report success in supporting individuals in achieving weight loss goals. One well-known example is Weight Watchers (www.weightwatchers.com/uk/). Groups such as Weight Watchers rely on the support that individuals can derive from social groups in helping them achieve and sustain weight loss. Although social support via groups is obviously not the only element to plans such as Weight Watchers (for example other elements focus on self-motivation, activity motivation and counting points for calories), it is one element which Weight Watchers itself acknowledges as fundamental to successful weight loss. Weight Watchers describes groups as "a place to learn golden nuggets of information on how to lose weight successfully . . . share top tips for following our plan and you can hear from other members living the plan" (*www.weightwatchers.co.uk/plan/?skipmap=1*). The impact of such groups is well documented: for example Madigan, Daley, Lewis, Jolly, and Aveyward (2014) conducted a prospective study with over 3,000 adults to compare the effectiveness of such commercial programs. They found that participants attending Weight Watchers lost on average 4.2kg at three months, reducing to 3.7kg at 12 months and that similar weight losses were achieved in participants attending other group based programs such as Rosemary Conley (www.rosemaryconley.com/) and Slimming World (www.slimmingworld.co.uk/). In contrast those attending NHS group programs, which are typically more expensive to run, lost a lower amount of weight. The effectiveness of these commercial schemes has been confirmed in other studies using randomised controlled trials, where participants assigned to commercial programs have been shown to lose about twice as much weight (-5.06kg on average) than those in standard care (Jebb et al., 2011), accompanied by reductions in waist circumference and fat mass which would reduce the risk of cardiovascular disease and type II diabetes (Knowler et al., 2002; Saaristo et al., 2010).

Virtual online support groups

For many individuals, attending group meetings such as those offered by commercial programmes can be difficult practically, physically or psychologically. Many people find attending group support sessions difficult due to time constraints, work constraints, and other commitments such as child-care, while others may prefer to avoid such groups for reasons such as shyness or concerns about the stigma attached to their condition (White & Dorman, 2001). For these reasons, internet-based support resources can offer a sustainable and viable resource either as an alternative to, or as an addition to, attending more structured group sessions. Internet health communities offer a potential alternative encouraging anonymous sharing of experiences, providing support, advice and motivation through online blogs, chat-rooms and discussion forums. Additionally, internet forums may appeal to people because they enable access to support across unrestricted geographical areas and allow participation at convenient times free from judgement or stigma. Wright, Rains, and Banas (2010) have described how the support gained from what they describe as 'weak' social ties can often be valuable for providing access to objective opinions, different perspectives and less demand in terms of reciprocal obligations than are often felt from stronger ties to family and friends. In this sense these weak ties, while transient, may actually be strong because they are maximally relevant to individual needs. Given the possible advantages of online support, it is notable that it is now often an associated element of many commercial weight loss programmes.

Despite some enthusiastic support for the benefits of online weight loss group programmes, some evidence presents a more complex account of their effects. Some studies have reported less weight loss in commercial online programmes when compared to those using a weight loss manual which provided 16 step-by-step lessons to modify eating, activity and thinking around weight (Womble et al., 2004), whereas others have found that online weight maintenance programmes are as effective for achieving weight loss compared to in-person support programmes, with 62 per cent of participants sustaining weight loss of at least 5 per cent after one year (Harvey-Berino, Pintauro, Buzzell, & Gold, 2004). In other randomised controlled trials, on-line interventions have been shown to be effective at achieving greater weight loss compared to education alone (Tate, Wing, & Winett, 2001). Differences likely reflect the different content of such sites, user motivation, and the support that is offered to users within the programmes; here social support from other users may be central in supporting and motivating participants to persist with their weight loss efforts. Indeed, online programmes with overweight and obese participants which provide structured, therapist-led behavioural interventions which explicitly encourage peer interaction and group support have been shown to result in impressive mean weight losses of 8.3kg after six months (mean starting weight = 92kg: Gold, Burke, Pintauro, Buzzell, & Harvey-Berino, 2007). Such findings suggest that group identity interactions may be critical to motivating successful weight loss.

Along similar lines, Hwang et al. (2010) have begun to explore how members interact in such groups and how the social support derived from them may motivate members to persist with weight loss efforts. In a mixed methods survey with 193 people about their experiences of a free internet weight loss community (www.sparkpeople.com), members reported using the online forums frequently with over 56 per cent of participants reading messages, 36 per cent responding to messages and 18 per cent posting discussions on at least a daily basis. In follow-up interviews, participants described how internet support forums gave them encouragement and motivation (88 per cent of respondents), information (59 per cent) and shared experiences (43 per cent) with 60 per cent of participants agreeing that other online members were more helpful than other people in supporting weight loss. As one member commented: "They're like a family. No one tears you down or believes your statements/questions are dumb. They're better than family, actually. A great support group" (p. 10).

Moreover, comments about the competitive nature of group interactions appeared to motivate some participants: "Being a part of a team, gives it somewhat of a competitive nature to try to exercise more to climb up the team leader-board for exercise minutes. That's definitely a help to my weight loss efforts" (p. 10).

Although there are concerns about the accuracy of what members may post online in terms of providing incorrect advice or counterproductive tips, Hwang et al. (2007) have shown that weight loss advice online is generally accurate and conforms with clinical guidelines. This reiterates the value of engaging those effected by the health condition themselves in contributing towards treatment (Coulter & Collins, 2011; Abraham & Gardner, 2009). Moreover, it may be that fellow sufferers can positively contribute in this way for the very reason that they are likely to be seen as ingroup members. In line with a social identity perspective (e.g., Tajfel & Turner, 1979; Turner et al., 1987), the sense of shared group identity and in-group derived support is more effective than that derived from outgroups because in-group members are more likely to be seen as supportive and well-intentioned (Haslam, Reicher, & Levine, 2012). Ballantine and Stephenson (2011) have explored individual differences in the ways that social support is offered and received by individuals using an online Weight Watchers Facebook page. Ballantine and Stephenson found that there were three main categories of styles that users adopted when interacting with the online support groups: Passive Recipients (47 per cent) who receive emotional support and the highest levels of information support, but do so by being passive members; Active Supporters (32 per cent) who also receive a high level of information and emotional support but are active in their communications; and Casual Browsers (21 per cent) who are passive in their communications and receive little social support. Interestingly there were no differences among support style according to gender, age, or internet ability but active supporters were more likely to have been members of the group for longer, whereas passive recipients were most likely to be satisfied with the support that they were receiving through the group. These findings demonstrate that there are important individual differences between the ways that people interact with groups which reflect their engagement, communication style and their access to support from the group. However little is known about how these differences impact on achieving weight loss goals, and how they can be used to best promote health through groups. This is clearly a challenge in groups where participation has been prescribed, for example by a clinician, and which will therefore likely contain people who, outside of the group, possibly would not identify with each other.

Although there are encouraging results from on-line weight loss support programmes, it is clear that much more research is needed into the long-term success of these group programmes. A particular challenge for these programmes is to maintain weight losses, with evidence across the board suggesting that participants on them tend to regain weight over longer term follow ups (Wing & Hill, 2011). Here internet based resources may present a viable solution to engage participants over longer periods of time to achieve sustained reductions in weight as a form of continuity of care. Perhaps programmes that promote long-term supportive relationships between members would be the most effective at achieving sustained weight loss, and a goal for further research may be to capitalise on these group-initiated interactions to improve engagement and support for users who are typically poorly engaged.

The impact of clinical weight management groups

The rise in the prevalence of obesity, and the concurrent increasing burden on health services, has meant that group based treatments are increasingly being prescribed by clinicians to deliver education, support and treatment for those with morbid levels of obesity for whom weight poses a very real risk to health. Weight management within the NHS is dealt with through four 'tiers', with each using different activities to approach weight loss. Local definitions vary but usually tier 1 includes universal services such as primary care and health promotion; tier 2 includes lifestyle interventions; tier 3 reflects services that specialise in weight management; and tier 4 comprises bariatric surgery. As a result of the reported effectiveness of commercial programs, the UK National Health Service (NHS) now funds referrals to programs such as Weight Watchers for tier 2 care. Such treatment programmes have reported some effectiveness for patients in achieving reductions in weight of on average 5.6 per cent for those completing a first course (Jebb et al., 2011), such weight loss is associated with clinical benefits such as a reduced risk of progression to type II diabetes (Jebb et al., 2011; Saaristo et al., 2010). Our own research has explored the function and impact of groups for improving health behaviours and achieving weight loss goals at a tier 3 NHS service operating in the South West of the UK. Patients are referred to this service for an intense programme of weight management for morbid obesity to reduce weight and unhealthy eating behaviours. Depending on their progression (and personal desire), patients may be referred on for bariatric surgery if their body mass index is above 40kg/m2 or above 35kg/m2 with co-morbidities such as type II diabetes. Funding for bariatric surgery is considered if patients do not have surgical contraindications and can demonstrate a sustained commitment to lifestyle change by achieving weight loss of at least 5 per cent across the programme. However, many participants engage with the programme but choose to not continue to surgery.

Between 2012 and 2015 we conducted a programme of research with these groups to explore patients' progression through the weight management programme, with a focus on whether and how participants' sense of social identity as group members structured their experiences and subsequent health. The group programme comprised six sessions delivered during a six-month period with group sizes typically ranging from four–12 patients according to attendance. The sessions are led by a dietician experienced in motivational interviewing and group facilitation, and are designed to provide dietary education and teach participants about mindful eating. In a qualitative study, we interviewed 20 patients (12 males and eight females, mean age = 52 years, range 34–77 years) who had been registered with the bariatric service for at least six months. Participants had attended between two and nine sessions ($M = 5$, $SD = 2$) at the time of interview. Interviews were semi-structured and addressed participants' perspectives on their experiences of the group sessions and the form and function of their psychological connections within groups. Interviews lasted between 17–50 minutes, for further details see Tarrant, Shah, Daly, Kos, Khan, & Farrow, (in preparation).

Thematic analysis was conducted using Braun and Clarke's six-step process (2006) and indicated that participants strongly valued their participation in the groups and viewed them as a resource for achieving lifestyle change. Beyond documenting this supportive influence, however, the research allowed us to build a picture of how new groups come together and to learn lessons about how new connections between group members can be facilitated. The broad content of the interviews reflected many of the messages coming out of the research discussed earlier, with participants viewing the groups as a resource which supported their achievement of lifestyle change goals. Participants reflected on the role of the group facilitator in establishing interaction and a sense of group culture through which participants could share information and advice. Participants described how this shared social identity was central to the success of the programme and to improvements in health.

> Yeah, well I think, I think, adopting that identity, within the, oh what's the word, within the context of the group, oh . . . I think, I can sort this out, I probably don't need to diet that much, because, this is what is putting all the weight on, yeah, and I want to identify with it, because, I've found some kindred spirits, and, I can see the positive, changes, that I think will happen as a result of having that identity.

Participants explored how they felt a stronger sense of ownership over the materials used and information gained from the group when they had collectively developed and contributed to group resources (for example through sharing tips for weight-loss). They described how forming new psychological connections with other patients who were also embarking on the same journey provided them with social support which motivated and sustained them in losing weight.

> I think it gives you support. It's good to know that there are other people going through the same thing . . . you get support and off you go again. It's the support mainly more than anything.

Often this would be through raising a sense of not being alone, but also practically by celebrating successes of other group members (i.e., weight loss), supporting each other when goals had not been achieved, and sharing ideas for how to stay on track with weight loss goals (e.g., sharing meal plans, motivational tips). As one group member described, the sense of shared identity was central to the group's cause:

> You're not alone, yes. And it's like a rallying cry isn't it, you know like the olden days, you get a rallying cry and everybody gets together. People have a common cause, that's what it's all about.

Group members also described how their new social identity motivated them and improved their sense of self-efficacy to make lifestyle changes, which was unique to the type of support that can be derived from family and friends:

> . . . support [at the group] I think is more beneficial because you are all in the same boat, you're all doing the same thing. You can learn from each other and you can you know you can bounce off each other that sort of thing. You know the support is there, you're all in the same wavelength so everybody knows what each other's going through, whereas family and friends sort of get the back end of it whereas they get to know exactly what you are going through, your family and friends just get the bits when you know you haven't lost much weight and you need a shoulder to cry on that sort of support but I feel that the group have more understanding.

Here it appears the cohesiveness of the group and sense of shared empathy and understanding is critical to group effectiveness, and group leaders likely have a central role to facilitating trust, empathy and a sense of shared group meaning.

> I mean I suppose because you've got two professional people taking the group and they've got a lot of expertise between them. So I mean they come up with some very good ideas and strategies and so I think having the two professional people there rather than just having the group of patients is very useful so I think that helps.

Further research is required to provide empirical evidence for group leaders about how to best capitalise on shared group experiences and promote a sense of culture to drive group support in this way in the context of weight management programmes. Quantitatively we also explored whether engagement with the group programmes impacted on actual weight loss and improved healthy eating behaviours. On average participants lost 5 per cent of their body weight after engaging with the group sessions in the obesity management programme, losses which are clinically meaningful to improve health and reduce the risk of type II diabetes by 58–69 per cent over one year (Knowler et al., 2002; Saaristo et al., 2010). Furthermore, we observed reductions in unhealthy eating behavioural tendencies such as binge eating, eating, shape and weight concern, as well as improvements in health related quality of life following engagement with group sessions. Scores between Time 1 (entry to the programme) and Time 2 (completion of the programme) significantly decreased for eating concern (M = 2.81 vs. 2.08); shape concern (M = 5.56 vs. 4.67); weight concern (M = 5.18 vs. 4.36); and binge eating episodes (M = 3.28 vs. .98) (all *ps* < .05). In terms of health related quality of life, participant scores increased from entry to completion of the programme (M = 2.71 vs. 3.41). These findings suggest that participating in group-based weight loss programmes of this nature can result in reducing unhealthy eating behaviours, improving overall quality of life and ultimately achieving the aim of reducing weight.

We were further able to explore whether and how social identity within the group facilitated these improvements in health. Participants reported general increases from Time 1 to Time 2 in their sense of social support both from within the weight loss group (M = 4.35 vs. 4.62, p =.07) and also externally from family and friends outside of the group (M = 5.54 vs. 5.77, p =.03). This may suggest that group participation increased participants' ability to draw on social support more generally. Furthermore, it appears that those who became most strongly identified with the group may have gained the most from participation in it: social identification was positively related to the sense of social support derived from the programme (r = .43, p = .007), and also to improvements in health related quality of life (r = .40, p < .05).

Overall these findings suggest that the quality of the group dynamic, and the psychological connections formed between members, are critical to the success of the group for achieving sustained improvements in health, and further they may be interpreted to suggest that social identity is one means through which self-efficacy is increased and information is accessed and used successfully by patients. Groups of this nature offer patients access to social support and shared social identification with other morbidly obese patients which is unlikely to be easy to access elsewhere, and these findings indicate that the effectiveness of group support of this nature could be maximised by encouraging and fostering social identity with groups early on in the formation of the group's identity.

Although patients in our research were registered for consideration as bariatric surgery candidates, many patients in our study did not progress to surgery and achieved changes that enabled them to continue to manage their weight without surgical intervention. However, group support arguably should be a central part of treatment for those patients who are awaiting or have undergone bariatric surgery, where many patients fail to lose sufficient weight post-surgery (e.g., Snyder et al., 2009 found that 15 per cent of patients in their study failed to lose 50 per cent of their target excess weight). Indeed, the Surgical Review Corporation (SRC) states that Bariatric Centres of Excellence must make supportive and supervised groups available to patients who may undergo or have undergone a bariatric procedure (Surgical Review Corporation, 2013). There is encouraging evidence about the potential impact of groups for helping to achieve sustained weight loss where patients have undergone surgery. In a systematic review Livhits et al. (2011) report that support groups were positively associated with the degree of weight loss post-surgery for bariatric patients. More specifically, Orth, Madan, Taddeucci, Coday, and Tichansky (2008) have found that patients who attended post-operative support group meetings after their bariatric surgery lost more weight post-surgery than those who had not attended support group meetings (42 per cent compared to 32 per cent decrease in BMI), while Song, Reinhardt, Buzdon, and Liao (2007) found that patients lost more weight after a gastric bypass if they attended more than 5 group support sessions post-surgery. Importantly in the Orth et al. study there were no differences between the two groups who chose to attend or not attend support group meetings in terms of distance from, or time to, the clinic, although non-attenders did report that family obligations made attending meetings more difficult, and that they felt the groups were not needed for them/ would not impact on their weight loss (Orth et al., 2008). This demonstrates how personal psychological variables such as self-efficacy, as well as practical influences such as family commitments may moderate the benefits that can be derived from group support. Of course, it may be that patients attending support groups are simply more motivated, both to lose weight and to comply with the group's meetings, and that this confounds the effectiveness of group attendance, but overall it appears that post-surgery groups can offer support and help to reinforce continued education, which is important as many patients report forgetting pre-operative known facts (Madan & Tichansky, 2005). Given that there is currently limited joined up provision of care for pre / post-surgery, a challenge is to not see surgery or successful progression through tier 3 as the end point for patients, but as part of the longer-term care needs of this vulnerable group.

Conclusions and recommendations

Groups are increasingly being used as a means to deliver healthcare with group based interventions being regularly prescribed in the UK to help reduce addictive behaviours such as smoking, drug use, alcohol use, as well as a range of health conditions including obesity. There is growing evidence that the psychological connections that exist between group members and the sense of shared social identity that is fostered by such groups are fundamental for shaping whether group experiences are positive or negative, and ultimately how successful the group is at achieving its health goals for individual members. Although many healthcare conditions have guidelines for the content of group information, there exists no current template for how to maximise social identity within groups. Given the implications for health, and the likely variability that exists between group provision, the development of such guidelines could be of considerable health benefit.

Future research is needed to extend our understanding of the social and psychological processes through which group based support promotes and fosters health behaviour, as well as the methods that are most effective for promoting group identification to support health. Ultimately the development of a tool-kit to offer guidance for group facilitators about how to generate and sustain social identity and promote common group-goals in support or intervention groups would be of considerable benefit. Such a manual would need to be condition specific to consider the unique influences on identification, discrimination and diversity that exist for different health conditions; accordingly, there are likely to be several strategies that would be effective for increasing identification across different conditions. For example, participants attending groups to achieve health goals will have different motivations, different goals and different past experiences (often negative) linked to their ill-health. Group facilitators can act to manage this diversity and utilise it to find common experiences that help to establish a sense of shared identity. The empathy and facilitation skills of group leaders are also central to developing a sense of inclusion and facilitating interaction between group members. Although group facilitators are likely to receive education and training about developing and leading groups, ongoing training about how to maximise trust, empathy and inclusion by promoting a sense of shared consideration of patient perspectives and individual needs is likely to facilitate group cohesion. In addition, training for group facilitators to develop effective group management skills which foster a sense of group specific identification and prevent the formation of dysfunctional groups (e.g., those comprising disruptive or unengaged patients), or the emergence of maladaptive group norms (e.g., which reinforce negative health behaviours) is likely to be beneficial. Some of the strategies explored in Tarrant et al. (2015) might prove useful in this regard. A challenge for future research is to focus upon developing theoretically-driven evidence which can be used to guide group leaders in how to effectively utilise social identity processes to facilitate behaviour change in the context of addictive ill-health behaviours.

Acknowledgements

This research was supported by a grant from Leverhulme Trust (RPG-368) and also by the National Institute for Health Research (NIHR) Collaboration for Leadership in Applied Health Research and Care of the South West Peninsula (PenCLAHRC). The views expressed in this publication are those of the authors and not necessarily those of Leverhulme Trust, NIHR, PenCLAHRC, NHS, or the Department of Health. We are grateful to Jenni Chater for her assistance with the transcription of interviews reported in the discussion of our research with clinical weight management groups.

References

Abraham, C. & Gardner, B. (2009). What psychological and behaviour changes are initiated by 'expert patient' training and what training techniques are most helpful? *Psychology and Health*, *24*, 1153–1165.

Anderson, P. M. & Butcher, K. E. (2006). Childhood obesity: Trends and potential causes. *Future Child*, *16*, 19–45.

Andreyeva, T., Puhl, R. M., & Brownell, K. D. (2008). Changes in perceived weight discrimination among Americans: 1995–1996 through 2004–2006. *Obesity (Silver Spring)*, *16*, 1129–1134.

Ballantine, P. W. & Stephenson, R. J. (2011). Help me, I'm fat! Social support in online weight loss networks. *Journal of Consumer Behaviour, 10*, 332–337.

BBC News (2006). *Parents feed pupils through gates*. Retrieved from http://news.bbc.co.uk/1/hi/england/south_yorkshire/5349392.stm.

Black, D. R., Gleser, L. J., & Kooyers, K. J. (1990). A meta-analytic evaluation of couples weight-loss programs. *Health Psychology, 9*, 330–247.

Black, D. R. & Lantz, C. E. (1984). Spouse involvement and a possible long term follow-up trap in weight loss. *Behaviour Research and Therapy, 22*, 557– 562.

Braun, V. & Clarke, V. (2006). Using thematic analysis in psychology. *Qualitative Research in Psychology, 3*, 77–101.

Coulter, A. & Collins, A. (2011). *Making shared decision-making a reality. No decision about me, without me*. The King's Fund. Retrieved from www.kingsfund.org.uk/sites/files/kf/Making-shared-decision-making-a-reality-paper-Angela-Coulter-Alf-Collins-July-2011_0.pdf.

Cruwys, T., Bevelander, K. E., & Hermans, R. C. (2015). Social modeling of eating: A review of when and why social influence affects food intake and choice. *Appetite, 86*, 3–18.

Davis, C. & Carter, J. C. (2009). Compulsive overeating as an addiction disorder. A review of theory and evidence. *Appetite, 53*, 1–8.

Epstein, L. H., Valoski, A., Wing, R. R., & McCurley, J. (1990). Ten-year follow-up of behavioral, family-based treatment for obese children. *Journal of the American Medical Association, 264*, 2519–2523.

Farrow, C. & Tarrant, M. (2009). Weight-based discrimination, body dissatisfaction and emotional eating: The role of social group norms. *Psychology and Health, 24*, 1021–1034.

Frings, D. & Albery, I. P. (2015). The Social Identity Model of Cessation Maintenance: Formulation and initial evidence. *Addictive Behaviors, 44*, 35–42.

Gearhardt, A. N., Grilo, C.M., Dileone, R. J., Brownell, K. D., & Potenza, M. N. (2011). Can food be addictive? Public health and policy implications. *Addiction, 106*, 1208–1212.

Gold, B. C., Burke, S., Pintauro, S., Buzzell, P., & Harvey-Berino, J. (2007). Weight loss on the web: A pilot study comparing a structured behavioral intervention to a commercial program. *Obesity, 15*, 155–64.

Harvey-Berino, J., Pintauro, S., Buzzell, P., & Gold, B.C. (2004). Effect of internet support on the long-term maintenance of weight loss. *Obesity Research & Clinical Practice, 12*, 320–329.

Haslam, S. A., Reicher, S. D., & Levine, M. (2012). When other people are heaven, when other people are hell: How social identity determines the nature and impact of social support. In J. Jetten, C. Haslam & S. A. Haslam (Eds.), *The social cure: identity, health, and well-being* (pp. 157–174). Hove, UK and New York: Psychology Press.

Hitchman, S. C. Fong, G. T., Zanna, M. P., Thrasher, J. F., & Laux, F. L. (2014). The relation between number of smoking friends, and quit intentions, attempts, and success: Findings from the International Tobacco Control (ITC) Four Country Survey. *Psychology of Addictive Behaviors, 28*, 1144–1152.

Higgs, S. (2015). Social norms and their influence on eating behaviours. *Appetite, 86*, 38–44.

Houldcroft, L., Haycraft, E., & Farrow, C. (2015). Social and individual influences on eating in preadolescents: The role of friends' eating behaviours and individual anxiety and depression. *Advances in Pediatric Research, 2*, 1–10.

Hwang, K. O., Farheen, K., Johnson, C. W., Thomas, E. J., Barnes, A. S., & Bernstam, E. V. (2007). Quality of weight loss advice on internet forums. *American Journal of Medicine, 120*, 604–609.

Hwang, K. O., Ottenbacher, A. J., Green, A. P., Cannon-Diehl, M. R., Richardson, O., Bernstam, E. V., & Thomas, E. J. (2010). Social support in an internet weight loss community. *International Journal of Medical Informatics, 79*, 5–13.

Jebb, S.A., Ahern, A. L., Olson, A. D., Aston, L. A., Holzapfel, C., Stoll, J., . . . Caterson, I. A. (2011). Primary care referral to a commercial provider for weight loss treatment versus standard care: A randomised controlled trial, *The Lancet*, *378*, 1485–1492.

Jetten, J., Haslam, C., & Haslam, A. (2012). *The social cure: Identity, health, and well-being*. Hove, UK and New York: Psychology Press.

Jeffery, R. W., Bjornson-Benson, W. M., Rosenthal, B. S., Lindquist, R. A., Kurth, C. L., & Johnson, S. L. (1984). Correlates of weight loss and its maintenance over two years of follow-up among middle-aged men. *Preventative Medicine*, *13*, 155–168.

King, A. C., & Frederiksen, L. W. (1984). Low cost strategies for increasing exercise behaviour. Relapse prevention and social support. *Behavior Modification*, *8*, 13–21.

Knowler, W. C., Barrett-Connoer, E., Fowler, S. E., Hamman, R. F., Lachin, J. M., Walker, E. A., & Nathan, D. M. (2002). Diabetes Prevention Program Research Group. Reduction in the incidence of type 2 diabetes with lifestyle intervention or metformin. *New England Journal of Medicine*, *34*, 393–403.

Latner, J. D., Ciao, A. C., Wendicke, A. U., Murakami, J. M., & Durson, L. E. (2013). Community-based behavioral weight-loss treatment: Long-term maintenance of weight loss, physiological, and psychological outcomes. *Behaviour Research and Therapy*, *51*, 451–459.

Latner, J. & Stunkard, A. (2003). Getting Worse: The Stigmatization of Obese Children. *Obesity Research*, *11*, 1550–8528.

Livhits, M., Mercado, C., Yermilov, I., Parikh, J.A., Dutson, E., Mehran, A., Ko, C.Y., Shekelle, P.G., & Gibbons, M.M. (2011). Is social support associated with greater weight loss after bariatric surgery? A systematic review. *Obesity Review*, *12*, 142–148.

Lloyd, J., & Wyatt, K. (2015). The Healthy Lifestyles Programme (HeLP) – An Overview of and Recommendations Arising from the Conceptualisation and Development of an Innovative Approach to Promoting Healthy Lifestyles for Children and Their Families. *International Journal of Environmental Research and Public Health*, *12*, 1003–1019.

McLean, N., Griffin, S., Toney, K., & Hardeman, W. (2003). Family involvement in weight control, weight maintenance and weight-loss interventions: A systematic review of randomised trials. *International Journal of Obesity and Related Metabolic Disorders*, *27*, 987–1005.

Madan, A. K. & Tichansky, D. S. (2005). Patients postoperatively forget aspects of preoperative patient education. *Obesity Surgery*, *15*, 1066–1069.

Madigan, C. D., Daley, A. J., Lewis, A. L., Jolly, K., & Aveyard, P. (2014). Which weight-loss programmes are as effective as Weight Watchers (R)?: Non-inferiority analysis. *British Journal of General Practice*, *64*, e128–e136.

Marquez, B. & Wing, R. R. (2013). Feasibility of Enlisting Social Network Members to Promote Weight Loss among Latinas. *Journal of the Academy of Nutrition and Dietetics*, *113*, 680–687.

Meule, A. & Gearhardt, A. N. (2014). Five years of the Yale Food Addiction Scale: Taking stock and moving forward. *Current Addiction Reports*, *1*, 193–205.

Ogden, C. L., Carroll, M. D., Kit, B. K., & Flegal, K. M., (2014). Prevalence of childhood and adult obesity in the United States, 2011–2012. *The Journal of the American Medical Association*, *311*, 806–814.

Orth, W. S., Madam, A. K., Taddeucci, R. J., Coday, M., & Tichansky, D. S. (2008). Support group meeting attendance is associated with better weight loss. *Obesity Surgery*, *18*, 391–394.

Oyserman, D., Fryberg, S. A., & Yoder, N. (2007). Identity-based motivation and health. *Journal of Personality and Social Psychology*, *93*, 1011–1027.

Perkins, W. H. (2002). Social norms and the prevention of alcohol misuse in college contexts.*Journal of Studies on Alcohol*, *14*, 164–172.

Perrri, M. G., McAllister, D. A., Gange, J. J., Jordan, R. C., McAdoo, G., & Nezu, A. M. (1988). Effects of four maintenance programs on the long-term management of obesity. *Journal of Consulting Clinical Psychology, 56*, 529–534.

Polivy, J. & Pliner, P. (2015). 'She got more than me': Social comparison and the social context of eating. *Appetite, 86*, 88–95.

Previte, J., Fry, M. L., Drennan, J., & Hasan, S. F. (2015). Friends or foes: Group influence effects on moderate drinking behaviors. *Journal of Business Research, 68*, 2146–2154.

Puhl, R. & Brownell, K. D. (2001). Bias, discrimination, and obesity. *Obesity Research, 9*, 788–805.

Randolph, T. G. (1956). The descriptive features of food addiction. Addictive eating and drinking. *Quarterly Journal of Studies on Alcohol, 17*, 198–224.

Reider, S. & Ruderman, A. (2007). The development and validation of the weight management support inventory. *Eating Behaviors, 81*, 39–47.

Rice, S. L. & Tonigan, J. S. (2012). Impressions of Alcoholics Anonymous (AA) Group Cohesion: A case for a nonspecific factor predicting later AA attendance. *Alcoholism Treatment Quarterly*, 30, 40–51.

Robinson, E. (2015). Perceived social norms and eating behaviour: An evaluation of studies and future directions. *Physiology & Behavior, 152*, 397–401.

Robinson, E., Benwell, H., & Higgs, S. (2013). Food intake norms increase and decrease snack food intake in a remote confederate study. *Appetite, 65*, 20–24.

Robinson, E., Fleming, A., & Higgs, S. (2014). Prompting healthier eating: testing the use of health and social norm based messages. *Health Psychology, 33*, 1057–1064.

Saaristo, T., Moilanen, L., Korpi-Hyovalti, E., Vanhala, M., Saltevo, J., Niskanen, L., Jokelainen, J., Peltonen, M., Oksa, H., Tuomilehto, J., Uusitupa, M., & Keinänen-Kiukaanniemi, S. (2010). Lifestyle intervention for prevention of type 2 diabetes in primary health care: One-year follow-up of the Finnish national diabetes prevention program (FIN-D2D). *Diabetes Care Volume, 33*, 2146–2151.

Shiffman, S., Li, X., Dunbar, M. S., Ferguson, S.G., Tindle, H. A., & Scholl, S. M. (2015). Social smoking among intermittent smokers. *Drug and Alcohol Dependence, 154*, 184–191.

Snyder, B., Nguyen, A., Scarbourough, T., Yu, S., & Wilson, E. (2009). Comparison of those who succeed in losing significant excessive weight after bariatric surgery and those who fail. *Surgical Endoscopy, 23*, 2302–2236.

Song, Z., Reinhardt, K., Buzdon, M., & Liao, P. (2008). Associations between support group attendance and weight loss after roux-en-y gastric bypass. *Surgery for Obesity and Related Disorders, 4*, 100–103.

Surgical Review Corporation (2013) Accreditation: Centre of Excellence. Retrieved from www.surgicalreview.org/facilities/accreditation/requirements/center-of-excellence/.

Tajfel, H. & Turner, J. C. (1986). An integrative theory of intergroup conflict. In S. Worchel & W. G. Austin (Eds.), *Social psychology of intergroup relations* (pp. 2–24). Chicago, IL: Nelson-Hall.

Tarrant, M. & Butler, K. (2011). Effects of self-categorization on orientation towards health. *British Journal of Social Psychology, 50*, 121–139.

Tarrant, M., Hagger, M., & Farrow, C. (2012). Promoting positive orientation towards health through social identity. In J. Jetten, C. Haslam & S. A. Haslam (Eds.), *The social cure: identity, health, and well-being* (pp. 39–54). Hove, UK and New York: Psychology Press.

Tarrant, M., Shah, P., Daly, M., Kos, K., Khan, S., & Farrow, C. (in preparation). *Patient experiences of a bariatric group programme for managing obesity in secondary care: A qualitative interview study.*

Tarrant, M., Warmoth, K., Code, C., Dean, S., Goodwin, V. A., Stein, K., & Sugavanam, T. (2015 in press). Nurturing psychological connections in healthcare: Towards a guidance framework for developing group-based interventions. *British Medical Journal Open*.

Tate, D. F., Wing, R. R., & Winett, R. A. (2001). Using Internet technology to deliver a behavioral weight loss program. *Journal of the American Medical Association, 285*, 1172–1177.

Terry, D. J. & Hogg, M. A. (1996). Group norms and the attitude-behavior relationship: A role for group identification. *Personality and Social Psychology Bulletin, 22*, 776–793.

Thomas, S. L., Hyde, J., Karunaratne, A., Kausman, R., & Komesaroff, P. A. (2008). 'They all work . . . when you stick to them': A qualitative investigation of dieting, weight loss, and physical exercise, in obese individuals. *Nutrition Journal*, 7, 34–41.

Turner, J. C., Hogg, M. A., Oakes, P. J., Reicher, S. D., & Wetherell, M. S. (1987). *Rediscovering the social group: A self-categorization theory*. Oxford: Blackwell.

Wang, C., Bleich, S. N., & Gortmaker, S. L. (2008). Reference to this increasing caloric contribution from sugar-sweetened beverages and 100% fruit juices among US children and adolescents, 1988–2004. *Pediatrics, 121*, e1604–e1614.

Wang, S. S., Brownell, K. D., & Wadden, T. A. (2004). The influence of the stigma of obesity on overweight individuals. *International Journal of Obesity, 28*, 1333–1337.

White, M. & Dorman, S. M. (2001). Receiving social support online: implications for health education. *Health Education Research, 16*, 693–707.

Wing, R. R. & Hill, J. O. (2001). Successful weight loss maintenance. *Annual Review of Nutrition, 21*, 323–341.

Wing, R. R. & Jeffery, R. W. (1999). Benefits of recruiting participants with friends and increasing social support for weight loss and maintenance. *Journal of Consulting and Clinical Psychology, 67*, 132–138.

Wing, R. R., Marcus, M. D., Epstein, L. H., Jawad, A. (1991). A 'family based' approach to the treatment of obese type II diabetic patients. *Journal of Consulting and Clinical Psychology, 59*, 156–162.

Womble, G., Wadden, T. A., McGuckin, B. G., Sargent, S. L., Rothman, R. A., & Krauthamer-Ewing, E. S. (2004). A randomized controlled trial of a commercial Internet weight loss Program. *Obesity Research, 12*, 1011–1018.

Wright, K. B, Rains, S., & Banas, J. (2010). Weak-tie support network preference and perceived life stress among participants in health-related, computer-mediated support groups. *Journal of Computer-Mediated Communication, 15*, 606–624.

5

GROUP IDENTIFICATION AND ADDICTIVE HEALTH BEHAVIOURS IN ADOLESCENTS

Kirsty Miller, Juliet R. H. Wakefield and Fabio Sani

Good habits formed at youth make all the difference
(Aristotle)

Adolescents are an important population to investigate when considering the nature and origins of addiction. Adolescence is a time when many risky health behaviours begin, with drugs, smoking, and alcohol use increasing dramatically during this period (Nielsen, Ringgaard, Broholm, Sindballe, & Olsen, 2002). Consistent with Aristotle's words, such behaviours have a strong tendency to persist into adult life (Degenhardt et al., 2008).

Individuals who abuse substances throughout their lives are damaging to society, to the economy, and to their own health. Within Scotland, smoking is still the primary preventable cause of ill health and premature death (NHS National Services Scotland, 2014), being responsible for around 13,000 deaths each year, and many more hospital admissions (Scottish Government, 2008a). Excessive drinking increases the risk of lasting health damage, with alcohol-related mortality more than doubling in the last 15 years and alcohol use being responsible for 40,000 hospital discharges per year (Scottish Government, 2009). Excessive alcohol use also has social consequences, (e.g., family breakdown, crime, disorder, and sickness-related absence from work), which cost the economy an estimated £2.25 billion every year (Scottish Government, 2009). In addition to this, Scotland has a long-standing and serious drug problem, with an estimated 52,000 drug users presenting an economic and social cost of £2.6 billion per annum. While these figures refer to the consequences of Scots using a variety of substances, cannabis is the most commonly used illegal drug in Scotland, with one in three citizens using cannabis at some point in their lives, and one in 10 doing so in the past year (Scottish Government, 2008b). With these costs in mind, it makes sense to examine issues around adolescent addiction and health-related behaviour, and explore how we might encourage adolescents to form the life-long 'good habits' of which Aristotle spoke.

Research indicates that adolescents are particularly prone to engaging in negative health behaviours for several reasons, some of which relate to individualistic factors, and some of which relate to socially-determined factors (e.g., group memberships). While interest in the latter is growing, there has been a lack of theoretically based perspectives from which to address such issues. This chapter considers how the social identity approach to group psychology (Turner, Hogg, Oakes, Reicher, & Wetherell, 1987) can offer a solution. Building upon previous research which focuses on social factors, the social identity approach suggests that group *identification* (rather than group contact) has implications for health behaviour. Identity processes are then considered in relation to recent research in treatment settings, and suggestions for prevention are discussed. The chapter concludes by suggesting that the social identity approach provides an informative and nuanced perspective from which to address addictive behaviours in adolescence and adulthood.

Examining adolescent addictive behaviours in social terms

It is important to bear in mind that adolescence is a time of transition, often coinciding with loss and change of social groups (e.g., school, friends, and peers). This has implications not only for an individual's social world, but also for their identity and sense of self. In societies where children finish primary/elementary school and begin secondary/high school, this transition usually occurs during the early period of adolescence (around 11 or 12), and generally involves moving from one school to another, with the resulting change of location, staff, and peers. This potentially entails the loss of several core identities, which can have a variety of negative consequences (Breakwell, 1986; Chandler & Proulx, 2008; Hopkins & Reicher, 1997; Thoits, 1983). There can also be resistance to identification with the new group/s if old identities cannot be relinquished or reconciled so that they fit into the new context (Ellemers, 2003; Haslam, Eggins, & Reynolds, 2003). This can lead to feelings of isolation, confusion, and uncertainty.

This uncertainty can be confounded by adolescents' tendencies to distance themselves from the childhood identities linked to their immediate families (Seidman & French, 2004). The opinions and values of parents/caregivers become less important at this time, and the influence of such individuals declines. As this happens, the influence of friends usually becomes stronger (Collins & Steinberg, 2006; Viner et al., 2012), with adolescents perceiving peer validation as increasingly important (Hogg, Siegel, & Hohman, 2011). Feeling that one 'belongs' and 'fits in' is particularly important at this time, as is feeling valued, liked, and accepted by peers (Coleman, 1974; Erikson, 1968; Newman & Newman, 2001). Unfortunately, attempts to achieve these goals can encourage adolescents to engage in risky behaviour. Indeed, it has been shown that alcohol and cigarette use are frequently used as a method to display commitment to a peer group and to gain the group members' approval (Dolcini & Adler, 1994; Luther & McMahon, 1996). Drug use may also be used as a way to promote one's social standing (Luthar & D'Avanzo, 1999), with socially active and socially attractive adolescents more likely to use drugs (Selnow & Crano, 1986) and initiate marijuana use at an early age (Smith & Fogg, 1978). Siegel, Alvaro, Patel and Crano (2009) found that adolescents believed that using inhalants increased their popularity with peers, and those who reported greater substance use experienced higher ratings of peer admiration (Becker & Luthar, 2007), with cigarette, alcohol, and marijuana use higher among those who believed that they received peer support for their substance use (Duan, Chou, Andreeva, & Pentz, 2009). Furthermore, Odgers, Houghton, and Douglas (1996) found that once this reputation was achieved, adolescents attempted to maintain it by continuing to engage in such behaviour.

Addressing socially motivated adolescent addictive behaviours

It has been argued that policy makers have not responded adequately to the knowledge that these socially-motivated behaviours can have a large and sustained negative impact on adolescents' present and future wellbeing (Sawyer et al., 2012). This is particularly problematic given that the current population of adolescents is the largest in history, comprising more than a quarter of the world's population (Sawyer et al., 2012).

However, it is promising that researchers who are interested in adolescent health and health behaviours are increasingly calling for professionals and policymakers to adopt a social approach towards such issues. In particular, a recent series of papers published in *The Lancet* (Sawyer et al., 2012; Viner, 2012; Catalano et al., 2012; Patton et al., 2012) drew attention to the health-related plight of adolescents, along with the importance of seeking to improve adult health through the use of the life-course theory, which focuses on how our childhood and adolescent experiences impact upon our adult health and wellbeing. Ultimately, the authors' recommendation was that the wellbeing of adolescents should be considered from a primarily social perspective.

This viewpoint echoes recent developments within the world health agenda (e.g., The Lancet, 2009) which suggest that traditional definitions of health and wellbeing need to be reconceptualised. Within our own country, Scotland's then-Chief Medical Officer, Sir Harry Burns, claimed in 2014 that traditional definitions of such terms fail to consider "the close and complex interrelationships between an individual's societal and environmental circumstances and their sense of well-being" (Burns, 2012, p. 4). In response, Burns referred to definitions of health that are firmly couched in social terms, such as an "ability to perform personally valued family, work and community roles" and an "ability to deal with physical, biologic, psychological and social stress" (Burns, 2012, p. 4). This definitional shift reflects a growing awareness among healthcare practitioners of the ways in which the social world and an individual's wellbeing are irrevocably entwined.

Such observations have encouraged an increasing number of health professionals to adopt a Social Determinants of Health (SDH) approach to adolescent wellbeing, which the World Health Organization defines as "the conditions in which people are born, grow, work, live, and age, and the wider set of forces and systems shaping the conditions of daily life" (WHO, 2015). The SDH consist of both structural and proximal determinants, both of which impact upon individuals' health (Viner et al., 2012). Structural determinants include national wealth, income and sex inequality, access to education and health care services, as well as employment opportunities. In the case of adolescents, proximal determinants refer to factors such as connectedness to family and school (Viner et al., 2012), and outcomes relating to the individual, their family, peers, and teachers are particularly important in relation to mental wellbeing and health behaviour. Consequently, it has been suggested that improving adolescent health requires an assessment of the nature of young people's interactions with their family, friends, peers, and teachers (Viner et al., 2012).

There are certain aspects of adolescents' relationships with these social groups that are particularly important for health behaviour. Elements that determine the quality of such relationships (e.g., having a sense of connectedness, good communication, support, involvement, and belonging within the group) can help protect against risky health behaviours and mental health problems. The family is one of the most important groups from this perspective, with adolescents who report high levels of family connectedness reporting lower levels of cigarette, alcohol, and marijuana use (Resnick et al. 1997). Smoking (Wang, Fitzhugh, Westerfield, & Eddy, 1995) and alcohol use (Bonnie & O'Connell, 2004) can be discouraged through healthy family norms and attitudes, as well as through healthy behaviour modeling. However, the nature of this influence depends entirely on the content of the norms, values, and behaviours in question: children of parents who smoke (Bauman, Carver, & Gleiter, 2001) and drink (Bonnie & O'Connell, 2004) are more likely to engage in these behaviours themselves.

The emotional component of group memberships is also important: in countries with greater family connections (versus countries with fewer family connections), adolescents were found to have fewer behavioural and mental health problems (Viner et al., 2012). They were also more likely to delay sexual initiation, and tended to report lower levels of cigarette, alcohol, and marijuana use (Resnick et al., 1997).

Quality of relationships with others at school can also influence wellbeing, but this is dependent on the degree to which young people feel a sense of connection with peers, friends, and teachers (Osterman, 2000). Strong emotional connections between students and teachers can lead to reductions in substance misuse, violence, and other antisocial behaviours (Patton et al., 2006).

Finally, peers are able to influence behaviour in either positive or negative ways. As with the family, healthy peer norms and values can protect against substance misuse (Donovan, 2004), and strong peer connections can reduce the risk of adolescents engaging in a wide range of risky health behaviours (Anteghini,

Fonseca, Ireland, & Blum, 2001; Resnick et al., 1997). However, as mentioned previously, adolescents' heightened sensitivity to peers can actually encourage their experimentation with addictive and risky behaviours, such as substance misuse (Patton et al., 2004; Trucco, Colder, & Wieczorek, 2011), smoking, and alcohol initiation and persistence (Beal, Ausiello, & Perrin, 2001; Donovan, 2004; Kaplan, Nápoles-Springer, Stewart, & Pérez-Stable, 2001; Salazer, Santelli, Crosby, & DiClemente, 2009).

This knowledge regarding the crucial role that social groups can play in adolescent health behaviour reflects professionals' growing interest in the SDH approach. Moreover, the idea of improving public health through socially framed interventions has received increasing amounts of interest from various governments and international agencies (Viner et al., 2012). This has been illustrated by numerous organisations commissioning national and international surveys in order to investigate the social elements that can influence young people's health and behaviour. For example, the Health Behaviour in School Aged Children study (HBSC: World Health Organization, Regional Office for Europe, 2012) is an international study spanning 43 countries that examines the health behaviours and contextual factors that are relevant to children aged 11–15 years. Across Scotland, several studies have also collected data on adolescent health, health behaviours, and social factors. For example, the Scottish Health Survey (Scottish Executive, 2005a), and the Scottish Schools Adolescent Lifestyle and Substance Use Survey (SALSUS: NHS Scotland, 2005) focus on themes such as mental health, substance use, and contextual factors (e.g., schools, general environment, family and friendships).

Indeed, recent Scottish Government policies have made young people's health a key priority. The *Getting It Right for Every Child* (GIRFEC: Scottish Executive, 2006) programme, launched in 2006, provides the supporting methodology for all Scottish Government policies concerning children. National and local targets for children and adolescents have focused on obesity, mental health, and sexual health, as well as smoking, alcohol, and drug use. This holistic approach speaks to the fact that getting to the root of individual risky health behaviours can be difficult, since there are complex relationships between them, and they rarely occur in isolation (Parkinson, 2012).

However, despite these promising developments, there are still some problems with the SDH approach. Although researchers have proposed various models explaining how social determinants impact upon health and health behaviour, the literature contains inconsistent and competing models which use a variety of complex concepts and terms (Viner et al., 2012). While experts within other disciplines (e.g., anthropology, quantitative sociology, and epidemiology; c.f. Berkman, Glass, Brissette, & Seeman, 2000) have also found consistent links between social factors and wellbeing, such individuals have encountered similar problems regarding inconsistencies in how concepts are defined and measured. It is argued that this inconsistency can influence theorizing, study design, and data interpretation, ultimately leading to confusion regarding how to conceptualise and measure key concepts such as social connectedness (Jetten, Haslam, Haslam, Dingle, & Jones,

2014). In time, this confusion can promote methodological weakness and a lack of theoretical clarity.

Ultimately, the SDH approach can best be thought of as a starting point from which to address adolescent health behaviours. In particular, insights can be drawn from the proximal determinants of health, and how these social groups have the potential to influence adolescent behaviour. However, it is possible that an alternative yet complementary approach – the social identity approach – can offer a coherent and consistent perspective from which to draw insights regarding the prevention and treatment of adolescent addictive behaviours.

The social identity perspective

The social identity approach (Turner et al., 1987) is founded on the idea that as well as having a personal identity, one also possesses multiple social identities, which are obtained through membership of social groups. In certain contexts, specific social identities will become salient (or prominent), meaning that (for instance), one might think of oneself as a woman in one context, or as a psychologist in another context. Crucially, these salient social identities effect cognitions and behaviour, as we attempt to think and act in ways that are consistent with the prevailing norms, values, and beliefs of our currently salient social identity. Moreover, we will attempt to help, support, and co-operate with people whom we consider to be fellow in-group members (Haslam, 2004). In this way, our social world provides us with a complex and dynamic sense of who we are and how we relate to those around us at any particular moment.

It is important to note, however, that these effects will be stronger when we feel psychologically invested in the group in question: in situations where the group and its members matter to us, and are central to our lives (e.g., Oakes, Haslam, & Turner, 1994). This means that there is an important distinction between simply being a nominal member of a group and actually *identifying* as a group member.

This subjective sense of *group identification* is a central tenet of the social identity perspective, but it can also provide a new dimension to the SDH approach. The sense of shared social identity that group identification fosters provides the psychological foundation for positive, meaningful, and supportive social interactions (Cruwys, Haslam, Dingle, Haslam, & Jetten, 2014). Group identification thus has the ability to influence both thoughts and behaviours in positive ways.

The remainder of the chapter will outline evidence which supports the idea that the social identity perspective can provide a coherent and theoretically-based approach to adolescent addictive and risky behaviours, thereby remedying some of the SDH perspective's shortcomings. Identifying with particular social groups can influence health behaviours, and there will be consideration of why such influence may occur. The future implications of this work will be investigated in relation to how group identification may influence the uptake and maintenance of various health behaviours, as well as how this knowledge could be used to improve adolescents' health.

Group identification and health behaviours

Social identity processes can influence health behaviours in complex ways, partly due to the role played by group norms. Norm adherence can be used to strengthen in-group cohesion and validate one's status as a group member (Hogg & Abrams, 2003; Turner et al., 1987), an effect that may be especially relevant for adolescents, who are susceptible to peer influence and have a strong desire to 'belong' (e.g., Hogg et al., 2011). Moreover, group identification increases one's likelihood of acting in accordance with the norms of that particular group (e.g., Turner, 1991). While this is helpful in the context of healthy norms (e.g., exercise, or getting vaccinated), adherence to unhealthy norms (e.g., smoking or binge drinking) can be harmful. This helps to explain why the health-related behaviours encouraged by group identification are not always positive.

Thus when a behaviour is seen as something 'we do' (i.e., normative), group members can be motivated to perform that behaviour because of its identity consequences. For example, Oyserman, Fryberg, and Yoder (2007) found that white middle-class participants were likely to associate health-promoting behaviours with their ingroup, while ethnic minority participants were more likely to associate health-harming behaviours with their ingroup. As a result, the ethnic minority participants were more likely to report negative attitudes towards health when their social identity was made salient, leading to reduced cognitive accessibility of health-related knowledge, more health fatalism, and weaker perceptions of the importance of engaging in healthy behaviours.

These findings were supported by a qualitative study by Stewart-Knox and colleagues (2005), who examined why adolescents start smoking. They found that smoking was used as a means by which to define group membership and differentiate between different groups. In a series of interviews with young people spanning three years, they found that rather than peers influencing smoking uptake through direct persuasion, peer influence occurred indirectly when young people tried to conform to the normative behaviour of the peer group with which they identified. The authors suggested that smoking was not a reason for group affiliation, but was rather a behaviour that signified one's membership of the group: both smoking and not smoking were used strategically as a means to accentuate similarities within the in-group and differences between the in-group and out-groups.

However, it is important to remember that these behaviours will only be found among those who identify highly with the group in question. Such individuals will tend to be strongly influenced by group norms, whereas those who identify to a lesser extent will be less likely to be influenced. There is thus an interaction between group norms and group identification, with identification moderating the extent to which group norms influence behaviour (see Figure 5.1).

This relationship has been illustrated with a variety of health behaviours. For example, Schofield and colleagues (2001, 2003) found that group identification increased conformity to peer group norms, and this led to increased smoking behaviour among adolescents who identified highly with a peer group that was associated with extensive smoking. Similarly, Åstrøm and Rise (2001) found that

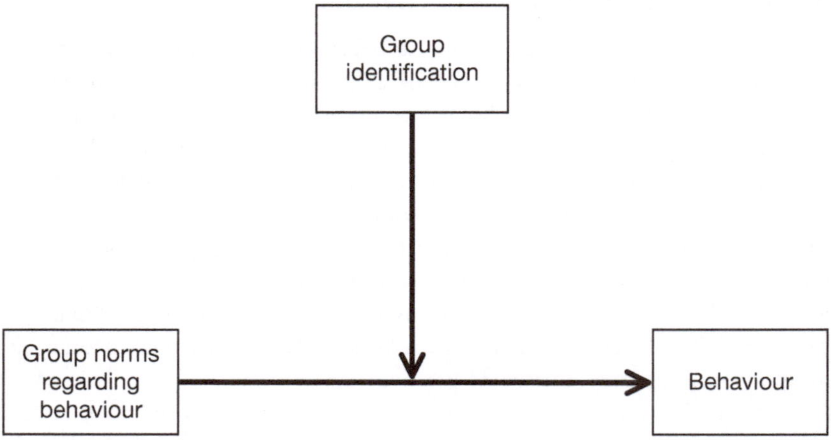

FIGURE 5.1 The relationship between group norms and behaviour, with group identification acting as a moderator.

group identification moderated the extent to which young people planned to eat healthily: those who identified highly were more likely to eat healthily (in accordance with the group norm) than those who did not identify strongly with the group. These results have been replicated with a number of other health behaviours, including exercise, sun-protective behaviour (Rivis & Sheeran, 2003; Terry & Hogg, 1996), and binge drinking (Johnston & White, 2003).

These studies illustrate that group identification can be a double-edged sword: although group identification is associated with many positive health outcomes, it also increases adherence to group norms, which can on occasion be negative. However, knowledge of these processes can be used to improve health behaviour. This can be achieved by altering the salience of different identities to encourage healthy normative behaviours. For example, Tarrant and Butler (2011) found that when an 'unhealthy identity' (student) was salient, participants were less likely to engage in healthy behaviours than when a 'healthier identity' (nationality) was salient. Similar outcomes for smoking were found when a family identity (vs. a peer-group identity) was made salient (Kobus, 2003; Schofield et al., 2003), while making a 'family man identity' salient (vs. a 'miners' masculine identity') has been shown to lead to safer sex behaviour (Campbell, 1997).

This knowledge is increasingly being used in treatment settings. For example, in a study with former substance users, Buckingham, Frings, and Albery (2013) revealed that possessing an 'addict identity' influenced subsequent substance use. However, more negative feelings towards the addict identity were associated with reduced substance use and lower rates of relapse among both former smokers and those who attended Alcoholics Anonymous/Narcotics Anonymous meetings. Similar results have been noted in an adolescent population with Kelly, Stout, Greene, and Slaymaker (2014) investigating how social networks can influence young people's recovery from substance use disorder (SUD). They found that a 12-Step Treatment Programme encouraged social network change, with 'high-risk' friendships having decreased and 'low-risk' friendships having increased at follow-up. Kelly and colleagues used these results to highlight the importance of social networks when treating young people with SUDs.

Dingle, Stark, Cruwys, and Best (2014) expanded upon these ideas by suggesting that relinquishing an addict identity would allow individuals to identify with a 'recovery identity'. They found that among those recovering from drug and/or alcohol abuse, treatment outcomes and wellbeing were influenced by identification with the therapeutic community (TC). Over the course of a treatment programme, identification with the TC increased. In contrast, participants' social identity as members of substance-using social groups was lower after entry to the TC and decreased throughout the programme, with substance-using identities and recovery identities increasingly diverging over time. Dingle and colleagues (2014) concluded that identity transition is an important step in recovery from alcohol and drug misuse. Those who continued to identify with their substance-using peers at follow-up experienced much poorer outcomes in terms of substance use and life satisfaction. In contrast, those who retained their recovery identity showed positive outcomes in terms of substance abstinence and life satisfaction.

Furthermore, when considering group norms, Cruwys, Haslam, Fox, and McMahon (2015) found that in a group intervention for disordered eating, normative change was able to influence both eating-related cognitions and eating intentions over time. One of the particularly noteworthy aspects of this intervention was that participants were encouraged to challenge previously accepted norms by means of a group discussion. This very quickly allowed the norms of the peer group to change from promoting unhealthy eating to promoting healthy eating. These insights could be used in-group settings with addicts, or those at risk of participating in addictive behaviours. Indeed, Cruwys and colleagues (2015) suggest that such mechanisms of normative change could be used with a variety of vulnerable people who are undergoing group therapy. In a study of recovering addicts, the authors found that normative change accounted for up to 26 per cent of patient improvement (Cruwys et al., 2015), thereby illustrating the substantial impact that social factors can have on an individual's behaviour.

This work is promising to the extent that it illustrates how identity processes can be used to change detrimental behaviour in both every-day and therapeutic settings. In recent years, such findings have been extended by research highlighting the important health-related outcomes that can be obtained from identification with *multiple* groups, and how multiple group identifications can be used to protect against the development of risky behaviours.

Impact of multiple group identifications on health behaviour

As previously discussed, group identification can have different implications for health depending on the norms of the different groups involved, and this is particularly important when considering multiple group identifications. For example, Verkooijen, de Vries, and Nielsen (2007) found that identification with several 'high risk' groups (that had norms associated with substance use) was associated with higher risks of substance use, whereas identification with 'low risk' groups (which did not have norms associated with substance use) was associated with lower risks, with this relationship being influenced by the nature of the perceived group norms. However, the most important aspect of their findings was that identifying with multiple groups with competing norms actually led to a weaker relationship between group norms and behaviour in general, thereby 'diluting' the behavioural impact of negative norms.

This research is consistent with recent work by Sani and colleagues (2015), who found that the more group identifications participants had, the less likely they were to participate in risky health behaviours (smoking and drinking heavily), and the more likely they were to have a good diet and to engage in physical exercise. The authors' explanation for these findings was that having more groups with which one identifies strongly can over-ride any negative effects of identifying with groups with negative norms. This is partly because group identification can provide a variety of psychological benefits, including a greater sense of meaning and purpose in life, as well as feeling that one is likely to receive support from fellow group members in times of crisis. These in turn can promote positive affect, as well as providing an incentive (and a sense of obligation) to look after oneself so that one will be healthy enough to help the group achieve its aims and goals.

These conclusions were supported by Miller, Wakefield, and Sani (2016), who examined the relationship between identification with three different groups (family, school, and friends) and health behaviours in over 1,000 secondary school pupils aged between 13 and 17. The authors found that the relationship between group identification and behaviour differed for the individual groups under study. Both family and school identification predicted reduced odds of smoking, binge drinking, and cannabis use. In contrast, friend identification predicted increased odds of smoking, binge drinking, and cannabis use. Furthermore, when the impact of multiple group identifications was considered, the results were consistent with those of Sani et al. (2015), showing that multiple group identifications predicted reduced smoking, binge drinking, and cannabis use.

These findings therefore support both Sani et al.'s (2015) and Verkooijen et al.'s (2007) conclusions that having multiple group identifications can 'cancel out' any negative behaviours associated with identifying with groups which possess unhealthy norms. When aiming to improve adolescents' health/risky behaviours, we should therefore encourage them to identify with as many groups as possible, thereby helping them to cultivate a social environment that protects them against unhealthy and addictive group norms.

Implications

When considering how to use these insights to help adolescents who engage in (or are at risk of engaging in) addictive behaviours, the suggestion is that professionals should encourage such individuals to identify with groups which possess healthy norms. This would have the benefit of increasing the likelihood of them engaging in positive behaviour, and would also protect against identification with groups which possess unhealthy norms. In turn, this would allow adolescents to draw a sense of identity from positive, healthy groups, rather than substance-using groups, the latter of which would provide both a substance-using identity and the desire to behave in accordance with these damaging norms (e.g., Best et al., 2016).

The onus is therefore on those interested in adolescent wellbeing to provide groups that possess healthy norms with which young people would be able to identify. Hogg and colleagues (2011) suggest (citing Carroll, Houghton, Durkin, & Hattie, 2009; Mosbach & Leventhal, 1988) that adolescents should be encouraged to identify with groups beyond the confines of immediate peers and other adolescents. In particular, they recommend groups which would enable adolescents to adopt adult responsibilities – perhaps grounded in the local community or organisations that would provide a distinctive, strong, and valuable sense of self. Such groups have the potential to protect young people against the uncertainty of adolescence, while still enabling them to garner respect from relevant others.

Furthermore, young people should be encouraged to identify with as many of these groups as possible. As outlined above, identifying with many groups can increase the likelihood of engaging with groups which possess healthy norms. While identification with several groups with healthy norms would be the ideal situation, and indeed, should be the aim, the most promising aspect of this work is that multiple group identifications have the ability to compensate for identification with groups with any unhealthy norms. This means that having these multiple group identifications can provide a useful 'safety net' to protect even those who identify with groups which encourage unhealthy behaviours.

Conclusion

The central importance of adolescent wellbeing to overall public health is gradually being accepted by healthcare practitioners, government bodies, international agencies, and researchers. There is growing awareness of the importance of addressing this group when considering ways to improve – and protect – population health. One of the most straightforward ways to do this is to prevent the development of risky health behaviours during adolescence. Doing so has long- and short-term benefits at both an individual and a societal level. For example, it will protect the health and wellbeing of the young people themselves, it will prevent the immediate and long-term social problems associated with substance use, and, finally, it will prevent these behaviours from becoming deeply-rooted addictions that continue into adulthood.

The social identity approach provides an integrated theoretical perspective which draws together and builds upon knowledge provided by other disciplines regarding health-related behaviour. The social identity approach, supported by a growing body of empirical research, allows consideration of the ways in which behaviours, and ultimately prevent these behaviours from occurring in the first place. Using a holistic approach, it is possible to utilise knowledge about social identities and group membership in order to address both psychological and behavioural outcomes, thus protecting all aspects of wellbeing. Doing this means that more resources are available to help prevent young people from becoming involved in risky health behaviours that could eventually evolve into harmful addictions. Thus, even millennia on, there is still truth in Aristotle's observation that 'good habits started in youth can make all the difference'.

References

Anteghini, M., Fonseca, H., Ireland, M., & Blum, R. W. (2001). Health risk behaviors and associated risk and protective factors among Brazilian adolescents in Santos, Brazil. *Journal of Adolescent Health*, 28, 295–302.

Åstrøm, A. N. & Rise, J. (2001). Young adults' intention to eat healthy food: Extending the theory of planned behaviour. *Psychology and Health, 16*, 223–237.

Bauman, K. E., Carver, K., & Gleiter, K. (2001). Trends in parent and friend influence during adolescence: The case of adolescent cigarette smoking. *Addictive Behavior, 26*, 349–361.

Beal, A. C., Ausiello, J., & Perrin, J. M. (2001). Social influences on health-risk behaviours among minority middle school students. *Journal of Adolescent Health, 28*, 474–480.

Becker, B. E. & Luthar, S. S. (2007). Peer-perceived admiration and social preference: Contextual correlates of positive peer regard among suburban and urban adolescents. *Journal of Research on Adolescence, 17*, 117–144.

Berkman, L. F., Glass, T., Brissette, I., & Seeman, T. E. (2000). From social integration to health: Durkheim in the new millennium. *Social Science and Medicine, 51*, 843–857.

Best, D., Beckwith, M., Haslam, C. Haslam, S. A., Jetten, J., Mawson, E., & Lubman, D. I. (2016). Overcoming alcohol and other drug addiction as a process of social identity transition: The social identity model of recovery (SIMOR). *Addiction Research & Theory, 24*, 111–123.

Bonnie, R. J., & O'Connell, M. E. (Eds.). (2004). *Reducing underage drinking: A collective responsibility*. Washington, DC: The National Academies Press.

Breakwell, G. M. (1986). *Coping with threatened identities*. London and New York: Methuen.

Buckingham, S. A., Frings, D., & Albery, I. P. (2013). Group membership and social identity in addiction recovery. *Psychology of Addictive Behaviors, 27*, 1132–1140.

Burns, H. (2012). *Chief Medical Officer annual report 2011 – Transforming Scotland's health*. Retrieved from Scottish Government website: www.scotland.gov.uk/Publications/2012/12/7521.

Campbell, C. (1997). Migrancy, masculine identities and AIDS: The psychosocial context of HIV transmission on the South African gold mines. *Social Science and Medicine, 45*, 273–281.

Carrol, A., Houghton, S., Durkin, K., & Hattie, J. A. (2009). *Adolescent reputations and risk. Developmental trajectories to delinquency*. New York: Springer.

Catalano, R. F., Fagan, A. A., Gavin, L. E., Greenberg, M. T., Irwin, C. E., Ross, D. A., & Shek, D. T. L. (2012). Worldwide application of prevention science in adolescent health. *Lancet, 379*, 1653–1664.

Chandler, M. J., & Proulx, T. (2008). Personal persistence and persistent peoples: Continuities in the lives of individual and whole cultural communities. In F. Sani (Ed.), *Self-continuity: Individual and collective perspectives*. New York: Psychology Press.

Coleman, J. S. (1974). *Relationships in adolescence*. London and Boston, MA: Routledge and Kegan Paul.

Collins, W. A. & Steinberg, L. (2006). Adolescent development in interpersonal context. In W. Damon, R. Lerner, & N. Eisenberg (Eds.), *The Handbook of Child Psychology*. Hoboken, NJ: Wiley and Sons.

Cruwys, T., Haslam, S. A., Dingle, G. A., Haslam, C., & Jetten, J. (2014). Depression and social identity: An integrative review. *Personality and Social Psychology Review, 18*, 215–238.

Cruwys, T., Haslam, S. A., Fox, N. E., & McMahon, H. (2015). 'That's not what we do': Evidence that normative change is a mechanism of action in group interventions. *Behaviour Research and Therapy, 65*, 11–17.

Degenhardt, L., Chiu, W. T., Sampson, N., Kessler, R. C., Anthony, J. C. Angermeyer, M., . . . & Wells, J. E. (2008). Toward a global view of alcohol, tobacco, cannabis, and cocaine use: Findings from the WHO World Mental Health Surveys. *PLOS Medicine, 5*, e141.

Dingle, G. A., Stark, C., Cruwys, T., & Best, D. (2014). Breaking good: Breaking ties with social groups may be good for recovery from substance misuse. *British Journal of Social Psychology, 54*, 236–254.

Dolcini, M. M. & Adler, N. E. (1994). Perceived competencies, peer group affiliation, and risk behavior among early adolescents. *Health Psychology, 13*, 496–506.

Donovan, J. E. (2004). Adolescent alcohol initiation: A review of psychosocial risk factors. *Journal of Adolescent Health, 35*, 529, e7–e18.

Duan, L., Chou, C. P., Andreeva, V. A., & Penta, M. A. (2009). Trajectories of peer social influences as long-term predictors of drug use from early through late adolescence. *Journal of Youth and Adolescence, 38*, 454–465.

Ellemers, N. (2003). Identity, culture and change in organisations: A social identity analysis and three illustrative cases. In S. A. Haslam, D. van Knippenberg, M. J. Platow, & N. Ellemers (Eds.), *Social identity at work: Developing theory for organizational practice* (pp. 191–203). New York: Psychology Press.

Erikson, E. H. (1968). *Identity: Youth and crisis*. New York: W. W. Norton.

Haslam, S. A. (2004). *Psychology in organizations: The social identity approach*. London: Sage.

Haslam, S. A., Eggins, R. A., & Reynolds, K. J. (2003). The ASPIRe model: Actualizing social and personal identity resources to enhance organizational outcomes. *Journal of Occupational and Organizational Psychology, 76*, 83–113.

Hogg, M. A., & Abrams, D. (1993). Towards a single-process uncertainty-reduction model of social motivation. In M. A. Hogg, & D. Abrams (Eds.), *Group motivation* (pp. 173–190). Hemel Hempstead, UK: Harvester Wheatsheaf.

Hogg, M. A., Siegel, J. T., & Hohman, Z. P. (2011). Groups can jeopardize your health: Identifying with unhealthy groups to reduce self-uncertainty. *Self and Identity, 10*, 326–335.

Hopkins, N. & Reicher, S. D. (1997). The construction of social categories and processes of social change: Arguing about national identities. In G. Breakwell & E. Lyons (Eds.), *Changing European identities* (pp. 69–93). Oxford: Butterworth-Heinemann.

Jetten, J., Haslam, C., Haslam, S. A., Dingle, G., Jones, J. M. (2014). How groups affect our health and well-being: The path from theory to policy. *Social Issues Policy Review, 8*, 103–130.

Johnston, K. L. & White, K. M. (2003). Binge-drinking: A test of the role of group norms in the theory of planned behaviour. *Psychology and Health, 18*, 63–77.

Kaplan, C. P., Nápoles-Springer, A., Stewart S. L., & Pérez-Stable, E. J. (2001). Smoking acquisition among adolescents and young Latinas: The role of socioenvironmental and personal factors. *Addictive Behaviors, 26*, 531–550.

Kelly, J. F., Stout, R. L., Greene, M. C., & Slaymaker, V. (2014). Young adults, social networks, and addiction recovery: Post treatment changes in social ties and their role as a mediator of 12-step participation. *PLOS One*, *19*, e100121.

Kobus, K. (2003). Peers and adolescent smoking. *Addiction*, *98*, 37–55.

The Lancet (2009). What is health? The ability to adapt. *The Lancet*, *373*, 781.

Luthar, S. S. & D'Avanzo, K. (1999). Contextual factors in substance use: A study of suburban and inner-city adolescents. *Development and Psychopathology*, *11*, 845–867.

Luthar, S. S., & McMahon, T. (1996). Peer reputation among inner city adolescents: Structure and correlates. *Journal of Research on Adolescence*, *6*, 581–603.

Miller, K., Wakefield, J. R. H., & Sani, F. (2016). Greater number of group identifications is associated with healthier behaviour in adolescents. *British Journal of Developmental Psychology*.

Mosbach, P. & Leventhal, H. (1988). Peer group identification and smoking: Implications for intervention. *Journal of Abnormal Psychology*, *97*, 238–245.

Newman, B. M. & Newman, P. R. (2001). Group identity and alienation: Giving the WE its due. *Journal of Youth and Adolescence*, *30*, 515–538.

NHS National Services Scotland, (2014). *Scottish schools adolescent lifestyle and substance use survey (SALSUS): Smoking among 13 and 15 year olds in Scotland 2013*. Retrieved from www.isdscotland.org/Health-Topics/Public-Health/Publications/2014–11–25/SALSUS_2013_Smoking_Report.pdf.

NHS Scotland. (2005). *Scottish schools adolescent lifestyle and substance use survey national report*. Retrieved from Drug Misuse Information Scotland: www.drugmisuse.isdscotland.org/publications/local/SALSUS_2008.pdf.

Nielsen, G. A., Ringgaard, L., Broholm, K., Sindballe, A., & Olsen, S. F. (2002). *Unges livsstil og daligdag 2000: Forbrug af tobak, alkohol, og stoffer* [Young people's lifestyle and daily life 2000: Use of tobacco, alcohol and drugs]. Copenhagen, Denmark: Danish Cancer Society and National Board of Health.

Oakes, P. J., Haslam, S. A., & Turner, J. C. (1994). *Stereotyping and social reality*. Oxford: Blackwell Publishing.

Odgers, P., Houghton, S., & Douglas, G. (1996). Reputation enhancement theory and adolescent substance use. *Journal of Child Psychology and Psychiatry*, *37*, 1015–1022.

Osterman, K. F. (2000). Students' need for belonging in the school community. *Review of Educational Research*, *70*, 323–367.

Oyserman, D., Fryberg, S. A., & Yoder, N. (2007). Identity-based motivation and health. *Journal of Personality and Social Psychology*, *93*, 1011–1027.

Parkinson, J. (2012). *Establishing a core set of national, sustainable mental health indicators for children and young people in Scotland: Final report*. Glasgow, UK: NHS Health Scotland.

Patton, G. C., Bond, L., Carlin, J. B., Thomas, L., Butler, H., Glover, S., . . . & Bowes, G. (2006). Promoting social inclusion in schools: A group-randomized trial of effects on student health risk behavior and well-being. *American Journal of Public Health*, *96*, 1582–1587.

Patton, G. C., Coffey, C., Cappa, C., Currie, D. Riley, L. Gore, F., . . . & Ferguson, J. (2012). Health of the world's adolescents: A synthesis of internationally comparable data. *Lancet*, *379*, 1665–1675.

Patton, G. C., McMorris, B. J., Toumbourou, J. W., Hemphill, S. A., Donath, S., & Cataano, R. F. (2004). Puberty and the onset of substance use and abuse. *Pediatrics*, *114*, e300–e306.

Resnick, M. D., Bearman, P.S., Blum, R. W., Bauman, K. E., Harris, K. M., Jones, J., . . . & Udry, J. R. (1997). Protecting adolescents from harm. *Journal of the American Medical Association*, *278*, 823–832.

Rivis, A. & Sheeran, P. (2003). Social influences and the theory of planned behaviour: Evidence for a direct relationship between prototypes and young people's exercise behaviour. *Psychology and Health*, *18*, 567–583.

Salazer, L. F., Santelli, J. S., Crosby, R. A. & DiClemente, R. J. (2009). Sexually transmitted disease transmission and pregnancy among adolescents. In R. J. DiClemente, J. S. Santelli, & R. A. Crosby (Eds.), *Adolescent health: Understanding and preventing risk behaviors* (pp. 274–302). San Francisco, CA: Jossey-Bass.

Sani, F., Madhok, V., Norbury, M., Dugard, P., & Wakefield, J. R. H. (2015). Greater number of group identifications is associated with healthier behaviour: Evidence from a Scottish community sample. *British Journal of Health Psychology, 20*, 466–81.

Sawyer, M. D., Afifi, R. A., Bearinger, L. H., Blakemore, S., Dick, B., Ezeh, A. C., & Patton, G. C., 2012. Adolescence: A foundation for future health. *Lancet 379*, 1630–1640.

Schofield, P. E., Pattison, P. E., Hill, D. J., & Borland, R. (2001). Youth culture and smoking: Integrating social group processes and individual cognitive processes in a model of health-related behaviours. *Journal of Health Psychology, 8*, 291–306.

Schofield, P. E., Pattison, P. E., Hill, D. J., & Borland, R. (2003). Youth culture and smoking: Integrating social group processes and individual cognitive processes in a model of health–related behaviours. *Journal of Health Psychology, 8*, 291–306.

Scottish Executive (2005). *The Scottish Health Survey, 2003*. Edinburgh, UK: Astron.

Scottish Executive (2006). *Getting it right for every child*. Edinburgh, UK: Astron.

Scottish Government, (2008a). *Scotland's future is smoke-free: A smoking prevention action plan*. Edinburgh, UK: Astron.

Scottish Government, (2008b). *The road to recovery: A new approach to tackling Scotland's drug problem*. Edinburgh, UK: Astron.

Scottish Government (2009). *Towards a mentally flourishing Scotland*. Edinburgh, UK: Astron.

Seidman, E. & French, S. E. (2004). Developmental trajectories and ecological transitions: A two-step procedure to aid in the choice of prevention and promotion interventions. *Development and Psychopathology, 16*, 1141–1159.

Selnow, G. W. & Crano, W. D. (1986). Formal vs. informal group affiliations: Implications for alcohol and drug use among adolescents. *Journal of Studies on Alcohol, 47*, 48–52.

Siegel, J. T., Alvaro, E. M., Patel, N., & Crano, W. D. (2009). '. . . you would probably want to do it. 'Cause that's what made them popular': Exploring perceptions of inhalant utility among young adolescent non-users and occasional users. *Substance Use and Misuse, 44*, 597–615.

Smith, G. M. & Fogg, C. P. (1978). Psychological predictors of early use, late use, and nonuse of marijuana among teenage students. In D. B. Kandel (Ed.), *Longitudinal research on drug use: Empirical findings and methodological issues* (pp. 101–113). New York: Wiley.

Stewart-Knox, B. J., Sittlington, J., Rugkåsa, J., Harrisson, S., Treacy, M., & Abaunza, P. S. (2005). Smoking and peer groups: Results from a longitudinal qualitative study of young people in Northern Ireland. *British Journal of Social Psychology, 44*, 397–414.

Tarrant, M. & Butler, K. (2011). Effects of self-categorisation on orientation towards health. *British Journal of Social Psychology, 50*, 121–139.

Terry, D. J. & Hogg, M. A. (1996). Group norms and the attitude-behaviour relationships: A role for group identification. *Personality and Social Psychology Bulletin, 22*, 775–793.

Thoits, P. A. (1983). Multiple identities and psychological well-being: A reformation and test of the social isolation hypothesis. *American Sociological Review, 48*, 174–187.

Trucco, E. M., Colder, C. R., & Wieczorek, W. F. (2011). Vulnerability to peer influence: A moderated mediation study of early adolescent alcohol use initiation. *Addictive Behavior, 36*, 729–736.

Turner, J. C., Hogg, M. A., Oakes, P., Reicher, S., & Wetherell, M. (1987). *Rediscovering the social group: A self-categorization theory*. Oxford: Basil-Blackwell.

Verkooijen, K. T., de Vries, N. K., & Nielsen, G. A. (2007). Youth crowds and substance use: The impact of perceived group norm and multiple group identification. *Psychology of Addictive Behaviors, 21*, 55–61.

Viner, R. M., Ozer, E. M., Denny, S., Marmot, M., Resnick, M., Fatusi, A., & Currie, C. (2012). Adolescence and the social determinants of health. *Lancet, 379*, 1641–1652.

Wang, M. Q., Fitzhugh, E. C., Westerfield, R. C., & Eddy, J. M. (1995). Family and peer influences on smoking behaviour among American adolescents: An age trend. *Journal of Adolescent Health, 16*, 200–203.

World Health Organization. Regional Office for Europe. (2012). *Social determinants of health and well-being among young people: Health behaviour in school-aged children (HBSC) study: International report from the 2009/2010 survey*. Retrieved from the World Health Organization, Regional Office for Europe: www.euro.who.int/__data/assets/pdf_file/0003/163857/Social-determinants-of-health-and-well-being-among-young-people.pdf.

World Health Organization (2015). *Social determinants of health*. Retrieved September 12, 2015 from www.who.int/social_determinants/en/.

6

ADDICTION TO CRIME AND A SOCIAL IDENTITY OF RECOVERY

Jacqueline Malton

Criminal offending and substance use disorder are closely related (Nurco, Hanlon, Kinlock, & Slaught, 1990). However, little research exists around the subject of the possibility of core social motives (Fiske, 2004) that may drive a social identity that is linked with criminal activity, with addiction or with a lifestyle that involves both. Being a member of the criminal fraternity may furnish individuals with social motives that have been previously absent and with a social status and a sense of belonging that are valued and valuable. Alternatively, being an addict may be a response (albeit not an intentional one) to a deficit in core social needs and addressing this need may necessitate criminal activity to fund this lifestyle and the substance use linked to it. However, single motives are unlikely and there is likely to be a complex interplay between motives and identities that evolve over the course of substance using and offending careers.

Fiske (2004) posits that core social motives describe how we interact with others via our behaviours, thinking and feelings in relations to others. She describes these five core social motives as: belonging, understanding, controlling, self-enhancing, and trusting. Therefore, for those who achieve this status through involvement in substance using and offending groups, there will be a strong bind to the group and its impact on identity, belonging and wellbeing.

The aim of the study that is described in this chapter is to explore these concepts with a group of offenders from a male addiction unit within Her Majesty's Prison, UK. This facility addressed substance dependency among offenders. The study deployed a method that involved in-depth qualitative interviews, which explored the subjective experiences of ten participants with regard to their background, substance misuse and criminal social identity, and linked these to their core social motives. The participants were serving terms of imprisonment at a prison in southern England, UK and undergoing treatment for substance dependency, having been previously diagnosed under the auspices of the Diagnostic Statistical Manual of Mental Disorders Fourth Edition (DSM 1V, 1991).

The study revealed a range of crimes that were committed to fund lifestyle and the users' drug and alcohol habits. These included drug-related crimes such as possession and supplying, as well as acquisitive crimes such as burglary, robbery and theft. Beyond this however is the suggestion that participants attempted to satisfy their core social motive via their criminal social identity and associated addictive behaviours, which had become the driving and most dominant force in their lives. Therefore, the study suggests how addiction treatment programmes may be utilised to begin the process of replacing these pervasive activities with more positive social identities and thus promoting core social motives that are more sustainable and altruistic, to enable programme participants to start a journey to addiction recovery and sustainable desistance from offending.

Currently the UK Ministry of Justice (2014) runs a number of accredited Substance Misuse Programmes as part of their Offender Behaviour Programmes (OBP's) founded on the published evidence based on what techniques and interventions help offenders to change, typically including cognitive programmes such as CBT and motivational interviewing. These programmes include the Alcohol Related Violence Programme (ARV), aimed at reducing alcohol related violence, The Drink Impaired Drivers Programme (DID; targeted at those found guilty of driving under the influence), and the FOCUS Substance Misuse Programme, which is a cognitive behavioural treatment programme designed to assist prisoners to address the issues between their substance misuse and offending behaviour. A drug intervention programme (Prison-Addressing Substance Related Offending [P-ASRO]) addresses how thought processes and socio-economic situations can contribute to problematic levels of substance use and crime in their lives. Generally, the programmes combine attempts at addressing faulty cognitions around substance use and offending and attempt to link these to generic life skills and competences. Many of the programmes (such as the Low Intensity Alcohol Programme [LIAP] and the Offender Substance Abuse Programme [OSAP]) use cognitive processes to change behaviour and attitudes in an effort to prevent relapse and will often embed evidence-based Relapse Prevention activities within their interventions.

Case study: RAPT and treatment delivery in UK prisons

Within the Offenders Behaviour Programme, the Rehabilitation of Addicted Prisoners Trust (RAPt) delivers substance dependency treatment programmes throughout a number of prisons within the UK, and has done so for a number of years.

The core programme consists of a 20-week programme divided into three phases: Motivational Enhancement Therapy, Primary Phase and Relapse Prevention. Its aims and objectives are to examine, in depth, core-using issues and to encourage examination and adoption of alternative lifestyles' not involving substances or crime. The RAPt accredited intensive treatment programme is based on the abstinent model of addiction adopted from the 12-step programme of the mutual help organisations (MHO) of Alcoholics and Narcotics Anonymous, but also incorporates a number of other evidence-based treatment approaches. The programme seeks to enable participants to examine how their life has become unmanageable as a result of their substance use (including alcohol) and the consequent relationship with criminal activity. Treatment is delivered by way of group and individual therapy, workshops, written assignments and weekly review by the treatment team. The key dynamic risk factors addressed within the programme are: criminal thinking, self-efficacy, motivation, and problem solving skills.

The RAPt reconviction analysis (2011) analysed data from the Police National Computer UK (PNC) of offending records for 973 male prisoners who had been released from prison between November 2004 and March 2010. The analysis examined three cohorts:

1 RAPt Completers: Prisoners who had completed the Substance Dependence Treatment Programme (SDTP) as described in the previous paragraph.
2 RAPt Non-Completers: prisoners who had engaged in the same 16–21 week SDTP but for a variety of reasons failed to complete the core programme.
3 Comparison completers: Individuals who had attended a lower intensity and shorter duration programme while in prison. This latter group had been assessed for their dependency on a particular drug although had not accessed the RAPT SDTP.

The cohorts were matched with respect to age group, ethnicity, severity of dependence, drug of choice, index offence (offences they were serving their sentence for when completing either intervention) and volume of previous offending. All the participants were followed up one year after release.

The study found that the percentage of male offenders who reoffended was as follows:

RAPt completers (n = 259): 31 per cent reoffended in the first year follow-up increasing to 44 per cent in the average period of two years to second follow-up

RAPt non–completers (n = 348): 50 per cent had reoffended in first year follow-up increasing to 66 per cent at an average of the two year follow up point

Comparison completers (n = 266): 51 per cent had reoffended during the first year follow-up increasing to 73 per cent at an average two year follow-up.

Within this 1-year follow-up period, the RAPT completers committed 0.8 re-offences on average (n = 259), the RAPt non-completers committed 1.5 re-offences on average (n = 348) and the comparison cohort committed 2.3 re-offences on average (n = 266). Therefore, even among those that did reoffend, the RAPt re-offenders were classified as having committed fewer re-offences per person.

This research indicates that intensive treatment is effective in tackling drug related crime and bringing about positive changes in the dynamic risk factors such as motivation, self-efficacy, criminal thinking, and social problem solving. It may also offer a linkage to external groups (i.e., AA and NA) for continuation of positive social influence through the recovery process.

The importance of social influence

Social influence as described by Fiske (2004) is characterised as: "any changes in beliefs, attitudes, or behaviour that results from personal interaction" (p. 508). These changes and beliefs in our thoughts, feelings and behaviours are influenced by imagined, implied or actual presence of others. Fiske suggests that the three concepts underpinning social influence are conformity, compliance and obedience.

Social influence is primarily determined by the core motive of belonging although all of the core social motives (belonging, understanding, controlling, enhancing self and trusting others) can be applied to social influence (Fiske, 2004). The mere exposure to behaviours (addictive or otherwise) within a family or an environmental setting can be interpreted as the norm and forms their attitudes. These norms become the unwritten rules for behaviour and over time the cognitions are developed from this exposure that supports the affect and behaviour. Through modelling by the family, environment or respected peers, social influence impacts upon the core social motives of belonging and understanding, and this approach has been acknowledged in the developmental perspective in criminology (e.g., Thornberry, 1997). These core social influences can be both positive and negative, and so in the prison context can take the positive form of protective social support or more negatively can involve violence, bullying and both drug use and drug dealing activities. It is suggested that social influence described by Fiske is closely aligned to the social identity approach (Tajfel & Turner, 1979; Turner, Hogg, Oakes, Reicher, & Wetherall, 1987) where significant others influence the behaviour of those around them by social comparison and social contagion within a social frame of reference (Turner et al., 1987). Thus, the influences in prison (inmates, warders and professionals including alcohol and drug treatment providers) are also an unavoidable component of the developmental pathway and learning model.

In his HM Inspectorate of Prisons Annual Report 2014/15 Nick Hardwick, Chief Inspector of Prisons, spoke of the rapid increase in the availability of new psychoactive substances (NPS), such as 'Spice' or 'Black Mamba', which has had an adverse impact on many of those who consumed the drug and has been associated with debt and associated violence. These drugs are developed or chosen to mimic the effects of illegal drugs such as cannabis, heroin or amphetamines and can have unpredictable and life threatening effects. Local prisons in particular have struggled to cope with the introduction of young adults, who are over-represented in violent incidents and the use of force by staff, some of which has been linked to the proliferation of substance use in prisons. The Inspectorate is concerned with increasing violence and since 2010 assault incidents have risen by 13 per cent to 16,196 and the rate of increase is accelerating (Annual Report 2014–15 HM Chief Inspector of Prisons for England and Wales).

As part of their routine collection of risks and incidents, RAPt has received reports of 54 serious NPS incidents from frontline staff in a three-month period of April, May and June 2015. Most of these incidents related to the use of Spice and were received from nine different prisons; 44 per cent resulted in an inmate being admitted as a healthcare patient, either inside the prison healthcare centre or at outside hospitals. Out of the 54 serious NPS related incidents; six featured an inmate acting violently and assaulting prison staff; four involved assaulting other prisoners; and five resulted in self-harm and/or a short term psychotic episode.

There are signs that prisoners dependent on Spice are able to benefit from RAPt's prison recovery programme to the same extent as those dependent on heroin or cocaine, based on a trans-diagnostic model for managing substance use problems and providing skills based solutions. One hundred and thirty-two prisoners who have engaged with the programme over the last three years have reported dependency on NPS. Data from RAPt's accredited prison programmes shows that participating prisoners who report NPS as one of their main substances are just as likely to complete the programme drug free as those that report 'traditional' illicit drug use (RAPt Research and Policy Briefing Series No. 4: Tackling the Issue of New Psychoactive Substances in Prison).

The aim of the second part of the study presented in this chapter was to explore and understand the social identity of criminals linked with addictive behaviour, incorporating Fiske's core social motives (2004) and the potential for behavioural change that may be sustained upon release.

Method

Design

Data for this study was collected using semi-structured interviews, aided by an interview guide to ensure that at the end of the interview major issues had been sufficiently covered (Howitt & Cramer, 2005). In preparing the interview schedule a number of questions were developed that related to the participant's personal history and lifestyle, the participant's substance misuse history and the participant's offending history. Specific questions were asked appertaining to the benefit and negative impact on substance misuse and offending, description of feelings relevant to substance misuse and offending, introduction into substances and criminal offending, and motivation for committing crime.

Participants

Participants were recruited from a HMP male facility in Southern England, UK (N = 10) who had been previously assessed as suitable for participation in the Rehabilitation Addictive Prisoners Trust (RAPt) treatment programme.

Interviews: The interviews were conducted using an official portable tape recorder, consent for which was received in writing from the Governor of the

HMP facility and from the ethics committee at London South Bank University. A pseudonym was used to protect the participant's identity. Data was coded according to the following categories: demographics, family history, violence within the family of origin, violence as means of offending, educational history including exclusion from school and pupil referral units, significant events in their lives, employment, substance misuse, criminal offending, motives for committing crime, and core social motives of belonging, understanding their environment, controlling, enhancing self, and trusting.

Demographics

The mean age of the participants was 33.5 years (range 20–43). The youngest participant was aged 20 years and the oldest 43 years. Eight of the participants were Caucasian and two were of mixed race heritage.

Three of the participants are serving Indeterminate Public Protection (IPP) sentences. These are life sentences imposed with a minimum tariff of imprisonment to be served before release. The offences for which these participants have been sentenced to an IPP relate to: two offences of robbery and one offence of Section 18 Wounding under the Offences Against The Person Act 1861. The offences for the remaining participants include: Kidnap, Conspiracy to supply Class A Drugs, Armed Robbery, Burglary (2), and Violence (2).

Eight out of the 10 participants did not receive full-time education. Six participants were excluded from mainstream schooling and sent to pupil referral units. Two of the participants were put into the care of the local authority due to their disruptive behaviours. Only two of the participants completed their education and Terry was the only one to leave school with educational qualifications in the form of GCSE's.

Analysis

Nine of the 10 participants identified the core social motive of belonging as relevant to their drug use and offending behaviours. Fiske (2004) suggests that the social motive of belonging underpins the remaining four social motives. For example, Terry specialised in committing bank frauds resulting in good feelings for him and a sense of being useful to others.

> "As time has gone on and I got involved in crime if I achieve what I am asked to do I like getting the praise for doing it you know . . . For example I've been involved in bank fraud for many years and you know if I met up with a group of guys I was going to do with on the day and I would go into a bank and get the money I'm like the hero for the hour and I used to get a bit of a boost from doing it, coz everybody is happy we've got the money and you know I'm the toast of the moment sort of thing."

Terry felt a 'boost'; praised, celebrated, happy; where everybody is happy in the moment and he had a sense of belonging and positive identity within the group. This sense of belonging for Terry appeared to accentuate the remaining four social motives. He understood his sense of belonging to these people in their shared goal. Terry felt in control and effective in getting the money through a fraudulent act. His sense of self is enhanced when seen by others as '*the hero of the hour*' and was trusted by his peers in their group activity without undue suspicion.

In a second example that illustrates a similar theme, Robert spoke of getting drunk and committing crime with his friends.

> "Basically we used to just get drunk on street corners and that and anyone we see we thought that might have money we used to mug 'em, hit 'em, attack 'em, mug at night, sometimes we used to do it on a bus or train. Sometimes there would be a gang of us – sometimes there would be two or three."

Nine out of the 10 participants spoke of needing a sense of belonging, to be part of, a liking to be liked, or to fit in with others. This core social motive of belonging, prescribed by Fiske (2004) as a need for basic survival, was reflected in all of the interviews bar one. This need to belong affected a number of behaviours and had a range of different origins; to prevent being bullied at school, the need for friendship, taking drugs, belonging to a gang or committing crime.

Alfie described his feeling part of a group in relation to committing football violence.

> "I felt like I belonged that's where I really felt I belonged to a group. I tried to fit into other groups it just didn't work that was 14 years ago . . . but I am not now but up to two years ago when I got arrested I was very much part of the crowd."

This conveys not only the importance of a sense of belonging to wellbeing but also the assumption that loss of the criminal identity would come at the cost of the loss of the belonging to the group. The importance of the group and its importance for identity is also reflected in the following exchange.

> **Terry** Q "Is that important to you what friends think of you?"
>
> R. "Yeah I've always yeah I like to be liked by people but it has not necessarily always been for the right reasons but I have always enjoyed being popular."

In the following quotation it is apparent that John had begun to formulate an identity with gangs whom he now saw as his family and his own emergence as a gang leader.

> **John** "I stopped talking to my mum and my family for a bit. I went to school living in a hostel coming up to my 16th birthday and all I had was these people from the street. That's when I started doing the gangs that's when I started making up my own gangs now . . . I started hanging around with guys from Brixton, Gypsy Hill, West Norwood and that and that's when I started understanding about weapons all this stuff that's when I got my first gun".

John clearly attributed his engagement in escalated offending with the sense of belonging and identity that resulted from gang membership. In contrast, Freddie felt bullied at school due to his lack of literacy skills and he was expelled. At his new school, in order to belong, he became the bully as illustrated below:

> "I didn't really do that good at school. I was kicked out of my first primary school coz of my bad behaviour. Basically my behaviour come from English classes, Geography, History coz I couldn't do the work . . . I was always getting tormented in class for not being able to read something or spell out something right – people used to take the mickey out of me so the more they done it the less I wanted to do it and yeah I just wanted to mess about . . . One day I kicked off I went a bit too far, started throwing chairs about and all that – I got expelled from the school. Got sent to a new school which was just up the road from where I was – it weren't a very good school, everyone who got sent to that school had been kicked out of another school and I went downhill from there."

Freddie goes on to explain how this evolution to offending continued:

> "I wanted to fit in with the others at me new school. I didn't want to get bullied – I wanted to fit in so we used to muck about – take the mick out of people basically. I became a bully in that school which I never thought I would do. I never used to think it was bullying. I just went with the crowd sort of thing."

Again, the explanation is social in terms of the development of a criminal offending career. Similarly, Wesley spoke of his long-term association with criminals in preference to living a 'straight life':

> "All my friends have been criminals. I moved away in 2008 when I come out of prison to another area. Couldn't do the straight life with straight people; got embarrassed being around normal people and I just went to the crime people in that new area I moved to, so its a good place to have actually experienced that coz I know what I've done wrong the last time. I just like the rough and tumble council estates. I associated with people similar to me unfortunately."

Wesley expressed a developmental experience that related to his sense of comfort and belonging and a form of social identification that was a significant barrier in his attempts at desisting from crime. Tyler's main previous convictions were for violence. It would seem, that rather than specialising in violent offences, he had internalised the same behaviours learnt from his father, as directed to him as a child.

> "I just think it's from when I was younger and when I used to do anything wrong my dad used to beat me up so I grew up with the mindset that if anyone does anything wrong I've got to beat them up. The last violent thing I done to someone was in 2005 – my first GBH and Section 18 and I sort of realised then that I don't have to do that just because my dad done it. I'm older now, I can make my own decisions . . . ."

Tyler was the victim of violence from his father while growing up. His behaviour of violence towards others appears to correspond with Bandura's (1977) social learning principles of learning through observing others. It appears that Tyler responded by committing violence for behaviours he believed to be wrongful, in a similar way to how his father behaved towards him. Thus, other people's behaviours and voices become assimilated to the point where they are internalised and normalised as a method of problem solving particularly if the source is perceived to be someone who has status and authority (see Buckingham this volume; Terry & Hogg, 1991).

The individual can struggle even more to find their own voice within a variety of social contexts and situations. However, Tyler began to come to a new level of understanding from his own learning on the RAPt recovery programme "*that I don't have to do that just because my dad done it*".

All of the 10 participants had experienced physical, emotional, or sexual abuse while growing up in their family environment or in the care system; this may point towards emotional deprivation and/or insufficient emotional support resulting in individual vulnerabilities. However, individual vulnerabilities linked to the development of offending are also consistent with those who have addictions (Brown, 1997).

Brown (1997) suggests that low frustration tolerance leads to excessive disappointment and anger. Six of the participants: John, Tyler, Wesley, Alfie, Paul and Freddie, spoke of inflicting violence upon others, revealing indicators of temperament and negative reaction to others. All of these participants reported being the victim of abuse, bullying and/ or sexual abuse during their childhood, either by parents or people known to them. Thus, the underlying experiences of abuse may provide a common cause factor for both offending and substance use and may also provide a social learning framework for the types of group that these individuals learn to engage with and experience reward from belonging to.

In his model of addictive offending, Brown (1997) describes the feature of a "powerful emotional reaction" experienced by the individual in association with the criminal act, which is mood-changing. Nine out of the 10 participants' responded that they had experienced this factor while committing criminal acts and reported feelings ranging from nervousness and fear to 'buzz'. Leigh, Terry and Robert spoke of their dominant emotional reaction as one of fear. Questioning evolved to include how they felt before, during and after committing the crime.

A number of the participants used the colloquial word 'buzz' in relation to the experience and how they were feeling which equates with Brown's (1997) description of this feature. Three of the participants spoke of the feelings of power and control which they attributed to their offending as a powerful emotional reaction. Feelings of control emerged which intensified the emotional feelings attached to their offending and criminal identity.

Linking crime and substance use

Six of the participants stated that their motivation for committing crime was to support their drug use and to support the related lifestyle. One participant (Wesley) stated his motivation for committing the crime was because he was addicted to it (offending), suggesting a step beyond the 'buzz' to something more compulsive. Alfie stated his motivation for committing crime was a sense of belonging while Freddie declared his motivation was about showing off to others.

Six of the participants also indicated that the majority of the offences had been committed under the influence of drink or drugs, suggesting that alcohol or drugs was not only a motive for committing crime but also a precipitant of crime while under the influence of substances. In relation to recovery, three of the participants spoke of the relevance of attending the RAPt programme which had helped them look at and change their behaviours, as outlined in the quotations below.

> **Terry:** "I'm thinking differently now and I am thinking what direction I want my life to go more of a positive direction than I have done for a long time."

> **John:** "then I started RAPt and it brought so much emotions back to me and feelings back and made me understand myself and my crimes and why I done things and it gave me the responsibility to own my problems and own my responsibilities."

> **Wesley:** "I've got to change I've got no option coz if I don't they might as well keep me in till the day I die."

Discussion

The five core social motives identified by Fiske (2004) applied fully to two of the participants (Tyler and John) in relation to their offending behaviours. The common denominator appears to refer to a breakdown in the relationship with the family and a renewed sense of loyalty and identity to their friends. This alliance within a gang or towards a friend involved establishing a framework which enveloped the core social motives and bound them into social group norms and social identities in which offending and substance use were embedded. In relation to their addiction and criminal activity, nine out of the 10 participants identified a sense of belonging as a crucial factor to their addiction and criminal behaviour, suggesting the strength of group identity in the perceived bind to the norms and values of offending and substance using groups, and the resultant challenges in attempting to sustain desistance and recovery. In addition, nine out 10 also describe a powerful emotional reaction as being significant in this process when attached to the subjective social identity relating to crime.

Fiske (2004) believes that this small number of core social motives enhances people's survival in groups and are unifying themes in social psychology. Evidence of these themes, detected in the qualitative data, provides useful knowledge in further understanding criminal behaviour and its links to addictive careers. Further research may be required to ascertain if positive role models and mentors would be a useful intervention in redirecting offenders away from committing crime incorporating work on social identity transition and positive social identities of recovery from criminality. As such, the more acceptable positive social construct of recovery may deliver resources (i.e., emotionally significant) that are sustainable and contribute toward being an active and engaged member of society. These themes are addressed in part in the Haslam et al. and Bliuc et al. chapters in this book.

An exploration of the developmental pathways of young people into crime and anti social behaviour (The Riots Communities and Victims Panel's Report, 2013) examined the evidence for interventions that exist for effectively addressing the behaviour of young people, in particular the cost effectiveness of such initiatives. A London-based charity, run by ex-offenders that offered a variety of intervention programmes in schools and pupil referral units relating to anti-social behaviours and criminal offending was highlighted in the report as "an example of an effective programme".

Positive interventions using mentors are a useful tool in changing thought distortions and behavioural responses, and can provide both a strong therapeutic ally and also the basis for a new form of social learning that can be extended through effective and assertive linkage to attractive and positive social groups. In the case of the RAPt programme, continuation of the 12-step programme through attendance at MHOs such as Offenders Anonymous would provide such opportunity. Evidence of positive change in those participants who completed the RAPt programme may indicate that a change has occurred in their cognitions and motivation. Therefore, this would enable individuals to remain abstinent from substance misuse and subsequently reduce the need for individuals to engage in acquisitive crime to sustain their substance misuse. The challenge is to establish how that initial change impacts on individual's social networks and social identities when returning to their communities and whether they have created a strong enough foundation to allow them to benefit from new forms of social engagement.

This change may also be persuasive in arguing a model for offender management which acknowledges that offender's core social needs and motives that may have driven their addictive behaviour and criminal activity and help guide and encourage prisoners towards a recovery orientated approach to such behaviour. What is clear from the data above is that social identity and social norms play a key role in initiating and sustaining addiction and offending careers and that to change these core components of identity is a process that requires both intervention programmes like RAPt and the subsequent pathways into pro-social and positive networks and identities.

Acknowledgement

This study was conducted as part of the MSc in Addiction Psychology, School of Applied Sciences, at London South Bank University, London, UK. Components of this study were previously published in Malton, J. (2013). Is it possible to be addicted to committing crime? *Addiction Today,* March/April 2013, 22–23

References

American Psychiatric Association (2000). *Diagnostic and Statistical Manual of Mental Disorders* (4th ed.). Arlington, VA: American Psychiatric Association.

Bandura, A. (1977). Self-efficacy: Toward a unifying theory of behavioral change. *Psychological Review, 34,* 191–215.

Brown, I. (1997). A Theoretical Model of Behavioural Addictions – Applied to Offending. In J. E. Hodge, M. McMurran and C. R. Hollin (Eds) *Addicted to crime?* (pp. 13–65). Hoboken, NJ: John Wiley & Sons.

Fiske, S. T. (2004). *Social beings: Core motives in social psychology* (2nd ed.). Hoboken, NJ: John Wiley & Sons.

HM Chief Inspector of Prisons for England and Wales (2014–2015). *Annual Report.* Retrieved from www.justiceinspectorates.gov.uk.

Howitt, D. & Cramer, D. (2005). *Introduction to research methods in psychology.* Harlow, UK: Pearson Education.

Nurco, D. N., Hanlon, T. E., Kinlock, T. W., & Slaght, E. (1990). *Variations in criminal patterns among narcotic addicts.* U.S. Department of Justice National Institute of Justice. Retrieved from www.ncjrs.gov.

RAPt (2011). Reconviction analysis: Avoiding the cycle of drug relapse reoffending. *Criminal Law & Justice Weekly.* Retrieved from www.criminallawandjustice.co.uk.

Tajfel, H. & Turner, J. (1979). *Integrative theory of intergroup conflict.* In W. G. Austin and Worchel, S. (Eds.). *The social psychology of intergroup relations* (pp. 33–48). Monterey, CA: Brooks/Cole.

Terry, D. J. & Hogg, M. A. (1996). Group norms and the attitude-behaviour relationship. A role for group identification. *Personality and Social Psychology Bulletin, 22,* 776–793.

The Riots Communities and Victims Panel's Report (2013). Retrieved from www.gov.uk/dclg.

Thornberry, T. P. (Ed.). (1997). *Developmental theories of crime and delinquency.* New Brunswick, NJ: Transaction Publishers.

Turner, J. C., Hogg, M. A., Oakes, P. Reicher, S. D., & Wetherall, M. S. (1987). *Rediscovering the social group: A self -categorisation theory.* New York: Basil Blackwell.

UK Ministry of Justice (2014). Offenders Behaviour Programmes (OBPs). Retrieved from www.justice.gov.uk/offenders/before-after-release/obp.

7

THE ASSOCIATIVE REFLECTIVE MODEL OF SOCIAL IDENTIFICATION (ARMS)

With a particular emphasis upon addiction, behavioural change and social identity

Sarah A. Buckingham

We could confidently state that positive social connections aid in the development of a functional neuronal system (see Eagleman, 2015). Initially, enculturation of the infant is predominantly dependent upon significant others where the development of positive social connections enables the individual to steer the course of daily challenges within a multifaceted world (Reynolds & Branscombe, 2015).

Poor social connections can be determinants for impoverished mental and physical health (Durkheim, 1897/2007) and be significant factors in the development of psychopathology. To feel isolated is one of the greatest of evils for man stated the psychologist, William James (1890/2007). In writing about sociability and shyness as instincts he wrote that; "As a gregarious animal, man is excited both by the absence and by the presence of his kind" (p. 430). Earlier in the chapter he described how man inhibits such instincts as sociability and shyness with the development of habit, until he becomes unaware of the former. Addiction has been described as a habit (West, 2005). Recent work has demonstrated how subjective intoxication reduced ostracism effects manipulated through Cyberball, (a virtual ball game that can be used for research on ostracism, social exclusion, rejection, prejudice and discrimination) and reduced feelings of distress and elevated feelings of social inclusiveness (Hales, Kipling, & Eckardt, 2015).

For many, the ability to socialise or reduction of uneasiness from the inability to do so may have been overridden at some stage, by the use of addictive substances and/or behaviours. In the final days of despair many find themselves isolated and ostracised by the very people they sought to impress and enjoy. The addiction-related identity may eclipse all other identities, for example being a mother, and lead the individual to pursue one aim, e.g., to drink. Within the literature of Alcoholics Anonymous, the authors highlight the difficulties they perceive to underlie the problems of addiction: "Since defective relations with other human beings have nearly always been the immediate cause of our woes, including our alcoholism" (AA 2007, p. 82). The alcoholic and addict have traditionally been perceived as delinquents of low social status and to exist outside of the mainstream of 'normative' behaviour refusing or unable to conform to the social norms of the day (Camus, 1942/2013).

It is suggested that the process of recovery from addictive practices and substances is long term. It is possible that personal goals for abstinence, cessation or reduction are more achievable when individuals allow themselves to become subjectively affiliated with a recovery group. Identification with similar others and the collective agency of this membership has the potential to provide a bridge to 'normalization'. As such, the social identity associated with recovery will be bound intrinsically with new behavior that is not related to addictive using and practices. Learning to become part of a group with higher status and the associated self-efficacy and self-esteem, has the potential to elevate the individual into a positive social identity that differentiates a new identity associated with recovery from the chronic maladaptive social identity associated with addiction (see Buckingham, Frings, & Albery, 2013).

Social identity theory (SIT)

The concept of the group as a collection of individuals has been the predominant Western perspective with a few notable exceptions (Durkheim, 1897/2007; Wundt, 1916/2011; McDougall, 1921; Mead, 1934; Sherif, 1936; Asch, 1952). These non-reductionist, collectivist theorists, conceived that the emergent group properties as non-individualistic and qualitatively distinct. Tajfel defined social identity as "the individual's knowledge that he belongs to certain social groups together with some emotional and value significance to him of this group membership" (Tajfel, 1972a, p. 292). It is not enough to be defined by others as belonging to social groups and being classified by others as belonging to such groups. It is an intrinsic part of this theory that individuals have internalised qualities of the group into their self-concept and are subjectively attached to it (see Jetten, Haslam, Haslam, & Dingle, 2014). The individual resides within the group and the group resides within the individual. The composition of an active, complex, multifaceted self (James, 1890/2007) is reflective of an individual's social relationships.

From the social identity perspective, the *content* of an individual's self-concept (Tajfel & Turner, 1979) are the parts of the self that have been developed, *a priori,* from the experience of memberships of social categories. The self-identity within this context incorporates traits, beliefs, behaviours and ideologies that have been accumulated from such experience (Brewer, 2001). At a societal level, the individual has internalised group elements that represent his belief system of group relations, e.g., social norms. Groups are subjectively represented by their norms and the level of prototypicality may predict how strongly identified an individual has become within a particular group. Intragroup differences are minimized through adherence to group norms and stereotypical group attributes. Normative behaviour is both descriptive (they describe how things are now) and prescriptive/injunctive (they are judgmental and expectancy based), (Cialdini, Reno, & Kallren, 1990; Prentice & Miller, 1996). These may be antagonistic or congruent, where the former may motivate behaviour change (Berkowitz, 2004). Group norms are both the spoken and un-spoken rules of how the group regulates itself. They provide a social frame of reference upon which group members can locate their own behaviour.

Social influence can be both emotionally and psychologically relevant, by significantly contributing to perception and behaviour (Oakes, 1987; Turner, 1982). Being part of a social group, and the strength of the identification with it and psychological attachment to it, influence attitude and consequent behaviour (Sani, 2012; Terry & Hogg, 1996). For example, social isolation and early-life maternal separation have been linked with increases in impulsive action (Lovic, Keen, Fletcher, & Fleming, 2011), lack of social norms and low sociability. In contrast, more creative thinking has been linked with multiple group memberships via cognitive flexibility (Steffens, Goclowska, Cruwys, & Galinsky, 2015). Turner (1985) stated that the way individuals internalise their group membership was through two main routes. The first was through a credible and esteemed social source, which was attractive to the individual (see Milner, 1975). The second route was through trusted fellow ingroup members, which would lead to an individual change in attitude. Heyes states that, "*we* may endow children with heightened social motivation by rewarding them from earliest infancy for doing what we do" (Heyes, 2011, p. 200). Approach and avoidant behaviour tendencies between ingroup and outgroup influence may be the direct effect of automatic processes that may even have been established in early childhood (Bargh, 2013; Chen & Bargh, 1999). The self is defined through comparison with significant others at varying levels of abstraction and inclusiveness and are available for categorization through prior social experience.

Self-categorisation theory (SCT)

Self-categorization theory (Turner, Hogg, Oakes, Reicher, & Wetheril, 1987) could be described as the cognitive and perceptual component behind social identity theory. This conceptualisation of the cognitive self attempts to describe a flexible, adaptive individual. It is emphasised that self-categorizations are not self-images that are static but more a cinematic action picture with behaviour and environment intrinsically linked in reflective action. They are creative, contemporary perceptual constructs. This theory attempts to portray the current psychological reality of the individual that is the result of interaction with the environment (internal or external) where a self-category becomes salient.[1] Amplified levels of identification and association with similar others (ingroup) in comparison with those seen as not similar (outgroup) create a social frame of reference and predominantly define the individual in a positive light through a process of positive distinctiveness. Therefore, perception and behaviour may change rapidly and with minimal conscious awareness, being characteristically automatic (Bargh, 1994, 1997) and dependent upon current goals and motivations.

Activation of behavioural representations within the environment may be triggered by acts of volition. However, what may appear as conscious choice may be motivated by on-the-spot associative evaluations from subtle cues within the environment (Bargh, 1994, 2006) in relationship to previous actions and prior experience. Bruner (1957) described a system where structural representations were formed through previous experience and had potential to shape future perception and behaviour. For example, implicit memory associations of parental alcohol use related to the onset of adolescents' alcohol use (Van Der Vorst et al., 2012).

Perception-behaviour link

The very act of perceiving an action or distinguishing feature of a group member has also been demonstrated to automatically activate the stereotypical behaviour of a group category (Bargh, 1994, 1999; Bargh, Chen, & Burrows, 1996; Brewer, 1988; Devine, 1989). A group of smokers (n = 77) were asked to photograph significant people in their lives, described as 'personal' smoking (PS) and non-smoking people (PN), and were compared with photographs of unknown people, described as 'standard' smoking (SS) and non-smoking people (SN). Investigators found that images of significant smokers (PS) increased levels of craving and excitement among this smoker participant group (Conklin, Salkeld, Perkins, & Robin, 2013).

Sophisticated attunement to social category similarities may activate a 'chameleon effect' (Chartrand & Bargh, 1999), promoting a positive link between similar others. This may be one basis for social learning (see Heyes, 2011) and successful social interaction. Individuals acquire knowledge of how to behave socially, where to find food, indeed how to navigate life normatively through observation, imitation and identification with significant and similar others who both react and collaborate within their social environment (see Heyes, 2011). We could state, "that perceiving is for doing" (Dijksterhuis & Bargh, 2001, p. 4). The 'perception-behaviour' link (Bargh et al., 1996; Chartrand & Bargh, 1999) describes environmental, semantic cues and simultaneous activation of behavioural schemata, leading to an outcome of behaviour; i.e., walking slowly, unless directly overridden. As such, there is an acknowledgement that behaviour may be consciously or unconsciously led where a spectrum through layers of preconsciousness may be evidenced.

Automatic cognitive processes

The acknowledgement that our everyday existence is guided by nonconscious processes has gathered momentum (see Bargh & Morsella, 2008; Fiske & Macrae, 2012; Hassin, Uleman, & Bargh, 2005) with empirical evidence of how automatic cognitive processes may direct behaviour (see Gawronski & Payne, 2010). Automatic cognitive processes are 'uncontrollable, fast and effective', (Bargh, 1997). They operate outside the control of conscious awareness, are not intentional and require minimal cognitive capacity. Such implicit cognitive processes are in contrast to explicit cognitive processes that are rule-bound, more effortful, prone

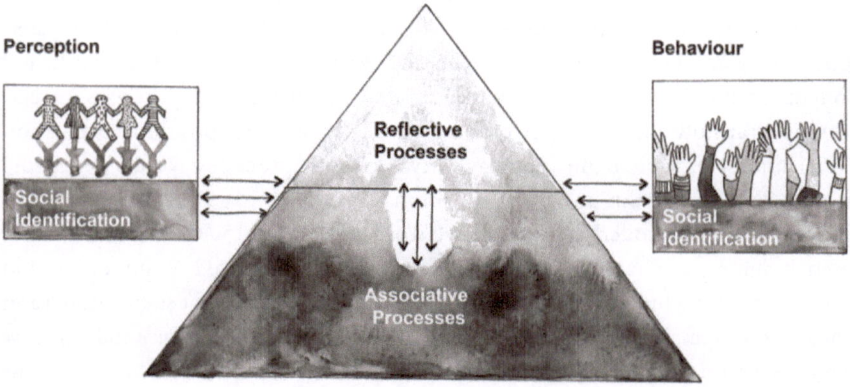

FIGURE 7.1 The Associative Reflective Model of Social Identification (ARMS).

to depletion and slower in activation. Automatic cognitive processes are described as being emotional, motivational, and behavioural reactions within context (Posner & Snyder, 1975).

For example, when students were given a lexical decision task involving the concepts of 'elderly' and 'forgetful' (Dijksterhuis, Aarts, Bargh, & van Knippenberg, 1998) the ones with more exposure to the elderly exhibited stronger association between the two. Following on from this was a memory task for the stimuli in the previous task, where the students with the stronger associations between 'elderly' and 'forgetful' exhibited poorer memory performance. Critically, the students were unaware of both the prime and their consequent behaviour that related to it.

To investigate more broadly how automatic cognitive processes may drive social behaviour, the social identity approach alongside social cognitive components (specifically regarding automatic cognitive processes) were synthesised to create a dual process model entitled, The Associative Reflective Model of Social Identification (ARMS), (see Figure 7.1).

As such, this model has been designed to explore the 'bottom-up' and 'top-down' dynamic psychosocial mechanics of social identity processes. Sheeran, Gollwitzer and Bargh (2013) have suggested that nonconscious processes may contribute to health behavior change. In line with this thinking, this dual process model, incorporating both associative and reflective modes of processing, was used to explore how social identities may be vehicles for health behaviour and health behavioural change. Behaviour may stem from differing levels of consciousness and this is portrayed synthetically in this dualistic model to test implicit and explicit routes of social identification.

Dual process models of memory storage and retrieval

Various dual process models of memory storage and retrieval (see Gawronski & Payne, 2010) have previously described how both nonconscious and conscious processes may originate from two differing memory systems that are bidirectional (see Gawronski & Bodenhausen, 2006; Moss & Albery, 2009; Smith & DeCoster, 2000; Strack & Deutsch, 2004; Wiers & Stacy, 2010). For example, Gawronski and Bodenhausen's (2006) model refers to *associative* and *propositional* processes in relationship to attitude change. They proposed the associative-propositional evaluation (APE) model in which the interplay between both processes would determine attitude change. In this model propositional processes have been described as negotiators for the underlying associative store and proceed with evaluative, rule-based judgments. The associative processes may be portrayed as impulsive and perceived to drive 'uncontrollable behaviour', thus suggesting that such automation is negative and unruly. Strack and Deutsch (2004) described *the reflective* and *impulsive* system where dominance also resides within the reflective mode. These previous synthetic models of duality emphasise the pathology of the nonconscious processes semantically, i.e., *impulsive*, and how conflict may arise between *reflective* logic and uncontrollable action (see Evans, 2009 for critique). Moss and Albery (2009) in their alcohol-behaviour link dual process model, proposed that when the propositional mode is in deficit, the associative mode offers efficient response through expectancy associations when cued perceptually, for example in alcohol myopia.

In line with their model, Moss and Albery (2009, p. 522.) state that "it is an important conceptual point that extreme responding is not necessarily synonymous with reckless or negative behaviour" Bargh (1997) described the associated action as being 'efficient' in contrast to 'impulsive', capturing the fast moving quality but in a more positive light. This would then enable the individual to become more adaptive and to utilise the limited conscious capacity for rule-based activities and considerations.

Contemporary research has demonstrated how addictive behaviour may not be volitional and may operate predominantly from the 'propositional' route (see Munafò & Albery, 2006; Stacy & Wiers, 2010) associated with automatic goal dependent processes. For example, Lindgren et al., (2013) demonstrated that the implicit association among current drinkers between concepts of 'drinking' and 'me' was a predictor of alcohol consumption, problematic drinking symptoms and alcohol cravings.

Addiction and addiction behavioural change

Addiction use disorder is a complex chronic problem with competing and confusing definitions and treatments. It is progressive and is associated with impulsivity. A key characteristic of addictive use disorder is the inability to cease addictive behaviour even though the individual may consciously desire to do so (see Wiers et al., 2010). Morbidity rates are high and are rising for alcohol related deaths (Institute of Alcohol Studies [IAS], 2014).

The process of addiction behavioural change is problematic. Withdrawal symptoms and cravings are characteristic and occur within individuals to greater or lesser degrees. Frequently individualistic (Prochaska & Velicer, 1997; see West, 2005 for critique) and brief in nature (e.g., weeks duration), treatment benefit can be overridden by recurring periods of relapse and remission (see Moos & Finney, 2011; West & Brown, 2013) and social network affiliations that support the undesired behaviour (Moos, 2011) and negate the new.

However, a more positive approach where new social pathways that offer alternative behavioural options (e.g., being sober) have potential to become activated automatically. By moving away from prior allegiances that have become unhelpful and creating psychological distance from these (see Buckingham et al., 2013) aids in this process. By developing new social pathways that promote the self in a positive light (in line with Tajfel and Turners original theory (1979) that people normatively strive for a positive self-construct) people can be encouraged to create new affiliations that may become automatic and efficient. The Social Identity Model of Cessation Maintenance (SIMCM) introduced by Frings and Albery (2015) (see Frings and Albery, this volume) highlights the positive role that implicit processes may play in cessation of addictive practices and behaviours.

Extending on from this, the Associative Model of Social Identification (ARMS) introduced in this chapter acknowledges how our active social identities can influence our daily behaviours both negatively (e.g., other problematic appetitive affiliations) and positively (e.g., being a member of a recovery group). Either way, subjective social norms are environmentally triggered and are accessible at differing levels of conscious awareness.

Study overview

As such, direct methods (e.g., questionnaire based survey) of explicit recall may not be so effective in capturing the relevant factors for effective addiction research and may also be susceptible to response bias (McCusker, 2001). This is particularly apparent in areas where certain identities (e.g., smoker) have become stigmatised and are therefore socially sensitive (Bayer & Stuber, 2006; Leas, Zablocki, Edland, & Al-Delaimy, 2014). Leas et al. (2014) reported how smokers reported smoking behaviour but did not self-label themselves with the smoker identity. Direct methods of measurement also demand introspection that is frequently limited by conscious accessibility (Schnabel, Asendorpf, & Greenwald, 2008). Individual, self-report of drinking behaviour for example, may be an unreliable mode of recall due to cognitive impairment caused by alcohol (see Moss & Albery, 2009). This method of direct measurement may therefore be less efficient than indirect measurement of implicit associations that have been described as being more precise (Houben & Wiers, 2006, 2008; Lindgren et al., 2013; Rooke, Hines, & Thorsteinsson, 2008; Waters & Leventhal, 2006), and may have greater predictive validity (Fazio & Olson, 2003).

To test the hypothesis that indirect methods of measurement (i.e., implicit) may be more predictive than direct methods of measurement (i.e., explicit) in relationship to health behavior and health behaviour change, both were included into a quasi-experimental correlation design.

The laboratory based study presented in this chapter used both an explicit self-report questionnaire alongside a variation of the Implicit Association Test (IAT, Greenwald, McGhee, & Schwartz, 1998) – the Single-Target Implicit Association Test (ST-IAT, Wigboldus, Holland, & van Knippenberg, 2006). The single-target IAT variant has been endorsed as a successful measure that is 'reliable' and 'effective' (Bluemke and Friese, 2007) and has previously been used in addiction research (i.e., smoking; Huijding & de Jong, 2006). This is a computerised reaction time task that measures associations (using response latencies) between one target category and two attribute categories.

The hypothesis was tested with a group of smokers who had all attempted to quit (N = 66), where some had been successful (n = 35) and some had not (n = 31). It was suggested that implicit associative processes linked with smoker social identities would be more predictive of successful or unsuccessful quitters, than reflective processes (explicit levels of ingroup identification, i.e., *I identify with being a smoker/ex-smoker*; Doosje, Ellemers, & Spears, 1995) obtained from self-report. It was suggested that current friends who also smoked and contemporary experience of other appetitive behaviour (measured in the self-report questionnaire) would be implicated in this process by providing a broader range of cues for addictive behaviour from where the individual might self-define.

For the indirect measurement, the implicit associations between the target category of 'self' and the attribute categories of 'smoker' and 'ex-smoker', were measured. Five words that represented each social category were chosen by a random selection of five ingroup category members, i.e., smokers and ex-smokers. The self-category was composed of three words that were representative of the individual, e.g., first name, and two photographic images of the participant. The faster the response between that target category and the attribute category would indicate more implicit association between them.

Results demonstrated that the unsuccessful quitters recorded significantly more friends in their social network who smoked, and recorded a significantly greater amount of problematic appetitive behaviours than the successful quitters. Importantly, implicit measures of identity association significantly differentiated between successful and unsuccessful quitters – and added significantly more predictive power than simply measuring explicitly reported identities. There was a significant but moderately sized relationship between explicit and implicit measures of identity, suggesting they are related but distinct constructs. Interestingly, unsuccessful quitters had more extreme explicit levels of identification with all categories than the successful quitters. The higher levels of explicit ex-smoker identity are highlighted.

A possible explanation for this effect is that overt identification with ex-smokers may be the start of the quit process (see Hendricks, Wood, & Hall, 2009). As such, this might be seen as pre-action for behavioural change and psychological, social mobility to a higher status group. Another possible explanation may be cultural, where smoking is now perceived as a stigmatised identity.

Implicit association with subjective membership categories has the potential to change perception and behaviour and yet not be evidenced in explicit identification. These processes are however related. Concordance between the two may produce moments of 'aha', where previous disassociation or preconscious elements come to the fore in the conscious mind of the individual. There are debates regarding the shared variance between implicit and explicit systems (Gawronski & Payne, 2010; Reich, Below, & Goldman, 2010). It is possibly that there are some shared elements and others that are independent of each other. Identification with similar others in a group setting may not only help alleviate social stigma surrounding certain identities, aid in motivation and goal achievement but also contribute to greater conscious awareness and more identification with one's actions and behaviours. The present results however, suggest that asking individuals to self-report on their health behaviour will not give a complete picture of the underlying dynamics involved in change, especially in the field of addiction and addiction behavioural change.

Motivational aspects within a social landscape may trigger self-definition at a current time-point. These may incorporate peer influence quoted as being a major factor for patterns of health behaviour (Mosback & Leventhal, 1988), especially in the adolescent population where the need for approval from esteemed ingroup members and the desire to be part of a group may enhance levels of ingroup identification (Milner, 1975; Phua, 2013; Turner, 1985). Chronic problematic health behaviour such as smoking is frequently activated when under pressure to conform to contemporary social norms, for example other people who smoke (Perkins & Berkowitz, 1986; Phua, 2013).

Individuals who are guided by appetitive impulses have been shown to display poorer executive control (Gawronski & Bodenhausen, 2006; Fillmore & Vogel-Sprott, 2006) and stronger implicit, appetitive associations (Field, Schoenmakers, & Wiers, 2008). This has a cumulative effect in active addiction. Moving away from friends who also participate in addictive behaviours and practices has been shown to reduce relapse rates and other appetitive behaviours (Buckingham et al., 2013). Less drinking behaviour within an individuals' close social network was shown to reduce personal levels of consumption in a prospective study (Rosenquist, Murabito, Fowler, & Christakis, 2010). Similarly, pro-drinkers and pro-abstainers network variables were primary predictors to alcohol outcome over a three-year period (Stout, Kelly, Magill, & Pagano, 2011). These social network predictors were more significant than the specifics of the routes of achievement, where considerations of severity and gender were controlled. Social influence impacts individual behaviour. For example, peer influence is cited as being the major factor in smoking initiation (Falomir & Invernizzi, 1999; Mosback & Leventhal, 1988), especially in the adolescent population. Such initiation coupled with alcohol for example, enhances attraction toward others and reinforces habitual use (Attwood, Penton-Voak, Goodwin, & Munafò, 2012). Attraction to peers may be more heightened within the addicted population, due to habitual reinforcement, substance use and heightened sensitivity toward salient cues (Attwood et al., 2012;

Robinson & Berridge, 2003). Peer influence is also a significant factor in successful addiction treatment (see Conklin et al., 2013). Moos (2011, p. 61) stated that "the social contents that underlie the initiation and maintenance of substance misuse may hold within them the potential for resolution of the problems they create".

This current study has demonstrated that the pool of social reference in the contemporary landscape of the individual may potentially impact implicit associations in memory and could also contribute to health behavioural change.

Common-fate and solidarity in the face of adversity are curative factors associated with positive group memberships (Jetten, Haslam, & Haslam, 2012) delivering collective resilience (Drury, Cocking, & Reicher, 2009). An experiment conducted by Jones and Jetten (2011) supports this claim. Participants who were primed for multiple group identities were able to hold their hand in cold water (0–2 degrees Celsius) for longer than those in the control condition. This lends credence to the conception that meaningful social memberships increase physical and mental resilience. Jetten et al. (2012) highlight how shared social identities in a variety of social settings and vulnerable populations may also have positive health outcomes.

Subjective affiliation with a group can significantly change a person's perception and behaviour. Social identity theory acknowledges the approach/avoidant influence of intergroup bias that is reflected in the main by a positive social identity that is achieved through active positive distinctiveness. This non-reductionist theory describes the group as a psychological entity, where individuals internalise qualities of significant group memberships. This may occur through repeated exposure or in a novel situation where components of group membership have become associated in memory. They may also derive from contemporary social influence (e.g., recovery group peers).

Addiction behavioural change may be achieved by learning from similar individuals where emotional and value-laden benefits lead to associations being forged in memory. For example, assertive linkages made by clinicians for individuals to be introduced to a mutual-help organisation (MHO) by an ingroup member may provide the first step in the recovery process (see Best, 2012, 2014; Day, this volume; Kelly & White, 2011). As such this begins a journey of positive connectedness where the resource from group membership potentially offers the individual a powerful associative resource – a sense of 'we', when cognitively compromised. Pattern activation may then link membership affiliation with behavioural representations, reflective of the group norms.

Group therapy however, has been a successful major long-term option for addiction treatment, with a particular emphasis upon MHOs and there has been a steady progress in contemporary research (e.g., Humphries, 2004; Kelly, Stout, Magill, & Tonignan, 2011; Kelly & White, 2011; Kelly et al., this volume; Moos, 2008) that has begun to address the social and psychological factors that underlie its effectiveness. Specific group norms of individual group membership are referred to being "key active ingredients" (Moos, 2008, p. 387). For individuals with problematic addictive behaviour, affiliation with a recovery group membership may offer an internal resource that could be utilised in times of stress and low cognitive capacity.

Relapse and remission may be more appropriately addressed by considering social identity processes that are both implicit and explicit. Automatic social cognitive processes have been described as impulsive but it is suggested that they may also be described as *efficient* when activated from a positive social identity of recovery that is distinct from a social identity that promotes addiction and the related health behaviours. It is suggested that the bottom-up top-down ARMS model of behaviour change enables a more intuitive approach (see Figure 7.1). Considering addiction behavior and behaviour change from the social identity perspective permits a perspective that does not pathologise. Describing behaviour as *efficient* in contrast with *impulsive* downgrades pejorative language and suggests that the psychosocial mechanisms connected with addiction can also offer a positive solution through the recovery process.

The ability to generalise these results to other forms of addictive behaviours and indeed health behaviour is possible for at least two reasons. First, investigation into identity and recovery (Dingle, Stark, Cruwys, & Best, 2015) suggests that similar processes operate among different samples in the population who have experienced recovery or who strive for this status. Second, to argue against generalisation would suggest that fundamental social identity mechanisms are different between groups. This does not preclude that the size of effects may vary between populations, or that they may contain relatively unique moderating and mediating factors. One interesting possibility is that the size of effects associated with implicit identities may be present in variable degrees dependent upon group characteristics and individual differences.

Future research

Future work could explore through the ARMS approach, the interplay between identities in a naturalistic prospective study to compare differing routes for addiction behavioural change, e.g., SMART Recovery (www.smartrecovery.org.uk), becoming a member of a recovery choir. In addition, monitoring conflicting and competing identities for an individual within their recovery landscape over a significant time period, (i.e., years) would deliver a more cohesive picture of the recovery process. This could include monitoring the social identity trajectories of close family members and close friends. The development of alternative methods of measurement for tracking differing levels of consciousness would be advantageous.

Into action

The application of the Associative Reflective Model of Social Identification would add more coherence and complexity to the emerging picture of how social categories that promote healthy lifestyle choices and their associated norms are vehicles for effective behavioural change through positive emotive connectivity.

By intelligent design of novel and traditional ways of accruing new social processes, architects of recovery models, for example, are *enabling* individuals to become prosocial and socially mobilised from their poor status of addiction and isolation (e.g., Best et al., 2016; Frings & Albery, 2015). Coming in from the cold is a reciprocal action. Social mobility for stigmatised groups may be difficult to attain but social creativity can also create change. Redefinition of boundaries and reciprocal action can be transformative and change lives.

Individuals who have sought treatment from others who offered limited insight may have been stigmatised because of lack of success from inefficient and simplistic models. It is conceivable that the impact of this would be self-stigmatisation (White, 2009) where individuals internalise the group consensus of failure and consequently lose hope for future change. Therefore, to suggest that personal choice will effect change is difficult. For those who sincerely strive for more positive health outcomes, in the footsteps of Asch the follow on from this work needs to be one of action, where empirical research findings become transformed into policy and practice (Jetten et al., 2014; Haslam, 2014; Haslam, Cruwys, Haslam, Dingle, & Chang, 2016; Haslam et al., this volume). Behavioural change in this context is part of a dynamic approach that is both contemporary and action-based where together individuals can shape their own and others futures by linking together to create new worlds.

Acknowledgements

This research was based in The School of Applied Sciences, London South Bank University, UK and formed part of a PhD thesis (completed 2014). Supervisory support provided by Professor Ian Albery (London South Bank University) and Dr Daniel Frings (London South Bank University) is gratefully acknowledged.

Note

1 The definition of the word *salient* (adj) is derived from the latin word *saliens* which means leaping. This is taken from the word *salire*; which means to leap. This is a perceptible quality of a stimulus, which has derived from stimuli, from within the individual organism (Coleman, 2009). Oakes (1987) stipulated that this meaning of stimulus salience is not the same as salient self-categorization that has been activated as a function of the psychological group membership to increase perception and influence the direction of behaviour. The latter meaning may only be relevant as a 'causal antecedent' (p. 119) to the associated group membership category.

References

Alcoholics Anonymous (2007). *Twelve steps and twelve traditions: How members of Alcoholics Anonymous recover and how the society functions*, (34th ed.). New York: Alcoholics Anonymous World Services, Inc.

Asch, S.E. (1952). *Social psychology*. Englewood Cliffs, NJ: Prentice-Hall.

Attwood, A.S., Penton-Voak, I.S., Goodwin, C., & Munafò, M.R. (2012). Effects of acute nicotine and alcohol on the rating of attractiveness in social smokers and alcohol drinkers. *Drug & Alcohol Dependence, 125*, 43–8.

Bargh, J.A. (1994). The four horsemen of automaticity: Awareness, intention, efficiency, and control in social cognition. In R.S. Wyer & T.K. Srull (Eds.), *Handbook of social cognition* (2nd ed., pp. 1–40). Hillsdale, NJ: Lawrence Erlbaum Associates.

Bargh, J.A. (1997). The automaticity of everyday life. In R.S. Wyer (1997). (Ed.), *Advances in Social Cognition: Volume X*. New Jersey: Lawrence Erlbaum.

Bargh, J.A. (2006). What have we been priming all these years? On the development, mechanisms, and ecology of nonconscious social behaviour. *European Journal of Social Psychology, 36*, 147–168.

Bargh, J.A. (2013). Early childhood is where many adult automatic processes are born. In M.R. Banaji and S.A. Gelman (Eds.), *Navigating the social world: What infants, children, and other species can teach us* (pp. 58–65). New York: Oxford University Press.

Bargh, J.A., Chen, M., & Burrows, L. (1996). Automaticity of social behavior: Direct effects of trait construct and stereotype priming on action. *Journal of Personality and Social Psychology, 71*, 230–244.

Bargh, J.A. & Morsella, E. (2008). The unconscious mind. Perspectives in *Psychological Science, 3*, 73–79.

Bayer, R. & Stuber, J. (2006). Tobacco control, stigma, and public health: Rethinking the relations. *American Journal of Public Health, 96*, 47–50.

Berkowitz, A.D. (2004). *The social norms approach*. Retrieved from www.alanberkowitz.com.

Best, D. (2012). *Addiction recovery: A movement for social change and personal growth in the UK*. Brighton, UK: Pavilion Publishing.

Best, D. (2014). *Strength, support, setbacks and solutions: The developmental pathway to addiction recovery*. Brighton, UK: Pavilion Publishing.

Best, D., Beckwith, M., Haslam, C., Haslam, S.A., Jetten, J., Mawson, E., & Lubman, D.I. (2016). Overcoming drug and alcohol addiction as a process of social identity transition: The Social Identity Model of Recovery (SIMOR). *Addiction, Research and Theory, 24*, 111–123.

Bluemke, M., & Friese, M. (2008). Reliability and validity of the Single-target Implicit Association Test (ST-IAT); Assessing automatic affect towards multiple attitude objects. *European Journal of Social Psychology, 38*, 977–997.

Brewer, M.B. (1988). A dual process model of impression formation. In T.K. Srull & R.S. Wyer, Jr. (Eds.), *Advances in social cognition* (Vol 1, pp. 1–36).

Brewer, M.B. (2001). The many faces of social identity: Implications for political psychology. *Political Psychology, 22*, 115–123.

Bruner, J.S. (1957). On perceptual readiness. *Psychological Review, 64*, 123–151.

Buckingham, S.A., Frings, D., & Albery, I.P. (2013). Group membership and social identity in addiction recovery. *Psychology of Addictive Behaviors, 27*, 1132–1140.

Camus, A. (1942/2013). *The outsider*. London: Penquin Modern Classics.

Chartrand, T.L. & Bargh, J.A. (1999). The chameleon effect: The perception-behavior link and social interaction. *Journal of Personality and Social Psychology, 76*, 893–910.

Chen, M. & Bargh, J.A. (1999). Nonconscious approach and avoidance behavioral consequences of the automatic evaluation effect. *Personality and Social Psychology, 25*, 215–224.

Cialdini, R.B., Reno, R.R., & Kallgren, C.A. (1990). A focus theory of normative conduct: Recycling the concept of norms to reduce lettering in public places. *Journal of Personality and Social Psychology, 58*, 1015–26.

Conklin, C.A., Salkeld, R. P., Perkins, K. A., & Robin, N. (2013). Do people serve as cues to smoke? *Nicotine and Tobacco Research, 15*, 2081–2087.

Devine, P.G. (1989). Stereotypes and prejudice: Their automatic and controlled components. *Journal of Personality and Social Psychology, 56*, 5–18.

Dijksterhuis, A., Aarts, H., Bargh, J.A., & van Knippenberg, A. (1998). *Intergroup contact and automatic behavior*. Manuscript submitted for publication, University of Nijmegen, The Netherlands.

Dijksterhuis, A. & Bargh, J.A. (2001). The perception-behaviour expressway: Automatic effects of social perception on social behavior. *Advances in Experimental Social Psychology, 33*, 1–40.

Dingle, G.A., Stark, C., Cruwys, T., & Best, D. (2015). Breaking good: Breaking ties with social groups may be good for recovery from substance misuse. *British Journal of Social Psychology, 54*, 236–254.

Doosje, B., Ellemers, N., & Spears, R. (1995). Perceived intragroup variability as a function of group status and identification. *Journal of Experimental Social Psychology, 31*, 410–436.

Drury, J., Cocking, C., & Reicher, S. (2009). The nature of collective resilience: Survivor reactions to the 2005 London bombings. *International Journal of Mass Emergencies and Disasters, 27*, 66–95.

Durkeim, E. (1897/2007). *On suicide*. London, UK: Penquin.

Eaglemann, D. (2015). *The brain: The story of you*. Edinburgh and London: Canongate.

Evans, J. St. B.T. (2009). How many dual-process theories do we need? One, two, or many? In J.St.B.T. Evans & K. Frankish (Eds.) *In two minds: Dual processes and beyond* (pp. 33–54). New York: Oxford University Press.

Falomir, J. & Invernizzi, F. (1999). The role of social influence and smoker identity in resistance to smoker cessation. *Swiss Journal of Psychology, 58*, 73–84.

Fazio, R.H. & Olson, M.A. (2003). Implicit measures in social cognition research: Their meaning and use. *Annual Review of Psychology, 54*, 297–327.

Field, M., Schoenmakers, T., & Wiers, R.W. (2008). Cognitive processes in alcohol binges: A review and research agenda. *Current Drug Abuse Review, 1*, 263–279.

Fillmore, M.T. & Vogel-Sprott, M. (2006). Acute effects of alcohol and other drugs on automatic and intentional control. In R.W. Wiers & A.W. Stacy (Eds.), *Handbook of implicit cognition and addiction*. Thousand Oaks, CA: Sage.

Fiske, S.T. & Macrae, C.N. (Eds.) (2012). *The Sage handbook of social cognition*. London, Los Angeles, New Delhi, Singapore, Washington, DC: SAGE.

Frings, D. & Albery, I. (2015). The social identity model of cessation maintenance: Fomulation and initial evidence. *Addictive Behaviors, 44*, 35–42.

Gawronski, B. & Bodenhausen, G.V. (2006). Associative and propositional processes in evaluation: An integrative review of implicit and explicit attitude change. *Psychological Bulletin, 132*, 692–731.

Gawronski, B. & Payne, B.K. (Eds.). (2010). *Handbook of implicit social cognition: Measurement, theory and applications*. New York and London: The Guilford Press.

Greenwald, A.G., McGhee, D.E., & Schwartz, J.L. (1998). Measuring individual differences in implicit cognition: The Implicit Association Test. Journal of *Personality and Social Psychology, 74*, 1464–1480.

Hales, A.H., Williams, K.D., & Eckhardt, C.H. (2015). A participant walks into a bar . . . Subjective intoxication buffers ostracism's negative effects. *Social Psychology, 46*, 157–166.

Haslam, C., Cruwys, T., Haslam, S.A., Dingle, G., & Chang, M.X-L. (2016). GROUPS 4 HEALTH: Evidence that a social identity intervention that builds and strengthens social group membership improves mental health. *Journal of Affective Disorders, 194*, 188–195.

Haslam, S. A. (2014). Making good theory practical: Five lessons for an Applied Social Identity Approach to challenges of organizational, health, and clinical psychology. *British Journal of Social Psychology*, *53*, 1–20.

Hassin, R.R., Uleman, J.S., & Bargh, J.A. (2005). *The new unconscious*. New York: Oxford University Press.

Hendricks, P.S., Wood, S.B., & Hall, S.M. (2009). Smokers' expectancies for abstinence: Preliminary results from focus groups. *Psychology of Addictive Behaviors*, *23*, 380–385.

Heyes, C. (2011). Automatic imitation, *Psychological Bulletin*, *137*, 463–483.

Houben, K. & Wiers, R.W. (2006). Assessing implicit alcohol associations with the Implicit Association test: Fact or artefact? *Addictive Behavior*, *31*, 1346–1362.

Houben, K. & Wiers, R.W. (2008). Implicitly positive about alcohol? Implicit positive associations predict drinking behaviour. *Addictive Behavior*, *33*, 979–986.

Huijding, J. & de Jong, P.J. (2006). Specific predictive power of automatic spider-related affective associations for controllable and uncontrollable fear responses toward spiders. *Behaviour Research and Therapy*, *44*, 161–176.

Humphries, K. (2004). *Circles of recovery: Self-help organizations for addictions*. Cambridge: Cambridge University Press.

Institute of Alcohol Studies (IAS) (2014). *Alcohol related health outcomes*. Retrieved from www.ias.org.uk/Alcohol-knowledge-centr/Health-impacts/factsheets/Alcohol-related-rates.aspx.

James, W. (1890/2007). *The principles of psychology*, volume 2. New York: Cosimo Classics.

Jetten, J., Haslam, C., & Haslam, S.A. (2012). *The social cure*. Hove and New York: Psychology Press.

Jetten, J., Haslam, C., Haslam, S.A., & Dingle, G. (2014). How groups affect our heath and well-being: The path from theory to policy. *Social Issues and Policy Review*, *8*, 103–130.

Jones, J.M. & Jetten, J. (2011). Recovering from strain and enduring pain multiple group memberships promote resilience in the face of physical challenges. *Social Psychological and Personality Science*, *2*, 239–244.

Kelly, J.F., Stout, R.L., Magill, M., & Tonignan, J.S. (2011). The role of Alcoholics Anonymous in mobilizing adaptive social network changes: A prospective lagged meditational analysis. *Drug and Alcohol Dependency*, *114*, 119–126.

Kelly, J.F. & White, W.L. (2011). *Addiction recovery management: Theory, research and practice*. New York, Dordrecht, Heidelberg, London: Humana Press.

Lease, E.C., Zablocki, R.W., Edland, S.D., & Al-Delaimy, W.K. (2014). Smokers who report smoking but do not consider themselves smokers: A phenomenon in need of further attention. *British Medical Journal, Tobacco Control*, *24*, 400–403.

Lindgren, K.P., Teachman, B.A., Neighbors, C., Wiers, R.W., Westgate, E., & Greenwald, A.G. (2013). I drink therefore I am: Validating alcohol-related implicit association tests. *Psychology of Addictive Behaviors*, *27*, 1–13.

Lovic, V., Keen, D., Fletcher, P.F., & Fleming, A.S. (2011). Early-life maternal separation and social isolation produce an increase in impulsive action but not impulsive choice. *Behavioral Neuroscience*, *125*, 481–491.

McCusker, C.G. (2001). Conceptualizing addiction: Cognitive biases and addiction: an evolution in theory and method. *Addiction*, *96*, 47–56.

McDougall, W. (1921). *The group mind*. London: Cambridge University Press.

Mead, G. H. (1934). *Mind, self, and society: From the standpoint of a social of a social behaviourist*. Chicago and London: Phoenix Books, The University of Chicago Press.

Milner, D. (1975). *Children and race*. Harmondsworth: Penquin Books.

Moos, R.H. (2008). Active ingredients of substance use-focused self-help groups. *Addiction*, *103*, 387–396.

Moos, R.H. (2011). Processes that promote recovery from addictive disorders. In J.F. Kelly & W.L. White (Eds.), *Addiction recovery management*, (pp. 45–66). Totowa, NJ, US: Humana Press.

Moos, R.H. & Finney, J.W. (2011). Commentary on Lopez-Quintero et al. (2011): Remission and relapse – the yin-yang of addictive disorders. *Addiction, 106*, 670–671.

Mosbach, P. & Leventhal, H. (1988). Peer group identification and smoking: Implications for intervention. *Journal of Abnormal Psychology, 97*, 238–245.

Moss, A. & Albery, I.P. (2009). A dual-process model of the alcohol-behavior link for social drinking. *Psychological Bulletin, 135*, 516–530.

Munafò, M. & Albery, I.P. (2006). *Cognition and addiction*. Oxford: Oxford University Press.

Oakes, P.J. (1987). The salience of social categories. In J. Turner et al., *Rediscovering the social group: A self-categorization theory* (pp 117–141). Oxford. Blackwell.

Perkins, H.W. & Berkowitz, A.D. (1986). Perceiving the community norms of alcohol use among students: Some research implications for campus alcohol education programming. *Substance Use & Misuse, 21*, 961–976.

Phua, J.J. (2013). The reference group perspective for smoking cessation: An examination of the influence of social norms and social identification with reference groups on smoking cessation self-efficacy. *Psychology of Addictive Behaviors, 27*, 102–112.

Posner, M.I. & Snyder, C.R.R. (1975). Attention and cognitive control. In R.L. Solso (Ed.) *Information processing and cognition: The Loyola symposium*, (pp. 55–85). Hillsdale, NJ: Erlbaum.

Prentice, D.A. & Miller, D.T. (1996). Pluralistic ignorance and the perpetuation of social norms by unwitting actors. In M. Zanna (Ed.), *Advances in experimental social psychology* (pp. 161–209). San Diego: Academic Press.

Proschaska, J.O. & Velicer, W.F. (1997). The transtheoretical model of health behavior change. *American Journal of Health Promotion, 12*, 38–48.

Reynolds, K.J. & Branscombe, N.R. (2015). *Psychology of change. Life contexts, experiences, and identities*. New York and London: Psychology Press.

Reich, R.R., Below, M.C., & Goldman, M.S. (2010). Explicit and implicit measures of expectancy and related alcohol cognitions: A meta-analytic comparison. *Psychology of Addictive Behaviors, 24*, 13–25.

Robinson, T.E. & Berridge, K.C. (2003). Addiction, *Annual Review of Psychology, 54*, 25–53.

Rooke, S.E., Hine, D.W., & Thorsteinsson, E.B. (2008). Implicit cognition and substance use: a meta-analysis, *Addictive Behaviors, 33*, 1314–1328.

Rosenquist, J.N., Murabito, J., Fowler, J.H., & Christakis, N.A. (2010). The spread of alcohol consumption behavior in a large social network. *Annals of Internal Medicine, 152*, 426–433.

Sani, F. (2012). Group identification and health. In J. Jetten, C. Haslam, & A. Haslam (Eds.), *The social cure* (pp. 21–38). Hove and New York: Psychology Press.

Schnabel, K., Asendorpf, J.B., & Greenwald, A.G. (2008). Assessment of individual differences in implicit cognition: A review of IAT measures.*European Journal of Psychological Assessment, 24*, 210–217.

Sheeran, P., Gollwitzer., P.M., & Bargh, J.A. (2013). Nonconscious processes and health. *Health Psychology, 32*, 460–473.

Sherif, M. (1936). *The psychology of social norms*. New York: Harper Bros.

Smith, E.R. & DeCoster, J. (2000). Dual-process models in social and cognitive psychology: Conceptual integration and links to underlying memory systems. *Personality and Social Psychology Review, 4*, 108–131.

Stacy, A.W. & Wiers, R.W. (2010). Implicit cognition and addiction: A tool for explaining paradoxical behaviour. *Annual Review of Clinical Psychology, 6*, 551–575.

Strack, F. & Deutsch, R. (2004). Reflective and impulsive determinants of social behavior. *Personality and Social Psychology Review, 8*, 220–247.

Steffens, N.K., Goclowska, M.A., Cruwys, T., & Galinsky, A.D. (2015). How multiple social identities are related to creativity. *Personality and Social Psychology Bulletin, 42*, 188–203.

Stout, R.L., Kelly, J.F., Magill, M., & Pagano, M.E. (2011). Association between social influences and drinking outcomes across three years. *Journal of Studies on Alcohol and Drugs*, May 2012, 489–497.

Tajfel, H. (1972). Social categorization. In S. Moscovici (Ed.), *Introduction a la psychologie sociale* (Vol. 1). Paris: Larouse.

Tajfel, H. & Turner, J.C. (1979). An integrative theory of intergroup conflict. In W.G.Austin & S. Worchel (Eds.). *The social psychology of intergroup relations* (pp. 33–48). Monterey: Brooks/Cole.

Terry, D.J. & Hogg, M.A. (1996). Group norms and the attitude-behaviour relationship. A role for group identification. *Personality and Social Psychology Bulletin, 22*, 776–193.

Turner, J.C. (1982). Towards a cognitive redefinition of the social group. In H. Tajfel (Ed.), *Social identity and intergroup relations* (pp. 15–40). Cambridge: Cambridge University Press.

Turner, J. (1985). Social categorization and the self-concept: A social cognitive theory of group behaviour. In J. Lawler (Ed.), *Advances in group processes* (Vol 2). Greenwich, CT: JAI Press. In T. Postmes & N.R. Branscombe, (Eds.) (2010). *Rediscovering social identity* (pp. 243–272). New York and Hove: Psychology Press.

Turner, J.C., Hogg, M.A., Oakes, P.J., Reicher, S.D., & Wetherill, M.S. (1987). *Rediscovering the social group: A self-categorization theory*. Oxford: Basil Blackwell.

Van Der Vorst, H., Krank, M.K., Engels, R.C., Pieters, S., Burk, J.W., & Mares, H.W. (2012). The mediating role of alcohol-related memory associations on the relation between perceived parental drinking and the onset of adolescents' alcohol use. *Addiction, 108*, 526–533.

Waters, A.J. & Leventhal, A.M. (2006). Clinical relevance of implicit cognition in addiction. In M. Munafo & I.P. Albery (Eds.), *Cognition & addiction*. UK: Oxford University Press.

West, R. (2005). Time for a change: Putting the Transtheoretical (Stages of Change) Model to rest. *Addiction, 100*, 1036–1039.

West, R. & Brown, J. (2013). *Theory of addiction*, (2nd edn). Oxford: Blackwell.

White, W. (2009). *Long-term strategies to reduce the stigma attached to addiction, treatment, and recovery within the City of Philadelphia (with particular reference to medication assisted treatment/recovery)*. Department of Behavioral Health and Mental Retardation Services. Retrieved from www.dev.facesandvoicesofrecovery.org/pdf/White/StigmaMedicationTreatment.pdf.

Wiers, R.W., Houben, K., Roefs, A., de Jong, P., & Stacy, A.W. (2010). Implicit cognition in health psychology: Why common sense goes out the window. In B. Gowronski & B.K. Paynes (Eds.), *Handbook of implicit social cognition: Measurement, theory, and applications*, (pp. 463–488). New York, London: The Guilford Press.

Wiers, R.W. & Stacy, A.W. (2010). Are alcohol expectancies associations? Comment on Moss and Albery (2009). *Psychological Bulletin, 136*, 12–16.

Wigboldus, D.H., Holland, R.W., & van Knippenberg, A. (2006). *Single target implicit associations*. Unpublished manuscript.

Wundt, W. (1916/2011). *Elements of folk psychology*. Lightening Source UK, Ltd.

8

DEVELOPING THE SOCIAL IDENTITY MODEL OF CESSATION MAINTENANCE

Theory, evidence and implications

Daniel Frings and Ian P. Albery

Overview

Many individuals use self-help groups and other forms of group therapy to achieve and maintain cessation from addictive behaviours. For instance, self-help group attendance has been shown to improve outcomes in a variety of studies (Kelly, Stout, Magill, Tonigan, & Pagano, 2012; Blonigen, Timko, Finney, Moos, & Moos, 2011; Kelly, Hoeppner, Stout, & Pagano, 2010). They are also popular – some estimates suggest that 80 per cent of US drinkers who are trying to cease alcohol use will attend Alcoholics Anonymous at some point (Dawson, Grant, Stinson, & Chou, 2006). In formal treatment settings such as residential treatments and therapeutic communities, some form of group therapy is an almost ubiquitous feature of the treatment regime. The current chapter suggests that the efficacy of such treatment modes can be understood in part by understanding the social identities (those identities which are associated with social groupings, see Tajfel, 1978 and Tajfel & Turner 1979) that develop around addiction – both those focused on addiction ('alcoholic', 'gambler') and those focused on cessation ('recovering addict', 'former gambler'). How these identities operate is described in the Social Identity Model of Cessation Maintenance (SIMCM, Frings & Albery, 2015) the mechanisms and implication of which are explored in the current chapter.

The social identity model of cessation maintenance

Drawing on broad definitions of addiction (i.e., including both substance and behavioural addictions) and cessation (from harm reduction/controlled use to abstinence) SIMCM argues that identities can operate to improve cessation outcomes in a variety of ways. They key pathways specified in SIMCM can be seen in Figure 8.1. These explicit (e.g., conscious and often controllable) and implicit (often unconscious and uncontrollable) processes are described below.

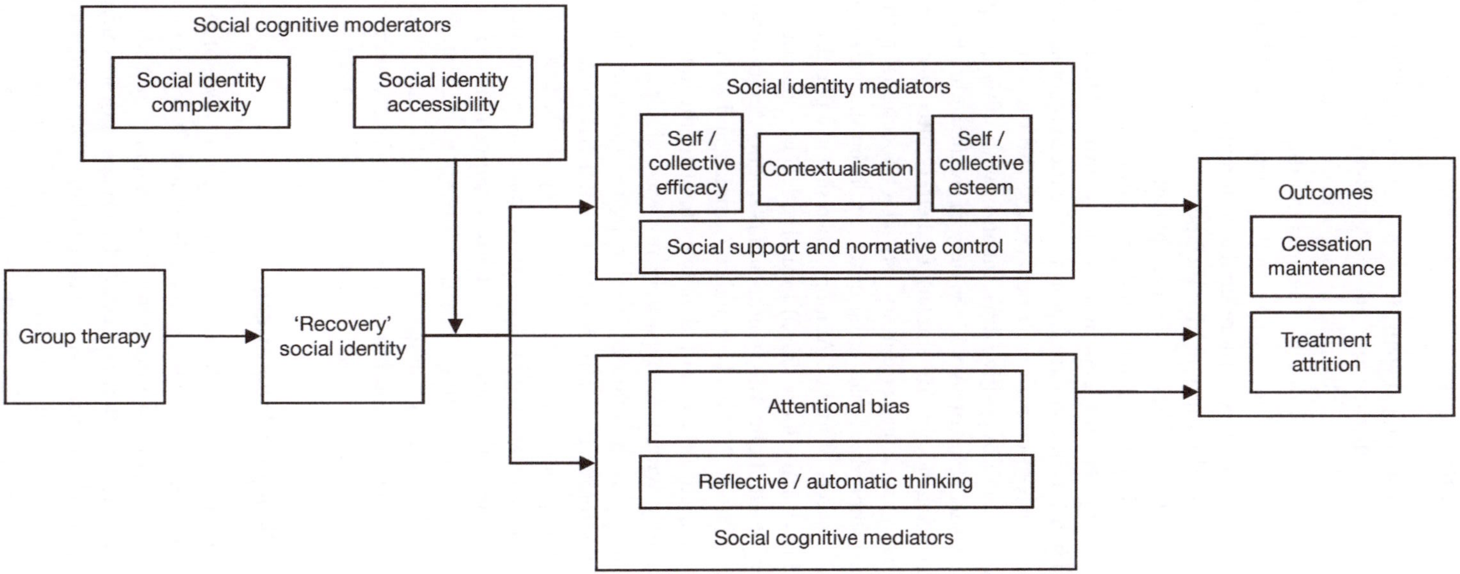

FIGURE 8.1 The Social Identity Model of Cessation Maintenance (SIMCM).

Explicit identity mediators

Briefly, SIMCM argues that group therapy is one form of activity which can generate an identity as a 'recovery addict identity' (or 'ex-smoker', 'former gambler', etc.). Once these identities are formed (by this, or other means) a number of processes are thought to follow. In line with self-categorisation theory (see Turner, Hogg, Oakes, Reicher, & Wetherell, 1987), when such an identity linked to recovery is salient, individuals see themselves as more similar to the prototype of the group – including holding more of the attributes that they perceive are typical to the group, to a greater extent (i.e., being efficacious in their quit attempts, or being increasingly resilient). Alongside this process, social influence from other group members (in terms of social support for cessation, social control when people break group standards of behaviour, contextualisation of the meaning of lapse and relapse and influence the perceived costs of such behaviours) also support. Finally, social identities may allow a sense of positive differentiation with other group members, resulting in increased self-esteem. A wide variety of evidence has linked a strong identity as a recovering addict (or similar) to better outcomes. For instance, although not directly measuring identity, social connections with a greater proportion of non-using others than using others has been shown to be linked to better outcomes in a variety of studies. Among non-residential populations, research by Buckingham, Frings and Albery (2013) measured levels of identity among two samples – members of Alcoholic Anonymous and Narcotics Anonymous [Study 1] and among smokers [Study 2]. Levels of addict / smoker and recovering addict / ex-smoker were measured. An index of identity preference (the difference between levels of each identity within each participant) was calculated. This identity preference correlated with the number of self-reported lapses in the recent past, and also efficacy for future cessation. Similar research has followed looking at residential treatment populations (Dingle, Stark, Cruwys, & Best, 2015). This work followed a number of clients staying in residential communities, measuring, among other variables, identities both as an addict and recovering addict. The difference in identification increased over time, and the difference in identities predicted treatment success. Beckwith, Best, Dingle, Perryman and Lubman (2015) observed identifying with a treatment community (and decreasing identity with being a user) at both baseline and a fortnight into treatment predicted treatment retention.

Social identity, efficacy and self-esteem

One mechanism identified by SIMCM as a driver of explicit effects of social identity is efficacy. Efficacy has been posited as a key predictor of success in a number of health related domains (see the Health Action Process Approach; Schwarzer, 2008, for more detail). Self-categorisation processes (the processes of identifying oneself as a member of a particular social group; Turner et al., 1987) suggest that when an identity is salient, an individual sees oneself and the social world from the perspective of that group. They also see themselves as embodying the prototype (i.e., the features and norms of the group which typify the group relative to a compactor (see, the meta-contrast principle) of the group to a greater extent than when such identities are not salient (Hogg, Hardie, & Reynolds, 1995)). If the group prototype contains being efficacious, then individuals will feel more efficacious when this group is active than when it is not. As noted above, the work by Buckingham et al. (2013) suggests a clear link between identity and efficacy, and this has been confirmed in more recent research (see Frings, Collins, Long, Pinto, & Albery, (under review, described below)).

Another important factor potentially linked to social identity is self-esteem. Higher self-esteem has been linked to decreased likelihood of engaging in an addiction (see e.g., Carvajal, Clair, Nash, & Evans, 1998). Similarly, being addicted to a behaviour has been linked with lower self-esteem. For example, both Niemz, Griffiths and Banyard, (2005) and Armstrong, Phillip and Sailing (2000) link pathological internet use with lower self-esteem. However, other evidence contra-indicates. Greenberg, Lewis and Dodd (1999) observed a link between positive self-esteem and over-exercise in relation to exercise addiction, but no links between esteem and other potentially addictive behaviours. In terms of treatment outcomes, Richter, Brown and Mott (1991) show that higher self-esteem is linked to better treatment outcomes. Higher self-esteem is also often an explicit or implied goal of addiction treatment. It should be noted that not all research shows that addiction treatment actually improves self-esteem – for instance, Graeven and Graeven (1983) showed lower self-esteem for a group of heroin addicts who had received treatment than those who had not. Although this review of the links between self-esteem is highly selective, it does show that the link between self-esteem and addiction is complex.

In the social identity literature, it is recognised that membership of a social group allows positive differentiation between the self-as-a-group member and members of other groups. This differentiation allows for the development of positive collective self-esteem (a feeling that ones group is good) which has positive implications for self-evaluation (see Rubin & Hewstone, 1998, for a detailed exploration of this argument). For addicts (whose potential to make such positive comparisons may be limited) such positive differentiation may be particularly impactful and valued. Thus, although increases in self-esteem may not directly link with cessation outcomes per se, it is expected that a positive identity related to cessation will itself be a source of self-esteem. Another possibility is that the fact such identities are likely to be highly valued by those attempting to maintain cessation may in itself be protective, if such identities may be lost as a result of engaging in addictive behaviour (see *Contextualisation* and also *Cost/reward appraisals*, below). Alongside these predictions, inconsistent links between esteem and outcomes may themselves be explained partly by SIMCM – self-esteem gains will only be observed to the extent that cessation related identities allow positive differentiation, and be both more measurable and influential at social identity levels (collective self-esteem) than an individual self-esteem level (personal self-esteem). If this is the case, self-esteem effects should only be observed when identities around cessation are salient.

Contextualisation

Identities associated with recovery are also likely to be effective to the extent that they contextualise situations in ways which are protective. As argued above, when an identity is salient, situations are viewed from the group's perspective. In addiction, this could be a powerful tool. Consider a situation in which a former gambling addict passes a casino, or an advert for an online gambling site. A gambling related identity may construe this situation as one in which an opportunity to gamble is presented. In contrast, consider the same individual who has a recovery identity salient. For such an individual, this situation would be one of risk, possible relapse etc. Both such perspectives are likely to lead to different cognitive and behavioural outcomes which will increase or decrease the chance of cessation – perhaps approach orientated in the former, and avoidance in the latter (see social cognitive mediators below).

Cost/reward appraisals

Contextualisation may also involve changing the nature of appraisals about a given behaviour or situation. Numerous models derived from a social cognitive understanding of health-related decision making and behaviour have consistently emphasised that individuals undertake a cost-benefit analysis of perceived outcomes associated with undertaking actions. In models such as the health belief model (Janz & Becker, 1984), protection motivation theory (Maddux & Rogers, 1983) and the prototype willingness model (Gerrard, Gibbons, Houlihan, Stock, & Pomery, 2008) these expectancy-outcome evaluations provide the impetus for the one's motivation to form an intention and then subsequently behave in a particular manner (see Abraham & Sheeran, 2015; Norman, Boer, Seydel, & Mullan, 2015; Gibbons, Gerrard, Stock, & Finneran, 2015). Some research suggests that cost/benefit analysis influences cessation success. For example, providing fiscal incentives for maintaining cessation has been shown to improve outcomes among pregnant women who smoke (Tappin et al., 2014). Similarly, confrontation of possible costs in terms of imminent negative health (or other) events can (but does not always) trigger cessation attempts, or maintain such attempts among those who have already quit (Dingle, Cruwys, & Frings, 2015; Meijer, Gebhardt, Dijkstra, Willemsen, & Van Laar, 2015). Identities may help shape such cost/benefit appraisals, and also feature in them.

Stories of hope and cost/benefit analysis

One activity group members undertake is sharing stories from their times as an active addict, or from their cessation journey. The stories, morals, lessons and reflections they contain convey social meaning for events such as lapses, or cessation milestones such as 'recovery birthdays'. They also provide hope and a positive vision of the future (see Banerjee & Greene, 2012; Jensen, 2000; Kaskutas, Ammon,

Delucchi, Room, Bond, & Weisner, 2005). One function of such stories may be that they contextualise what a lapse or relapse means in terms of cost to the self and others. Such stories may point to examples of the personal costs of lapsing (in terms of damaged relationships, loss of control etc). They may also explore the cost of such behaviours to others including the friends, family, and the group itself. Unfortunately, groups who have a longer collective history may also have experienced the relapse of a central member or one who is in some other way prototypical (i.e., is a highly representative member of the group). This could include a senior member or one 'in service' in the fellowships and / or a previously successful fellow group member. The direct cost(s) experienced by group members as a result of this may re-enforce contextualisation effects. Cost/benefit analysis may also be affected by levels of perceived social support and control.

Social support, control and outcomes

Both efficacy beliefs and contextualisation processes rely on the group possessing a coherent set of norms and identity. In general, to maintain such attributes, groups are motivated to both maintain both group locomotion (the ability of the group to achieve its shared goals) and social reality (the legitimacy of differentiation between the group and other groups) (Festinger 1950; Festinger & Thibaut, 1951; Abrams, Marques, Randsley de Moura, Hutchinson, & Bown, 2004). One way this takes place is through the creation of, and adherence to, social behavioural norms – prescriptive ways of behaving in a specific context, or prescriptive attitudes towards an attitude object. For self-help groups, such norms are considered 'an active ingredient' of self-help groups (Moos, 2008).

When group members break rules in the group, they will often attract attempts to correct their behaviour. Such responses can be either inclusive or exclusive (e.g., Israel, 1956; Levine, 1989; Orcut, 1973). Such 'social control responses' can include communication with the rule-breaker (Schachter, 1951; Festinger, Gerard, Hymovitch, Kelley, & Raven, 1952). These may often include attempts to persuade rule breakers to resume normative behaviours (Frings & Abrams, 2010; Frings, Abrams, Marques, & Randsley de Moura, 2010). In the addiction areas, such attempts may be communicated via inter-personal 1–1s, or be supported by formal structures within the group (such as sharing tales of hope, see Banerjee & Greene, 2012). When rule-breakers are seen as accountable for their actions, are well established members of a group and or have engaged in multiple / serious deviations from the norm, more exclusionary responses are likely. These include responses such as social isolation or the threat of, or actual, expulsion from the group (see Jacobs & Kent, 2007; Moreland, Levine, & Cini, 1993; Pinto, Marques, Levine, & Abrams, 2010; Frings & Pinto, under review).

Although there is a rich tradition of research into normative support and control in the social identity literature, little has directly investigated what norms addiction treatment groups hold, nor how they respond to violations. One study which addresses this (and describes the nuances of how and when social control responses of various kinds may be employed by group members more fully) is reported in Frings, Collins, Long, Pinto and Albery, (under review). In this paper we report a study in which we ask participants to list a variety of group goals and individual behaviours which they felt supported or violated group norms and also to rate the likelihood of a variety of supportive, inclusionary and exclusionary norms in response to these behaviours. Group members reported goals which reflected social reality aims (e.g., staying clean), but also reported individual behavioural violations which more often revolved around threats to group locomotion (e.g., participating intoxicated, sexual contact between senior and new members). Group members who identified highly with the group also perceived higher levels of social support and control being likely responses to norm violations. Generally, supportive and inclusive responses were seen as more likely than exclusionary ones – however, a notable exception was when participants saw such violations as costly to the group. Such perceived cost was linked with higher levels of expected punitive and exclusionary / avoidance behaviour. This initial evidence suggests that groups are generally supportive, but also that they manage non-normative behaviour punitively when it costs the group. Importantly, having a higher identity linked with the group was linked to increased perceptions of cost of relapse, suggesting that the group identity can affect cost/benefit appraisals.

Implicit processes in SIMCM

Contemporary research in social cognitive accounts of behaviour and addiction psychology distinguishes between two types of processing modalities, implicit processing and explicit processing, that may (may not) operate in parallel when one is perceiving environmental stimuli (see Sherman, Gawronski, & Trope, 2014; Gawronski & Payne, 2011; Tiffany, 1990). Explicit processes are characterised as slow acting, requiring more cognitive effort and draw upon more limited capacity resources. They are intentional, controllable and modifiable and are available to conscious awareness. An implicit process, or automatic cognitive process, requires little cognitive effort and is not as demanding on limited cognitive resources. Such processing is effortless, performed without intention or control, is relatively stable and resistant to change. Finally, implicit cognitive processes operate without the conscious awareness of the perceiver (Shiffrin & Schneider, 1977; Bargh, 2005). In social cognitive research there has been significant progress in understanding the implicit and explicit processing of attitude and belief-based environment stimuli (e.g., Gawronski & Bodenhausen, 2006), and how these processes predict social behaviour and socially relevant responding (e.g., Ackerman, Nocera, & Bargh, 2010). This same dissociation has been applied in understanding health behaviour (see Sheeran, Gollwitzer, & Bargh, 2013; Wiers, Houben, Roefs, de Jong Hofman, & Stacy, 2010; Friese, Hofman, & Wiers, 2011; Gerrard et al., 2008) and, for our purposes, addictive behaviours (Stacy, 1997; Sheeran et al., 2005; Field, Munafo, & Franken, 2009; Wiers et al., 2007; Rivis & Sheeran 2013). Across a number of theoretical and empirical accounts there appears to be agreement that in any given context exposure to a relevant stimulus has the effect of producing an automatic evaluation, that this evaluation will manifest itself in a motivational orientation to approach or avoid the stimulus and that this processing will include the activation of associated behavioural schemas (see Wiers et al., 2010; Strack & Deutch, 2004; Moss & Albery, 2009; Gerrard et al., 2008). Importantly this type of initial processing is characteristic of an associative or impulsive system. A controlled or reflective system may also operate which reflects the formation of a more conscious intention to behave governed by executive control (such as working memory capacity, inhibitory control), weighing up the cost and benefits of enacting a behaviour in terms of realising outcome expectancies associated with a course of action and the activation of conscious beliefs related to the activity. It appears, however, that in all likelihood the initial cognitive activity associated with a perceived stimulus is likely to be that characterised by implicit processes (Strack & Deutsch, 2004) and that more explicit processes act in response to this initial processing pattern.

Increasingly, evidence is being produced which supports both the existence and importance of identities held at an implicit level in both cessation maintenance and behavioural engagement. For example, implicit measured associations between self and alcohol predicts both alcohol use intentions and craving among students (e.g., Gray et al., 2011; Lindgren et al., 2013). Wolff, von Hippel, Brener and von Hippel (2015) show that among a sample of residential treatment programs clients, implicit associations between the self and drug alcohol/drug use predicted treatment retention. Recent research by Lindgren et al., (2013) and Lindgren, Foster, Westgate and Neighbors (2013) suggests that implicit associations between the self and being a drinker predicted scores on a daily drinking scale (suggesting implicit identities are linked to self-reported drinking habits and risk of alcohol related harm). Recent work from our own lab group (Frings, Melichar, & Albery, 2016) suggests these identities may also influence in-the-moment alcohol consumption (at least among populations not in treatment). In this study, we asked participants to rate their identity with being a 'drinker' using an explicit scale of social identity. Prior to this, participants completed an implicit identity measure (comprising an IAT measuring associations between the categories of 'self' and 'social drinker'). Both implicit and explicit identity predicted the amount of placebo alcohol participants both poured and subsequently consumed in a pouring taste preference task (see Albery et al., 2015). Although in its infancy, this body of research provides strong evidence of the importance of implicit identities. SIMCM makes some novel and testable predictions as to how these identities may be activated, and also how they may function.

Social cognitive moderators

Group memberships have to be activated to influence perception. Social cognition research into the implicit nature of higher mental processes for social behaviours (see Sherman et al., 2014) predicts how and when such influence occurs using the concept of automaticity. Automaticity occurs when environmental cues trigger cognitive constructs (e.g., identities, behavioural norms, expectations) which influence perception and behaviour. For instance, activating stereotypical traits of the elderly (by subliminally priming words associated with old age) has been shown to lead to participants walking slower down a corridor (Bargh, Chen, & Burrows, 1996). In addition, activating the 'socialising' representation has been shown to have effects on the accessibility of the concept 'drinking' alcohol and subsequent drinking related behaviour in people who report increase drinking habits (Sheeran et al., 2005). Other work has shown that unobtrusively activated the binge drinker stereotype has the effect of producing self-reported binge drinking measured prospectively in current binge drinkers (Rivis & Sheeran, 2013). Social cognitivists explain this by arguing that activation of specific constructs through the perception of environmental stimuli simultaneously activates associated semantic representations and behavioural schemas (e.g., Moss & Albery, 2009). Given the potential for implicit identities to help or hinder cessation, it is fruitful to consider when they become activated. In SIMCM, two factors are hypothesised to increase or decrease the likelihood that a given identity will be activated in a given situation. These factors (represented by the social cognitive moderators box in Figure 8.1) are the *complexity* and *accessibility* of the identity.

One assumption of the automaticity literature is that some constructs are more *accessible* than others. In other words, when creating a semantic interpretation on incoming stimulus-specific perceptions some constructs will be activated more easily and by a wider range of other weaker stimuli (Gawronski & Bodenhausen, 2006). One determinant of accessibility is *complexity*. More complex cognitive constructs are sensitive to a greater range of cues. For example, a representation of the 'elderly' which contains 'grandchildren, bingo, wise' will be activated in more contexts than one which contains only 'bingo'. The concept 'drinking' which is high in its complexity through association with other nodes like 'sociable, friendly, fun' will be more easily activated. Representations also become increasingly accessible through familiarity or frequency of use. In this way, repeated exposure to a stimulus will over time have the effect of making the associated representation more accessible via sustained activation. Constructs which are primed more often subsequently become more accessible and this accessibility may be a function of consistency of activation (Dijksterhuis, Aarts, Bargh, & van Knippenberg, 2000).

Over time, constructs representing the recovering addict identity should become increasing complex (as more information and experience is gathered) and should be activated more frequently (during group discussion, and due to their complexity). This should lead to increased accessibility. Eventually the behaviours, attitudes and perceptions linked to the recovering addict identity construct will become more accessible than those held pre-treatment. At this point, exposure to addiction related cues should activate the recovering addict sematic representation containing abstinence related behaviours beyond the immediate group treatment context.

Social cognitive mediators

Implicit identities may have a number of features and functions that differ from those explicitly experienced. The original formulation of SIMCM (Frings & Albery, 2015) pointed towards a number of effects of implicit identities, but did not specify what these may be, or how they may operate. The current chapter expands this aspect of the model by specifying a number of potential processes (represented by the social cognitive mediators pathway in Figure 8.1). In particular and in line with dual process models, we argue that implicit identities may affect behaviour by influencing the activation readiness of various associated concepts for a semantic interpretation, including behavioural enactment sequences, of a stimulus experience. This type of processing will be reflected in how far the stimulus automatically captures the attention of the perceiver (see Franken, 2003; Field et al., 2009) and the activation of stimulus-related memory-based associations (see Rooke, Hine & Thorsteinsson, 2008, for meta-analysis; e.g., De Houwer, Custers & De Clercq, 2006). Explicit identities, through reflective processing, are more likely to operate when the individual is more motivated to engage with their current thinking. It has been argued that this more 'aware' mode of thought is evolutionary adaptive to the extent that it may provide a system of control over more associative or implicit mechanisms in the enactment of the goal-directed behaviour.

From an implicit processing point of view, an identity can be viewed as a node in an associative network which contains other groups, representations of group members, group norms, self-construal such as efficacy and, to a greater or lesser extent, all other nodes with some identity relevant content. The activation readiness of these connected nodes sequences will be facilitated by the strength of activation of the associated identity, while also perhaps being simultaneously dampened by the strength of activation of the competing identity (and its competing nodes). As argued above, access to feelings of efficacy, an awareness of group norms and situational construal may all protect cessation. Thus, for instance, when an individual with an ex-smoker identity active, nodes which reflect self-efficacy, behavioural norms around cessation and linkages between the stimuli and the concepts of danger/risk will also be simultaneously activated and, in many cases, be open to conscious awareness. Such processes should help maintain cessation. However, in addition to these consciously accessible constructs, the identity node network is likely to contain automatic behavioural enactment sequences linked to addiction relevant stimuli. According to dual process approaches, once initiated such behavioural sequences need to run to completion and, as such, resistant to reflective thought (see Tiffany, 1990). The enactment sequences associated with a particular stimuli may differ between addict identities and recovering addict identities. For instance, an online gambler seeing a banner ad (stimuli) may then log into a gambling site and play poker (behavioural enactment). In an ex-gambler, the same stimuli may lead to a more protective behavioural enactment (e.g., turning off the computer and speaking to a supportive other). This interpretation supports the finding that often those attempting to cessate simply 'find themselves in a bar/in a strip club/smoking' without prior cravings or without making a clear decision to engage in the behaviour or not (see e.g., Tiffany, 1990; Franken, 2003).

Importantly, this reasoning suggests that implicit identities are, first and foremost, a measure of self-categorisation which may or may not be consciously accessible. It also suggests that, when either motivation or cognitive resource are low, such self-categorisations may have much greater effects. One prediction SIMCM therefore makes is that implicit identities will be particularly influential when these resources are limited. The current formulation also leads to a propositional implication as follows – Should associations that are contained within an associative identity network change, its effects on cessation will change also. Thus, replacing, for instance, feelings of low self-efficacy associated with addicts with a sense of efficacy, or replacing harmful behavioural enactment sequences with helpful ones, will have the same effect as shifting the activation level of the identity (or generating a new identity). In contexts such as AA (which make re-definition of what it means to be an addict a routine part of meetings) the effects of such a re-definition may be manifest. It also explains findings from various studies which show a positive correlation between addict and recovery identities at an explicit level, with higher recovery identities predicting cessation maintenance (e.g., Buckingham et al., 2013; Beckwith et al., 2015; Dingle et al., 2015). Future research could directly test this by measuring the implicit associations between various dimensions (e.g., efficacy) and identities through the course of engagement with the group.

Attentional bias

Attentional bias refers to the observation that with repeated exposure a stimulus may capture the attention of an individual in comparison to other types of stimuli. Using various approaches to measure this type of bias, including the modified Stroop, flicker induced change blindness, dot probe task and eye-tracking technology, a substantial body of research has linked attentional biases for addiction relevant stimuli to be related to increased engagement with that behaviour (see, Munafò & Franken, 2009, for meta analysis). Attentional biases for concern-related stimuli have been identified in a variety of habitual and compulsive behaviours including alcohol use (e.g., Sharma, Albery, & Cook, 2001), cannabis use (e.g., Cane, Sharma, & Albery, 2009), smoking (e.g., Attwood, O'Sullivan, Leonards, Macintosh, & Munafo, 2008), dieting behaviour (Wilson & Wallis, 2013) and sex-related activity (Fromberger et al., 2012), among others. For instance, among heavy but not light drinkers, performance on a modified stroop test (which involves naming the ink colour of words which are either neutral or alcohol related, but ignoring the meaning) is impaired when alcohol related words are presented (e.g., Sharma et al., 2001). Recent research has also shown that those who abstain from alcohol (for instance, for religious reasons) also show an attentional bias towards alcohol related stimuli (Moss, Albery, Siddiqui, & Rycroft, 2013). Attentional bias is thought to be a primarily automatic and unconscious process. SIMCM makes a prediction that implicit identities as both an addict and recovering addict will be related to differential types of attentional bias. In other words, the behavioural effects of these biases will differ, to the extent that they are linked to different behavioural enactment scripts. For those for whom an addiction identity is activated, an associated attentional bias will lead to an increased risk of lapse or relapse when such individuals are presented with addiction related cues (for instance, a side bar ad for online gambling for a gambling addict) (Franken, 2003). However, for those with a recovery identity, attentional bias towards the same cues may be linked with reduced risk of lapse or relapse (see Moss et al., 2013). As well as generating testable hypotheses, this differentiation highlights the role that identities have on shaping our perceptions of the environment. As attentional bias processes are seen to be primarily automatic processes, outside of conscious control, SIMCM also predicts that both attentional biases and the attentional bias-behaviour link will be related more to implicitly reported than to explicitly reported identities.

Persistence of old identities at an implicit level

One interesting question raised by SIMCM is the relationship between old and new identities. In the evidence to date, notable differences in the correlations between identities have been seen between samples. For instance, in both Buckingham et al., (2013) and Frings et al., (under review), identities as a therapy group member and a recovering addict were positively correlated. In Buckingham et al., no relationship was observed between smoking and ex-smoking identities. This latter observation may be an artefact of the fellowship practice of re-affirming one's status as an addict at meetings, however other evidence suggests that identities associated with addiction can persist at an explicit level for some time (Vangeli & West, 2012). From an implicit perspective, it would be expected that identities never truly 'vanish'. Rather, their presence and impact on the associative networks they are linked to may diminish over time (and, perhaps, the number of links with other stimuli may decay). However, the readiness of this identity to be activated may always be present, and given the right level of stimulation or activation thresholds, may well occur (particularly if competing activations from other identities are somehow depressed). From this perspective, an identity will always remain with an individual, but its effects on cognition and behaviour (and levels of conscious accessibility) may decrease.

Equally, identities associated with recovery may be relatively transient. Vangeli and West (2012) observed that smokers who cessated found group membership a powerful motivator during treatment, but did not see this identity as important when followed up (although a 'non-smoker' identity was often retained, which from an associative point of view may have similar content). Similarly, Dingle, Cruwys and Frings (2015) also observed that relationships (although not necessarily the associated *identities*) built up in residential treatment communities were not expected to last beyond the treatment setting. One question that arises from these studies is whether identities *actually* disappear or whether they lie dormant but ready for activation when the necessary conditions arise. Even though this evidence argues for a transient explicit identity activation, work to date has not empirically tested the possibility that implicit addict/recovery identities may remain in place and potentially accessible.

SIMCM and other theories and models around addiction

SIMCM also provides insight into other models that explain addiction and addiction treatment success. In this section we discuss how SIMCM speaks to stages of change models and another perspective on the links between identity and recovery, the Social Identity Model of Recovery (SIMOR, Best et al., 2016).

Stages of change models

Stages of change models, e.g., the transtheoretical model (Prochaska & Velicer, 1997), postulate that those attempting to cessate pass linearly through various stages (i.e., pre-contemplation, contemplation, preparation, action and maintenance). A key prediction of these models is that cessation is more likely to be achieved and maintained if treatment or interventions that aim to move people to a new stage in their recovery (e.g., preparation to action) are matched to the factors shown to be influential for the specific transition (e.g., Dijkstra, Conijn, & De Vries, 2006). A quitter's current stage is usually derived from self-report. SIMCM suggests that a better understanding may be gained by looking at their implicit identity as an addict and as an ex-addict. Moreover, predictions can be made about the levels of accessibility of recovery identities at each stage. Pre-contemplative addicts may have an accessible identity as an addict, but will be unlikely to have one as a recovering addict. Those in states of contemplation and preparation may have a recovery identity, but it will be low in accessibility (and meaning) relative active addict identities. Thus, the former will only operate infrequently relative to other identities. During the action period, the two identities will likely be in active competition, and as such exercises such as mindfulness may well be important to decrease the activation threshold of identities associated with recovery. When maintenance is reached, it would be hoped that a recovery identity would be activated readily and in a wide range of contexts, whereas addict identities may be related only rarely. If such predictions are supported, knowing the relative balance of identities may indicate how ready an individual is to move from, for instance, preparation to action, or action to maintenance. Implicit identity measures are likely to be preferable to explicit ones for such evaluations. For instance, a gambler may explicitly report feeling like an ex-gambler, or that they would like to become one. However, their implicit identity may still be rooted strongly as being a gambler and only weakly as an ex-gambler. For such an individual, a transition from contemplation to preparation may be possible, but a transition from preparation to action is likely to fail (as the behavioural enactment associated with being a gambler will not be countered by activation of an ex-gambler identity). A related avenue for future research is to link changes in the relationship between implicit identities with processes associated with successful transitions between particular stages (e.g., positive expectancies of quitting smoking in pre-contemplators, perceived negative outcomes of quitting in contemplators and heightened self-efficacy in the action stages). One implication of this relationship between stages and identity is that practitioners should ensure sufficient work is done on identity issues prior to attempting behavioural change.

SIMOR

Since SIMCM's inception a similar, largely complimentary, model has emerged which also uses social identity principles to understand the Recovery movement (e.g., AA, NA, etc.). The Social Identity Model of Recovery (Best et al., 2016) focuses upon the interplay of using and non-using groups within a recovering addicts network. It argues that the social influence of groups allow a series of identity transitions to take place – between being an active addict, a recovering addict and one in maintenance. Similar to SIMCM, SIMOR postulates that others in an addict's social circle provide either recovery capital, or increased risk of relapse. It conceptualises 'recovery' as an identity journey which entails changes in social networks and social activities (e.g., who recovering addicts see, and what they do with them). As addicts proceed through their transition from being an addict to an ex-addict, SIMOR argues that the balance of these social influences toward recovery pushes addicts towards sobriety. SIMOR's focus on transitions is couched in classic social categorisation terms, and in this respect, SIMCM sheds some light on the underlying processes that may be involved in such a transition (for instance, outlining some of the implicit processes that may underpin SCT concepts such as perceiver readiness, and also elucidating how social identities may lead to automatic behavioural enactment). SIMOR in turn describes some of the social network changes an addict may experience (and the importance of these) more explicitly than does SIMCM and also highlights in particular that recovering addicts are both receivers and generators of social influence.

Thoughts for practitioners

Although the development of SIMCM is in its early days, it still offers a number of suggestions for practitioners on how to harness the processes it describes to improve the chances of group members. Here, we discuss a few of the manifold issues SIMCM raises with direct relevance to practitioners – specifically around the role of implicit identities, contextualisation and social support. Perhaps most importantly SIMCM, as it takes a dual process approach, argues that in order for identities based on recovery to be effective in maintaining cessation they must be more accessible than addict-identities at an implicit level. It also argues that an identity's accessibility will be partly derived from its complexity and repetition of use. Thus, identity work that aims to increase the richness of recovery identities and broaden the scope in which they are applicable will likely show an increase in the adaptive effectiveness of such identities.

SIMCM's suggestion that contextualisation effects (i.e., recognising potentially risky situations as such, or defining the meaning of lapses and relapses) are based in part on perceptions of similarity driven by self-categorisation. As such, priming recovery identities in some way prior to discussing shared experiences is likely to make the exercise more impactful. This practice is widely incorporated in some paradigms (i.e., AA) but may well be absent in others. Equally, facilitators of such groups should be acutely aware that the various group processes, discussions and 'meaning-making' will shape such contextualisation, and should, where appropriate, be steered towards those that are compatible with treatment goals, and away from those that may hinder them.

SIMCMs focus on social support and control (and the initial evidence presented in Frings et al., under review) highlights that self-help groups can be very supportive when group members are struggling – offering advice and support. However, it also highlights that members of such groups are aware that other, more punitive, forms of social control exist. This slightly darker side of the group process may have some protective qualities (for example, by affecting cost/reward appraisals). However, group facilitators should also be aware that, should such sanctions be enacted, the loss of a group membership (particularly when opportunities for other positive group memberships are limited) could be devastating for the excluded parties. Thus, clear boundaries of acceptable, unacceptable and, perhaps 'grey' behaviours are important. Also important is an understanding of acceptable (and unacceptable) sanctions that can be enacted. Although research in this area is limited to a handful of studies, it is clear social support and control can be a double-edged sword.

Areas for future research

SIMCM is a theoretical model built (and increasingly being supported by) empirical evidence. As such there is scope for the testing of predictions and refinement of the model. Alongside this, there are two areas in particular that merit further discussion – the role of non-formal therapy and also the differences in identity among those who are treatment naïve and those who have experienced multiple cessation attempts.

Although SIMCM can be used as an explanation for how and why group therapy works, it is also an explanation of identity effects more generally. Conceptually, the content of an implicit identity developed outside group therapy can contain the same nodal links, behavioural enactments and other features as those developed in group work. However, it may be that they are less actively developed, less complex and less accessible. Similarly, identities linked to recovery (or similar) may well lack one or more aspect of the explicit effects that SIMCM postulates (e.g., social support/control or contextualisation). Such difference may only be short-term (e.g., it may be that these same features develop, but take longer) or more fundamental. Much will depend on the work the individual client does, and the social interactions they have during their cessation.

SIMCM could also be seen as assuming those in cessation approach their identity development as a 'blank slate'. However, most people ceasing an addiction may well have had interactions and/or hold stereotypes about others that have gone ahead of them. From a conceptual point of view, these may affect explicit processes. However, such processes are reasonably amenable to change. More importantly, they may have laid the groundwork of the cognitive architecture that underpins implicit identities (including behavioural enactments, links between nodes, etc.). These effects are likely to influence even those who are treatment naïve. Moreover, many individuals will have attempted to cessate on multiple occasions before. For these individuals, identities may already be firmly established. This may increase the speed with which recovery based identities become accessible (and dominant) but may also bring unwanted associations, beliefs and social norms which will require work to overcome. Empirically, little or no work has directly addressed these issues, so the extent to which they affect an individual's immediate quit attempt remains an open question.

Conclusions

To conclude, SIMCM presents a comprehensive theoretical account of how identities related to both addiction and addiction recovery function at both explicit and implicit levels of processing. The conditions under which addiction vs. cessation identities are active are defined using concepts such as identity complexity and accessibility. When recovery oriented identities are activated, a number of processes operating at both explicit (self-esteem, self-efficacy, contextualisation and social support and control) and implicit (attentional bias, reflective vs. automatic thinking) levels are thought to mediate their effects. An increasing body of empirical evidence is beginning to support the various aspects of the model. SIMCM has implications for models commonly used to understand recovery (i.e., stages of change approaches) and compliments other approaches to identity in addiction (e.g., SIMOR). Although the model has not been validated fully it has a number of implications for practice – in particular, around the development of identities and the management of 'meaning-making'.

References

Abraham, C. & Sheeran, P. (2015). The health belief model. In M. Connor & P. Norman (Eds.). *Predicting and changing health behaviour: Research and practice with social cognition models.* (pp. 30–69). Maidenhead: Open University Press.

Abrams, D., Marques, J., Randsley de Moura, G., Hutchison, P., & Bown, N. J. (2004). The Maintenance of Entitativity: A Subjective Group Dynamics Approach. In O. Corneille, V. Yzerbyt, & C. M. Judd (Eds.) *The psychology of group perception: Perceived variability, entitativity, and essentialism.* (pp. 361–379). New York: Psychology Press.

Ackerman, J. M., Nocera, C. C., & Bargh, J. A. (2010). Incidental haptic sensations influence social judgments and decisions. *Science*, *328*, 1712–1715.

Albery, I. P., Collins, I. S., Moss, A. C., Frings, D., & Spada, M. (2015). Habit predicts in-the-moment alcohol consumption. *Addictive Behaviors*, *41*, 78–80.

Attwood, A. S., O'Sullivan, H., Leonards, U., Mackintosh, B., & Munafò, M. R. (2008). Attentional bias training and cue reactivity in cigarette smokers. *Addiction*, *103*, 1875–1882.

Banerjee, S. C. & Greene, K. (2012). 'I quit' versus 'I'm sorry I used': A preliminary investigation of variations in narrative ending and transportation. *Psychology & Health*, *27*, 1308–1322.

Bargh, J. A. (2005). Bypassing the will: Toward demystifying the nonconscious control of social behavior. In R. L. Hassin, J. S., Uleman, J. A. & J. A. Bargh (Eds.) *The new unconscious* (pp. 37–58). Oxford: Oxford University Press.

Bargh, J. A., Chen, M., & Burrows, L. (1996). Automaticity of social behavior: Direct effects of trait construct and stereotype activation on action. *Journal of Personality and Social Psychology*, *71*, 230–244.

Beckwith, M., Best, D., Dingle, G., Perryman, C., & Lubman, D. (2015). Predictors of flexibility in social identity among people entering a therapeutic community for substance abuse. *Alcoholism Treatment Quarterly*, *33*, 93–104.

Best, D., Beckwith, M., Haslam, C., Haslam, A. S., Jetten, J., Mawson, E., & Lubman, D. I. (2016). Overcoming alcohol and other drug addiction as a process of social identity transition: The social identity model of recovery (SIMOR). *Addiction Research & Theory*, *24*, 111–123.

Blonigen, D. M., Timko, C., Finney, J. W., Moos, B. S., & Moos, R. H. (2011). Alcoholics Anonymous attendance, decreases in impulsivity and drinking and psychosocial outcomes over 16 years: moderated-mediation from a developmental perspective. *Addiction*, *106*, 2167–2177.

Buckingham, S., Frings, D., & Albery, I. P. (2013). Group membership and social identity in addiction recovery. *Psychology of Addictive Behaviors*, *27*, 1132–1140.

Cane, J. E., Sharma, D., & Albery, I. P. (2009). The addiction Stroop task: Examining the fast and slow effects of smoking and marijuana-related cues. *Journal of Psychopharmacology*, *23*, 510–519.

Carvajal, S. C., Clair, S.D., Nash, S. G., & Evans, R. I. (1998). Relating optimism, hope, and self-esteem to social influences in deterring substance use in adolescents. *Journal of Social and Clinical Psychology*, *17*, 443–465.

Dawson, D. A., Grant, B. F., Stinson, F. S., & Chou, P. S. (2006). Estimating the effect of help-seeking on achieving recovery from alcohol dependence. *Addiction*, *101*, 824–834.

De Houwer, J., Custers, R., & De Clercq, A. (2006). Do smokers have a negative implicit attitude toward smoking? *Cognition and Emotion*, *20*, 1274–1284.

Dijksterhuis, A., Aarts, H., Bargh, J. A., & van Knippenberg, A. (2000). On the relation between associative strength and automatic behavior. *Journal of Experimental Social Psychology*, *36*, 531–544.

Dijkstra, A., Conijn, B., & De Vries, H. (2006). A match–mismatch test of a stage model of behaviour change in tobacco smoking. *Addiction*, 101, 1035–1043.

Dingle, G., Cruwys, T., & Frings, D. (2015). Social identities as pathways into and out of addiction. *Frontiers in Psychology*, *6*, 1795.

Dingle, G. A., Stark, C., Cruwys, T., & Best, D. (2015). Breaking good: Breaking ties with social groups may be good for recovery from substance misuse. *British Journal of Social Psychology*, *54*, 236–254.

Festinger, L. (1950). Informal social communication. *Psychological Review*, *57*, 271–282.

Festinger, L., Gerard, H. B., Hymovitch, B., Kelley, H., & Raven, B. H. (1952). The influence process in the presence of extreme deviates. *Human Relations, 5*, 327–345.

Festinger, L. & Thibaut, J. (1951). Interpersonal communication in small groups. *The Journal of Abnormal and Social Psychology, 46*, 92.

Field, M., Munafò, M. R., & Franken, I. H. (2009). A meta-analytic investigation of the relationship between attentional bias and subjective craving in substance abuse. *Psychological Bulletin, 135*, 589–607.

Friese, M., Hofmann, W., & Wiers, R. W. (2011). On taming horses and strengthening riders: Recent developments in research on interventions to improve self-control in health behaviors. *Self and Identity, 10*, 336–351.

Franken, I. H. (2003). Drug craving and addiction: Integrating psychological and neuro-psychopharmacological approaches. *Progress in Neuro-Psychopharmacology and Biological Psychiatry, 27*, 563–579.

Frings, D. & Abrams, D. (2010). The effect of Difference Oriented Communication on the subjective validity of an in-group norm: DOC can treat the group. *Group Dynamics: Theory, Research & Practice, 14*, 281–291.

Frings, D., Abrams, D., Marques, J., & Randsley de Moura, G. (2010). The effects of cost, normative support, and issue importance on motivation to persuade in-group deviants. *Group Dynamics: Theory, Research and Practice, 14*, 80–91.

Frings, D. & Albery, I. P. (2015). The Social Identity Model of Cessation Maintenance: Formulation and initial evidence. *Addictive Behaviors, 44*, 35–42.

Frings, D., Collins, M., Long, G., Pinto, I., & Albery, I. P. (in press). A test of the Social Identity Model of Cessation Maintenance: The content and role of social control. *Addictive Behaviours Reports*. doi:a0.1016/j.abrep.2016.02.003.

Frings, D., Melichar, L., & Albery, I. P. (2016). Implicit but not explicit drinker identity predicts in-the-moment alcohol placebo consumption. *Addictive Behaviors Reports, 3*, 86–91.

Frings, D. & Pinto, I. (in prep). They did it again! Social control responses to repeated incidences of deviance in small groups.

Fromberger, P., Jordan, K., von Herder, J., Steinkrauss, H., Nemetschek, R., Stolpmann, G., & Müller, J. L. (2012). Initial orienting towards sexually relevant stimuli: Preliminary evidence from eye movement measures. *Archives of Sexual Behavior, 41*, 919–928.

Gawronski, B. & Bodenhausen, G. V. (2006). Associative and propositional processes in evaluation: an integrative review of implicit and explicit attitude change. *Psychological Bulletin, 132*, 692–731.

Gawronski, B. & Payne, B. K. (Eds.). (2011). *Handbook of implicit social cognition: measurement, theory, and applications*. New York: Guilford Press.

Gerrard, M., Gibbons, F. X., Houlihan, A. E., Stock, M. L., & Pomery, E. A. (2008). A dual-process approach to health risk decision making: The prototype willingness model. *Developmental Review, 28*, 29–61.

Gibbons, F. X., Gerrard, M., Stock, M. L., & Finneran, S. (2015). The Prototype/Willingness Model. In M. Connor & P. Norman (Eds.). *Predicting and changing health behaviour: Research and practice with social cognition models*. (pp. 189–224). Maidenhead: Open University Press.

Graeven, D. B. & Graeven, K. A. (1983). Treated and untreated addicts: Factors associated with participation in treatment and cessation of heroin use. *Journal of Drug Issues, 13*, 207–218.

Gray, H. M., LaPlante, D. A., Bannon, B. L., Ambady, N., & Shaffer, H. J. (2011). Development and validation of the Alcohol Identity Implicit Associations Test (AI-IAT). *Addictive Behaviors, 36*, 919 –926.

Greenberg, J. L., Lewis, S. E., & Dodd, D. K. (1999). Overlapping addictions and self-esteem among college men and women. *Addictive Behaviors, 24*, 565–571.

Hogg, M. A., Hardie, E. A., & Reynolds, K. J. (1995). Prototypical similarity, self-categorization, and depersonalized attraction: A perspective on group cohesiveness. *European Journal of Social Psychology*, *25*, 159–177.

Israel, J. (1956). *Self-evaluation and rejection in groups*. Stockholm: Almqvist & Wiksell.

Jacobs, D. & Kent, S. L. (2007). The determinants of executions since 1951: How politics, protests, public opinion, and social divisions shape capital punishment. *Social Problems*, *54*, 297–318.

Jensen, G. H. (2000). *Storytelling in Alcoholics Anonymous: A rhetorical analysis*. Carbondale, IL: Southern Illinois University Press.

Kaskutas, L. A., Ammon, L., Delucchi, K., Room, R., Bond, J., & Weisner, C. (2005). Alcoholics Anonymous careers: Patterns of AA involvement five years after treatment entry. *Alcoholism: Clinical and Experimental Research*, *29*, 1983–1990.

Kelly, J. F., Hoeppner, B., Stout, R. L., & Pagano, M. E. (2012). Determining the relative importance of the mechanisms of behavior change within Alcoholics Anonymous: A multiple mediator analysis. *Addiction*, *107*, 289–299.

Kelly, J. F., Stout, R. L., Magill, M., Tonigan, J. S., & Pagano, M. E. (2010). Mechanisms of behavior change in Alcoholics Anonymous: Does Alcoholics Anonymous lead to better alcohol use outcomes by reducing depression symptoms? *Addiction*, *105*, 626–636.

Levine, J. M. (1989). Reaction to opinion deviance in small groups. In P. B. Paulus (Ed.) *Psychology of group influence* (2nd ed.) (pp. 187–231). Hillsdale, NJ: Lawrence Erlbaum Associates.

Lindgren, K. P., Foster, D.W., Westgate, E. C., & Neighbors, C. (2013). Implicit drinking identity: Drinker + me associations predict college student drinking consistently. *Addictive Behaviors*, *38*, 2163–2166.

Lindgren, K. P., Neighbors, C., Teachman, B. A., Wiers, R. W., Westgate, E., & Greenwald, A. G. (2013). I drink therefore I am: Validating alcohol-related implicit association tests. *Psychology of Addictive Behaviors*, *27*, 1–13.

Maddux, J. E. & Rogers, R. W. (1983). Protection motivation and self-efficacy: A revised theory of fear appeals and attitude change. *Journal of Experimental Social Psychology*, *19*, 469–479.

Meijer, E., Gebhardt, W. A., Dijkstra, A., Willemsen, M. C., & Van Laar, C. (in press). Quitting smoking: The importance of non-smoker identity in predicting smoking behaviour and responses to a smoking ban. *Psychology & Health*, (just-accepted), 1–39.

Meijer, E., Gebhardt, W. A., Dijkstra, A., Willemsen, M. C., & Van Laar, C. (2015). Quitting smoking: The importance of non-smoker identity in predicting smoking behaviour and responses to a smoking ban. *Psychology & Health*, *30*, 1387–1409.

Moos, R. H. (2008). Active ingredients of substance use-focused self-help groups. *Addiction* *103*, 387–396.

Moreland, R. L., Levine, J. M., & Cini, M. A. (1993). Group socialization: The role of commitment. In M. Hogg & D. Abrams (Eds.). *Group motivation: Social psychological perspectives*. (pp. 105–129). Hertfordshire: Harvester Wheatsheaf.

Moss, A. C. & Albery, I. P. (2009). A dual-process model of the alcohol–behavior link for social drinking. *Psychological Bulletin*, *135*, 516–530.

Moss, A. C., Albery, I. P., Siddiqui, I., & Rycroft, N. (2013). Attentional bias for alcohol-related stimuli among belief based and non-belief based non-drinkers. *European Addiction Research*, *19*, 299–302.

Niemz, K., Griffiths, M., & Banyard, P. (2005). Prevalence of pathological Internet use among university students and correlations with self-esteem, the General Health Questionnaire (GHQ), and disinhibition. *CyberPsychology & Behavior*, *8*, 562–570.

Norman, P., Boer, H., Seydel E.R., & Mullan, B. (2015). Protection motivation theory. In M. Connor & P. Norman (Eds.). *Predicting and Changing Health Behaviour: Research and Practice with Social Cognition Models*. (pp. 70–106). Maidenhead: Open University Press.

Orcutt, J. D. (1973). Societal reaction and the response to deviation in small groups. *Social Forces, 52*, 259–267.

Pinto, I. R., Marques, J. M., Levine, J. M., & Abrams, D. (2010). Membership status and subjective group dynamics: Who triggers the black sheep effect? *Journal of Personality and Social Psychology, 99*, 107–119.

Prochaska, J. O. & Velicer, W. F. (1997). The transtheoretical model of health behavior change. *American Journal of Health Promotion, 12*, 38–48.

Richter, S. S., Brown, S. A., & Mott, M. A. (1991). The impact of social support and self-esteem on adolescent substance abuse treatment outcome. *Journal of Substance Abuse, 3*, 371–385.

Rivis, A. & Sheeran, P. (2013). Automatic risk behavior: Direct effects of binge drinker stereotypes on drinking behavior. *Health Psychology, 32*, 571–580.

Rooke, S. E., Hine, D. W., & Thorsteinsson, E. B. (2008). Implicit cognition and substance use: A meta-analysis. *Addictive Behaviors, 33*, 1314–1328.

Rubin, M. & Hewstone, M. (1998). Social identity theory's self-esteem hypothesis: A review and some suggestions for clarification. *Personality and Social Psychology Review, 2*, 40–62.

Schachter, S. (1951). Deviation, rejection and communication, *Journal of Abnormal and Social Psychology, 41*, 190–207.

Schwarzer, R. (2008). Modeling health behavior change: How to predict and modify the adoption and maintenance of health behaviors. *Applied Psychology, 57*, 1–29.

Sharma, D., Albery, I. P., & Cook, C. (2001). Selective attentional bias to alcohol related stimuli in problem drinkers and non-problem drinkers. *Addiction, 96*, 285–295.

Sheeran, P., Aarts, H., Custers, R., Rivis, A., Webb, T. L., & Cooke, R. (2005). The goal-dependent automaticity of drinking habits. *British Journal of Social Psychology, 44*, 47–63.

Sheeran, P., Gollwitzer, P. M., & Bargh, J. A. (2013). Nonconscious processes and health. *Health Psychology, 32*, 460–473

Sherman, J. W., Gawronski, B., & Trope, Y. (Eds.). (2014). *Dual-process theories of the social mind*. New York: Guilford Press.

Shiffrin, R. M. & Schneider, W. (1977). Controlled and automatic human information processing: II. Perceptual learning, automatic attending and a general theory. *Psychological Review, 84*, 127–190.

Stacy, A. W. (1997). Memory activation and expectancy as prospective predictors of alcohol and marijuana use. *Journal of Abnormal Psychology, 106*, 61–73.

Strack, F. & Deutsch, R. (2004). Reflective and impulsive determinants of social behavior. *Personality and Social Psychology Review, 8*, 220–247.

Tajfel, H. E. (1978). *Differentiation between social groups: Studies in the social psychology of intergroup relations*. Oxford. Academic Press.

Tajfel, H. & Turner, J. C. (1979). An integrative theory of intergroup conflict. In W. G. Austin. & S. Worchel (Eds.) *The social psychology of intergroup relations*. (pp. 33–48). Monterey, CA: Brooks/Cole.

Tappin, D. et al., (2014). Financial incentives for smoking cessation in pregnancy: randomised controlled trial, *British Medical Journal, 250*, H134.

Tiffany, S. T. (1990). A cognitive model of drug urges and drug-use behavior: role of automatic and nonautomatic processes. *Psychological Review, 97*, 147–168.

Turner, J. C., Hogg, M. A., Oakes, P. J., Reicher, S. D., & Wetherell, M. S. (1987). *Rediscovering the social group: A self-categorization theory*. Oxford: Basil Blackwell.

Vangeli, E. & West, R. (2012). Transition towards a 'non-smoker' identity following smoking cessation: An interpretative phenomenological analysis. *British Journal of Health Psychology, 17*, 171–184.

Wiers, R. W., Bartholow, B. D., van den Wildenberg, E., Thush, C., Engels, R. C., Sher, K. J., Grenard, Ames, S.L., & Stacy, A. W. (2007). Automatic and controlled processes and the development of addictive behaviors in adolescents: A review and a model. *Pharmacology Biochemistry and Behavior, 86*, 263–283.

Wiers, R. W. H. J., Houben, K. M. P. I., Roefs, A. J., Jong, D. P., Hofmann, W., & Stacy, A. (2010). Implicit cognition in health psychology: Why common sense goes out of the window. In B. Gawronski & B. K. Payne (Eds.). *Handbook of implicit social cognition: Measurement, theory, and applications*, (pp. 463–488). New York: Guilford Press.

Wilson, C. & Wallis, D. J. (2013). Attentional bias and slowed disengagement from food and threat stimuli in restrained eaters using a modified Stroop task. *Cognitive Therapy and Research, 37*, 127–138.

Wolff, N., von Hippel, C., Brener, L., & von Hippel, W. (2015). Implicit identification with drug and alcohol use predicts retention in residential rehabilitation programs. *Psychology of Addictive Behavior, 29*, 136–141.

9

ONLINE SUPPORT COMMUNITIES IN ADDICTION RECOVERY

Capturing social interaction and identity change through analyses of online communication

Ana-Maria Bliuc, David Best, Melinda Beckwith and Muhammad Iqbal

Introduction

As contemporary approaches to addiction treatment are evolving from models predominantly focused on acute bio-psychosocial stabilisation to models similar to managing chronic diseases such as diabetes and high blood pressure (White, 2009), the importance of communities of support becomes more central. The role of social support groups in recovery from addiction (Best et al., 2016), and other health conditions (Jetten, Haslam, & Haslam, 2012) has long been recognised and extensively researched. There has been a move from models predicated on an 'individual struggle' to a shared recovery process, that is, from an individual-focused approach to change to more socially oriented alternatives, not only regarding treatment per se, but also in how support for recovery is conceptualised (Beckwith, Bliuc, & Best, 2016; White, 1998). Recent definitions of recovery from addiction characterise recovery as a "process of change through which individuals improve their health and wellness, live self-directed lives, and strive to reach their full potential" (Substance Abuse and Mental Health Services Administration, 2012). SAMHSA's working definition of recovery encompasses four dimensions necessary to support recovery – health, home, purpose and community – incorporating the recognition that, during this process, social support is paramount (Betty Ford Institute, 2007).

In terms of empirical evidence, there is a vast amount of research on the effectiveness of recovery support groups, with much of this research based in the US and focused on Alcoholics Anonymous (AA; e.g., Kaskutas, 2009). Findings from a systematic review of the literature on AA conducted by Kelly and colleagues (Kelly, Magill, & Stout, 2009) indicates that such communities of support help people in recovery through what they refer to as "common processes", which are activities that facilitate the development of self-efficacy, coping skills, motivation and, importantly, adaptive changes in social networks through a move to health-promoting social networks (Kaskutas, Bond, & Humphreys, 2002; Kelly et al., 2009). Complementary literature from outside the US argues that recognition of the importance of these activities comes with the recognition that a successful recovery journey is often contingent upon people being able to develop and sustain a functional *recovery social identity* that is aligned to norms of non-using behaviour (Best et al., 2015; Buckingham, Frings, & Albery, 2013).

More recently, due to the proliferation of new technologies enabling a wide range of different modes of online communication, a new phase in how people go about gaining social support in their recovery has begun. The social element of recovery can be seen as being both amplified and diminished through the use of new technologies. In a sense, social support is easier to access through online communication, and this is particularly useful in cases of social, geographical or mobility-related isolation (Rodham, McCabe, & Blake, 2009), or where there is personal preference for online support, which may be due to any number of reasons, such as dissatisfaction with offline sources of support (Chung, 2013), or simply lack of availability of other sources of support at the time of need (Savic, Best, Rodda, & Lubman, 2013). Online peer support has also been shown to hold significant value to participants (Stewart Loane, Webster, & D'Alessandro, 2015), and it can be used to expand on existing support networks in a range of populations (e.g., Chung, 2013; Stewart Loane & D'Alessandro, 2014; Savic et al., 2013). For example, in a review on outcomes regarding smoking cessation, online support was shown to provide similar outcomes to face-to-face programs (Shahab & McEwen, 2009). Online groups may be also accessed with relative anonymity, low cost and minimal inconvenience, and withdrawal is easy if the experience is not deemed to be positive (Galston, 2000).

New technologies provide not only alternatives to access social support for recovery, but they can also be used to mobilise support from the broader community to counter stigma (Gee & McGarty, 2013), and research into the content of such support groups can inform professionals in healthcare and social services about the needs of their client group. With the increased role of online communication in the recovery process, there is emerging interest in examining whether new communication platforms are indeed supporting the recovery process in meaningful ways (Moorhead et al., 2013; White & Dorman, 2001). Recovery is a long-term and dynamic process, which online platforms may be capable of supporting through providing low-cost and easy access to both therapeutic interventions and online recovery communities as and when they are needed (Savic et al., 2013). On the other hand, one consequence of relying predominantly on new communication technologies to access support may be a diminished ability to seek support face-to-face (Chung, 2013), with the full range of implications of this gap not yet fully understood (Finfgeld, 2000). The Internet opens a lot of opportunities including seeking help and social support (but also trolling and gaining pleasure from manipulating other people). At present we have little evidence of sufficient quality to determine 'net' effects on personal and group wellbeing in recovery.

These new ways of accessing support that incorporate the use of technology have also opened new possibilities for conducting research in the field of addiction recovery. Changes in how recovery is conceptualised and how people engage with the process of recovery (bringing into the focus the key role of social networks and support) need to be captured and investigated through innovative approaches in research methodology. As Ben Shneiderman points out in a 2008 article titled 'Science 2.0', "traditional scientific methods need to be expanded to deal with complex issues that arise as social systems meet technological innovation" (Shneiderman, 2008, p. 1349). That is, traditional scientific methods such as the use of surveys, interviews, and laboratory experiments need to be supplemented with approaches that capture the rich context of online interactions and are able to deal with the challenges that access to 'big data' can create. Here we apply this idea to the field of addiction recovery by suggesting a combination of methods and approaches to examine data obtained from online support communities.

More specifically, we discuss potential ways in which the dynamic process of addiction recovery can be examined through an analysis of the online interactions within recovery support communities. We argue that the interaction and communication which happens on these platforms provides us with rich data that can be analysed in a variety of ways to advance our understanding of the phenomenon of recovery from addiction, in particular in relation to psychological dimensions of recovery that are expressed through both use of language and online social interaction patterns. Key psychosocial aspects of recovery, such as changes in social identity, are particularly well-suited to be investigated through these approaches.

In psychology, and social sciences more generally, the idea that language can be seen as a 'window into basic social and psychological process' (Chung & Pennebaker, 2014), reflecting states, social processes, personal concerns and traits, is not new. Analyses of 'text and talk' have been long employed to investigate psychosocial phenomena ranging from the human psyche (through Freud's free association technique), to attitudes to ethnic minorities (Verkuyen, 2001), and constructions of national identity (Wallwork & Dixon, 2004). Recent developments in computerised methods of analysing and categorising language enable researchers to capitalise on the access to large amounts of data that are now available online. For example, various existing linguistic analysis software systems/approaches can be used to analyse large online texts to locate identity markers and track changes in these identity markers across time (Pennebaker, Booth, & Francis, 2007; for a review of research using the methods please see Tausczik & Pennebaker, 2010). In this chapter we explore how specific analyses, including analysis of language, can be used to gain insights into the process of recovery from addiction, beyond changes in identity and recovery pathways. We conclude by suggesting ways in which we can best make use of large amounts of online data generated by participants in online recovery support groups to further understand the social network and social identity processes underpinning recovery from addiction.

Online communities of support

Online interactions are becoming a part of mainstream modes of communication for many people in industrialised societies. That is, we now shop, date, play games, work and socialise online (Preece, 2001). When we are worried, sick or need support we also frequently turn to the Internet. Online communities of support are increasingly playing a vital role in the process of recovery from a range of curable health issues as well as for coping with chronic conditions. There is extensive research on the positive role of online support in a range of health conditions including AIDS and HIV (Mo & Coulson, 2010), diabetes (Gustafson et al., 1999), cancer-related anxiety and depression (Winzelberg et al., 2003), Crohn's disease (Stewart Loane & D'Alessandro, 2013), and smoking cessation (Shahab & McEwen, 2009).

Online communities of support started to become popular in the early 1990s, mostly in the form of discussion forums about coping with a range of conditions including asthma, autism, cancer, and social anxiety. Nowadays, there are online support groups for the majority of health or other distressing conditions, with people joining these groups primarily to obtain and disseminate information about the particular condition that they are dealing with, provide and receive emotional support, form social relationships, and share experiences, coping strategies and challenges (Barak, Boniel-Nissim, & Suler, 2008). In the context of recovery from addiction, data from a recent UK report on experiences of recovery (Best et al., 2015) indicate that some of the key groups that people are likely to join online to seek support in their recovery journey include Facebook groups (e.g., Sober Nation Facebook group, AA Facebook group, etc.), SMART Recovery's online community, and other online groups such as Breaking Free Online, Soberistas, Intuitive Recovery, as well as Twitter accounts and blogs.

Although reviews of existing research identified mixed findings regarding the effectiveness of online support groups in relation to direct outcomes (i.e., participating in a cancer support group is not necessarily linked to higher remission rates; Eysenbach, et al., 2004), there is agreement on the positive role of participating in such groups for fostering general well-being, and more diffuse positive psychological outcomes through providing participants with a sense of belonging and personal empowerment (Bakardjieva, 2003; Barak et al., 2008; Tanis, 2007). There is mounting evidence that joining online support groups to help people cope with health and other conditions has become less about seeking information and more about sharing experiences and developing a sense of connectedness and belonging to a (psychological) community made up of people dealing with similar issues (Stewart Loane & D'Alessandro, 2013), that is developing a sense of shared social identity (Best et al., 2015; Jetten, Haslam, Haslam, Dingle, & Jones, 2014; Haslam, O'Brien, Jetten, Vormedal, & Penna, 2005). These online interactions represent an opportunity for group members to construct a shared representation of the recovery process (Edwards, 1997), and a shared narrative that further endorses a sense of social identity (Rappaport, 1993; Rafalovich, 1999).

Social identity and the recovery process: the role of online support groups

The recovery journey can be conceptualised as a process of *social identity change*, the emerging sense of self as 'in recovery' being shaped by the shared norms, values and expectations of a group made up of people going through similar experiences of recovery (Best et al., 2015; Buckingham et al., 2013). According to the recently developed Social Identity Model Of Recovery (SIMOR, Best et al., 2015), recovery is framed as a process of "social identity change in which a person's most salient identity shifts from being defined by membership of a group whose norms and values revolve around substance abuse to being defined by membership of a group whose norms and values encourage recovery" (p. 3). As in other contexts, a salient and relevant social identity (in this case, the developing recovery identity) is likely to shape the behaviour of group members through a process in which group values and norms are internalised by individual members (see Buckingham, Chapter 7 in the current volume; Haslam, 2014), and so shape self-concept and expectations and beliefs about substance use. That is, a shared sense of selfhood as 'us in recovery' will promote behaviours, which are aligned with the group's norms, such as avoiding environments and people that could compromise the recovery process (Best et al., 2015). Group normative behaviour is not merely restricted to substance abuse-avoiding behaviour, but can also include active participation in a shared process of recovery via online contexts (as captured, for example, through contributions in online forums) and further advocacy activities aimed at countering social stigma (Livingston, Milne, Fang, & Amari, 2012).

In turn, online interactions with like-minded individuals within the recovery support networks are likely to strengthen group members' sense of shared recovery identity, in ways that very much mirror the dynamics in face-to-face contexts (Spears, Postmes, Lea, & Wolbert, 2002). Existing evidence would suggest that belonging to an online community was shown to be particularly important for people who felt socially excluded and unable to talk openly about their condition (Bargh & McKenna, 2004; McKenna & Bargh, 1999; Stewart Loane & D'Alessandro, 2013), reflecting the internalisation of stigma, which research suggests people recovering from addiction continue to be subjected to by the general public (Phillips & Shaw, 2013). Moreover, group membership may become important to people who internalise a stigmatised identity making them more likely to influence their behaviour more strongly than in the case of other group members (Crabtree, Haslam, Postmes, & Haslam, 2010; McKenna & Bargh, 1998). Research on the variation in support seeking patterns for different health conditions (including diabetes, cancer, alcoholism, chronic fatigue syndrome, AIDS, depression, migraine, etc.) also shows that the *amount* of support sought in both face-to-face and online contexts is positively correlated to interpersonal dimensions of the experience of the health condition. That is, according to this research, people are more likely to seek support from people sharing the same challenges as themselves if they are suffering from a stigmatising condition (Davison, Pennebaker, & Dickerson, 2000).

By examining online social interactions in recovery support groups we can understand how new (recovery) social identities emerge, evolve and become crystallised. By accessing longitudinal data, we can examine the different phases of identity formation, from the initial emergence of these new recovery identities (closely aligned to the point in which individuals join a particular support group), to being fully-fledged online community members, often acting as influential agents of change within the groups. By mapping and analysing patterns of online interaction during the recovery process we can identify particular opportunities, challenges and barriers in the recovery process.

Exploring online interactions underpinning the recovery process

Addiction researchers have the opportunity to complement evidence based on self-report instruments to examine the process of recovery as captured by the digital footprint of online interactions (Davison et al., 2000). By examining the language of recovery as it occurs spontaneously in the realm of online communica-tion, we can identify how changes in identity are reflected in the language used when participating in conversations in online support groups. However, there is no research that we have identified so far that focuses on the recovery process (reflected in the quality and quantity of online interactions and changes over time). Thus, key questions about the relationship between people's progress through their recovery from addiction and changes in their social identity can now be explored by analysing patterns of online interactions of people going through the recovery journey.

Most existing research on recovery is based on data collected through self-reported research questionnaires (e.g., Groshkova, Best, & White, 2012) and clinical tools (e.g., Maudsley Addiction Profile, Marsden et al., 1998; Addiction Severity Index, McLellan et al., 1992; Opiate Treatment Index, Darke, Hall, Wodak, Heather, & Ward, 1992). However, with the proliferation of online groups and increased participation in these groups, there is an impressive quantity of online data that can be extracted from public forums where individuals are sharing their experience of recovery. This data can prove extremely valuable to researchers in the addiction field, but to be able to make the most out of this data, we need to adopt a systematic approach to its analysis. One of the key aims of this chapter is to propose and discuss such an approach.

The approach that we propose breaks down the study of online interactions into specific elements, coded in terms of specific online behaviours of participants, the way language is used, and the ways in which interactions unfold (see Figure 9.1). By measuring level of engagement (defined by length and frequency of online contributions), and level of disclosure (i.e., how much a person reveals about themselves and their recovery journey), we can quantify conversational behaviours aimed at social connection. Language used can be analysed in terms of its content (through identifying themes), and function (through identifying underpinning

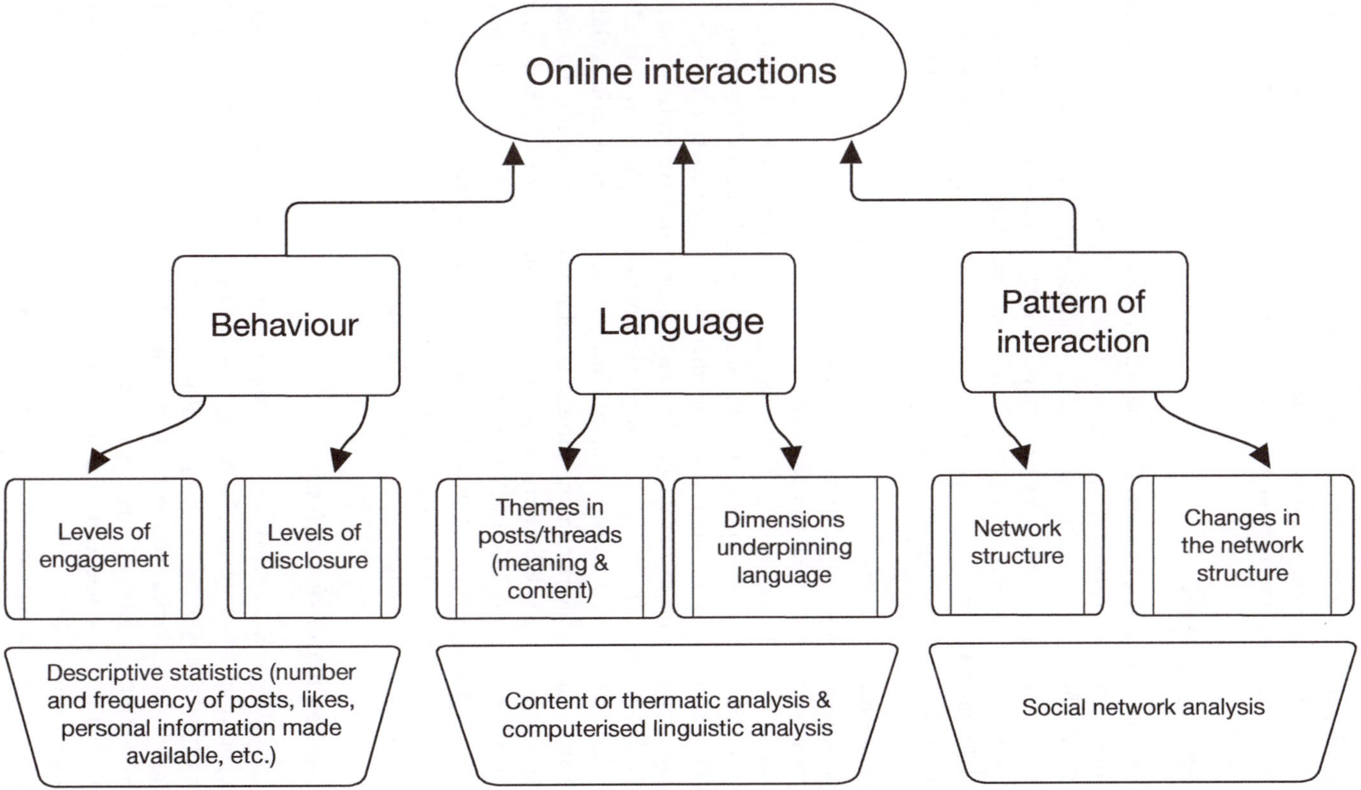

FIGURE 9.1 Mapping ways to research online social interactions in the context of recovery.

psychological drivers of particular language use). Finally, the pattern of interactions can be examined through conducting social network analysis that can tell us how the internal structure of the group looks, and how it evolves over time. By integration analyses of connectedness, language and specific patterns of interaction we can map out more precisely the process of identity change in recovery.

Qualitative techniques

Online textual data can of course be analysed by using traditional methods of text analysis such as thematic analysis (Braun & Clarke, 2006) or discourse analysis (Potter & Wetherell, 1987). Thematic analysis – identifying reoccurring themes within text – is often seen as the default option to analyse qualitative data from a theoretically neutral perspective, where a fairly structured approach to analysis is preferred (Braun & Clarke, 2006). Conversely, discourse analysis is particularly useful when researchers are seeking to uncover specific socially relevant functions of language use (Billig, 1991). However, it has been suggested that online text represents a variation of classic text, as its objective is often seeking or providing social support, rather than merely providing information (Walther & Boyd, 2002), so analysis of online text needs to reflect this social dimension of communication. Thus, a more suitable methodology in this case is conversation analysis (Goodwin & Heritage, 1990), a generic approach to the study of social interactions through an analysis of ordinary conversation as well as other forms of conversation including political speech, and organisational talk. Conversation analysis is particularly suited to capture the dynamics of language used in interactions by identifying how different messages are placed in the conversation and how contributors take turns within the exchange. This is important to the current model as an essential aspect of online social support, is the match between what the users expect or require and what the group offers (Cutrona & Russell, 1990; Cutrona & Suhr, 1992). For example, Vayreda and Antaki (2009) used conversation analysis to examine how social support is sought in an online forum on bipolar disorders, focusing on the way in which new members introduce themselves to the other group members.

Computerised linguistic analysis

An increasingly popular approach to analysing online qualitative data is through using linguistic analysis software. Recently, a number of different programs have been developed and perfected with a particular focus on uncovering more implicit expression of psychological constructs as they are reflected in language. One of the main advantages of using this type of software is that very large amounts of online data can be objectively analysed in a relatively short space of time, so these tools are often used to make sense of 'big data' collected through social media sites, such as Twitter and Facebook. Another benefit is that these software methods were specifically developed by psychologists to capture a range of psychological dimensions and processes, as well as individual differences. That is, one example of such software is the Linguistic Inquiry Word Count (LIWC) developed by James Pennebaker and colleagues (Pennebaker, Francis, & Booth, 2001; Pennebaker, Booth, & Francis, 2007; Pennebaker, Boyd, Jordan, & Blackburn, 2015). The latest version of the software (LIWC 2015) includes over 80 categories that tap into various domains including psychological processes (affect, cognition, drives, social processes, etc.), and personal concerns (work, home, leisure, etc.). LIWC has been previously used for textual analysis in a variety of contexts, ranging from clinical concerns, such as predicting depression and postpartum changes in emotion and behaviour (through an analysis of social media contributions, De Choudhury, Counts, & Horvitz, 2013; De Choudhury, Gamon, Counts, & Horvitz, 2013), and distinguishing between online language use of self-identified pro-anorexia patients (who defend anorexia as a lifestyle choice) and self-identified recovering anorexia patients (Lyons, Mehl, & Pennebaker, 2006), to community concerns, such as identifying markers of psychological change around the September 11 terrorist attacks in the US (Cohn, Mehl, & Pennebaker, 2004).

One example of recent research using LIWC that is particular relevant in the context of recovery is a study by Van der Zanden and colleagues (Van der Zanden, Curie, Van Londen, et al., 2014). In this study, LIWC was employed to analyse language used in group chat sessions by young adults suffering from depression. It was found that certain words used in those chats predicted successful treatment outcomes in a six-session online cognitive behavioural group course. For example, increased use of particular function words (such as 'should' and 'would', discrepancy words that express a misalignment between current reality and desired reality) predicted improved depression scores. Other recent linguistic analyses of client communications in Internet-delivered CBT (ICBT) for general anxiety disorders sufferers confirm that use of language (as captured by the same linguistic analysis software) changes as therapy progresses and symptoms improve (Dirkse, Hadjistavropoulos, Hesser, & Barak, 2015). That is, progressively fewer words reflecting negative emotion, anxiety, and causation were used over the course of the ICBT treatment. Finally, Zinken and colleagues (Zinken, Zinken, Wilson, Butler, & Skinner, 2010) used LIWC to conduct an analysis of the narrative style of people suffering from generalised anxiety disorder and depression in order to identify predictors of successful participation in a self-guided self-help program. Although they only found partial support for their hypothesis that reflection language would predict completion of the self-help program, one of their most exciting aspects of this research is that text analysis can be a useful tool for assessing likelihood of program completion (Zinken et al., 2010), which in turn is associated with behaviour change.

As these examples suggest, the use of LIWC can be readily adapted to analyse online text generated by addiction recovery groups. The existing categories can be used to map out changes in emotions, cognitive and social processes, and use of function words, but also new categories can be specifically constructed to capture identity change and other dimensions that are unique to the recovery process. For example, social and personal identities can be captured through the use of 'social orientation' words (Cohn et al., 2004). In LIWC, the social-orientation index was computed to reflect the use of words such as *talk*, *share*, or *friends* and personal pronouns other than first-person singular. Social identification with more specific groups can be captured through the use of the categories such as 'affiliation' that are now included in the 2015 version of LIWC (Pennebaker et al., 2015). A 'recovery identity' category can be also computed based on an analysis of texts that are representative of the language of recovery (following the procedure described for example in Slatcher, Chung, & Pennebaker, 2007).

Social network analysis

Given the central role of social connectedness is the process of recovery, social network analysis as a research methodology is a particularly useful tool that can help uncover the aspects of the recovery process that are influenced by specific configurations of social networks, and which support or hinder recovery. For example, social network analysis can help us unpack intra-group dynamics such as identifying those members of the group who have the most influence on the rest, in other words the group leaders. That is, by analysing the structure of a social group in terms of connections between members and positioning of members within the network (centrality versus periphery) we can capture degrees of prototypicality of those group members. Prototypicality refers to how well a particular group member embodies the group prototype, or in other words 'the ideal representation of the group's identity' (Giessner & van Knippenberg, 2008). This ideal representation fulfils the role of describing and prescribing those attributes that are most aligned to the norms of the group. The more prototypical a member is, the more they identify with the group, the more central they are likely to be within the group, and the more likely it is that the other members of the group will attempt to emulate them (Hogg, 2001; Giessner & van Knippenberg, 2008). Thus, it is particularly important in the context of recovery to be able to identify those group members who are the most likely to influence other members and drive changes in behaviours, and to understand the ways in which this shapes the group's ability to achieve and maintain their recovery goals.

Longitudinally mapping out changes in social networks can help us better understand both the positive and negative role (depending of the configuration of individual social networks) of belonging to social groups in the process of recovery (Gordon & Zrull, 1991). Analyses of the social networks of recovering alcoholics found that support from co-workers not regularly drinking with the person in recovery and the perceived support of co-workers (regardless of their drinking patterns) were influential in recovery, with positive and respectively negative effects; regarding family and friends, it was found that non-drinking network members positively influenced, and drinking network members negatively influenced, the drinking behaviour of recovering alcoholics (Gordon & Zrull, 1991).

In an online context, social network analysis can help us understand intra-group dynamics of support groups, again helping identify changes in the structure of the group and linkages between the group members that are associated with recovery or relapse. However, most research to date looking at online social networks was conducted in the field of information technology and consequently aims to understand networks and their dynamics from structural points of view (Cha, Mislove, & Gummadi, 2009; Mislove, Marcon, Gummadi, et al., 2007), rather than to examine their underpinning social and psychological dimensions.

Through adopting an intragroup perspective to understanding recovery, social network analysis can also be employed to identify those members of the online community that are likely to exert the most social influence on the other group members, in other words those key group members who are the most likely to become 'agents of change' in these groups.

Integrating different methodologies to capture the dynamic changes in the process of recovery

While all these methodologies represent very useful tools that can be used in addiction recovery research, by adopting a triangulation approach we can achieve a more complete understanding of the recovery process as reflected in participation in online support groups. That is, social network analysis can be complemented by the use of a linguistic software such as LIWC to examine not only changes in social networks, but also changes in language and in its underpinning psychological structures. The combined use of these tools can enable researchers to make comparisons between changes in social networks and psychological changes in network members and, based on this, identify correlates of positive outcomes.

To illustrate this argument we refer here to Jobs, Friends and Houses (JFH), a recent recovery initiative in the UK, and we detail how this integration of methodological approaches can be used to examine recovery processes in this specific case. JFH is a social enterprise that engages addicts in early recovery in an apprenticeship in a building profession while they work on the renovation and construction of recovery housing in the town of Blackpool. Participants in the programme are thus actively engaged in paid work, are provided with housing, and many also attend recovery mutual aid meetings together as a part of a lifestyle change programme. They are also encouraged to view their participation as 'giving back' to the recovery community and the wider community. JFH also has a Facebook page, which was originally set up so that staff could inform the group about recovery and social events but which now performs two primary functions: a) to create a recovery-supportive online community for staff and participants, and b) to allow the outside world to engage with JFH. What is presented here is an illustration of how the technique will work and is intended only to describe the method as this work remains at an early stage.

By conducting a social network analysis (SNA) based on the first five months of online interactions on the group's Facebook page, we can identify those group members who are the most central in the configuration of the network, and therefore the most likely to influence the behaviour of the other group members. For the purposes of this discussion, we focused on the network created by interaction between the individuals who posted on the JFH Facebook page and those who comment on these posts. As Figure 9.2 illustrates, particular group members become central from early on. Here it is clear that member number 55, already occupies a central position in the network within Month 1, due to the high number of linkages to the other members. Other members, such as member number 305, gradually becomes more connected as the months go by and eventually plays a more central role in the network. From a social identity perspective, the trajectories of the two members can help us examine different stages in establishing group leadership and social influence within the groups as they occur. By further analysing the content of communication in the case of these members we can identify specific 'prototypicality markers' for this particular group. By examining communication content in conjunction with network configuration and changes we can understand how over time group norms emerge, are validated and endorsed.

While this network focused solely on the post-comment network to quantify connections between group members, other units of analysis such as 'likes' on both posts and comments can be also used depending on the aim of the analysis, and it can be supplemented by analysis of language, either by employing traditional qualitative analysis approaches (such as thematic, conversation, or discourse analyses), or computerised linguistic analysis software such as LIWC. These analyses can not only help pinpoint differences in the language used by the most prototypical group members, but also identify psychological structures that underpin the use of language. We can, for example, examine whether group leaders (those members who occupy central positions in the structure of the social network) are likely to use language that more cohesively represents the group's values compared to more 'peripheral' members of the group. We can also identify whether these values evolve over time and how that affects the group structure, various group members' locations within the network, and overall group cohesion. We can also identify changes in social identity markers, group emotions and concerns by mapping out how those psychological dimensions evolve over time, using the different analytic options available.

Finally, we can interpret these results more broadly to uncover key psychosocial processes in recovery from addiction, as well as to compare how people conceptualise recovery in language in different online recovery groups and what holds constant across groups, in other words what it is to be 'in recovery'. This approach can be applied to evaluating levels of effectiveness of various recovery programs to help identify the most relevant aspects for successful individual behavioural change. In an ongoing study, we are interviewing some of the key figures in the online network to allow us to assess the relationship between their online activities and their personal recovery narratives.

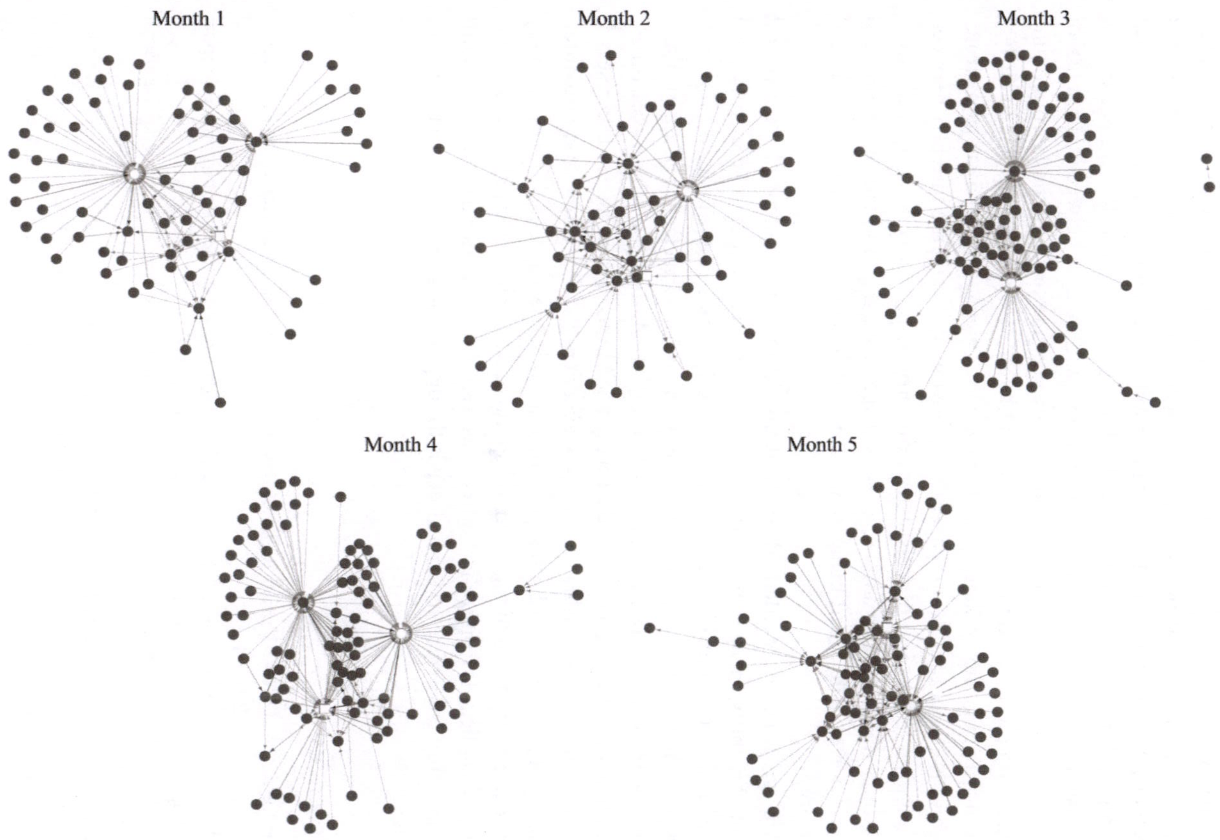

FIGURE 9.2 Representations of the social network configuration of the 'Jobs, Friends and Houses' Facebook page over 5 months.

Conclusion

Online recovery groups can allow us to utilise the available technology to take a novel approach to the naturalistic observation of recovery communities. In particular, we are now able to draw on new techniques and software in the analysis of an enormous amount of spontaneously generated 'data', a feat that would not be achievable using traditional research methods. By employing different analytical techniques, we can now triangulate findings to gain a broader perspective on psychosocial processes and group behaviour within and between members of recovery communities that have an online presence, and test hypotheses from online forums with more traditional forms of research follow-up. By being able to analyse the structure of groups' online interactions and the language used we can gain greater insights into the meaning of recovery for these members and the interplay between social and psychological process within the process of recovery, specifically how the groups norms, values and behaviours shape changes in individuals' expression of their norms, values and behaviours, hence their sense of social identity around recovery.

This gives us unprecedented levels of insight into the content of identity and extent of identity changes in the process of recovery. This needs to be corroborated against more traditional scientific methods to determine the impact on recovery trajectories in terms of health and wellbeing, and other social factors that contribute to recovery, such as jobs, friends, and housing. It also suggests the use of mixed methods approaches where online data analysis are tested against face to face research both quantitative and qualitative to assess experiences, perceptions and outcomes. By being able to pinpoint both aspects that act as barriers and enablers of recovery (that emerge from an integration of spontaneous, self-generated data and information collected from other sources) we can provide better designed programs that are more tailored to individual needs to support long-term positive behaviour change.

References

Bakardjieva, M. (2003). Virtual togetherness: An everyday-life perspective. *Media, Culture & Society*, 25, 291–313.

Barak, A., Boniel-Nissim, M., & Suler, J. (2008). Fostering empowerment in online support groups. *Computers in Human Behavior, 24*, 1867–1883.

Bargh, J. A. & McKenna, K. Y. (2004). The Internet and social life. *Annual Review of Psychology, 55*, 573–590.

Beckwith, M., Bliuc, A.-M., & Best, D. (2016) What the recovery movement tells us about prefigurative politics. *Jounal of Social and Political Psychology, 4*, 238–251.

Best, D., Alberson, K., Irving, J., Lightowlers, C., Mama-Rudd, A., & Chaggar, A. (2015). UK Life in revovery survey 2015. *The first national UK survey of addiction recovery experiences*. Helena Kennedy Centre for International Justice, Sheffiled Halam University, UK.

Best, D., Beckwith, M., Haslam, C., Haslam, A. S., Jetten, J., Mawson, E., & Lubman, D. I. (2016). Overcoming alcohol and other drug addiction as a process of social identity transition: The social identity model of recovery (SIMOR). *Addiction Research & Theory, 24*, 111–123.

Betty Ford Institute Consensus Panel (2007). What is recovery? A working definition from the Betty Ford Institute. *Journal of Substance Abuse Treatment, 33*, 221–228.

Billig, M. (1991). *Ideology and opinions: Studies in rhetorical psychology*. London: Sage.

Braun, V. & Clarke, V. (2006). Using thematic analysis in psychology. *Qualitative Research in Psychology, 3*, 77–101.

Buckingham, S. A., Frings, D., & Albery, I. P. (2013). Group membership and social identity in addiction recovery. *Psychology of Addictive Behaviors, 27*, 1132–1140.

Cha, M., Mislove, A., & Gummadi, K. P. (2009, April). A measurement-driven analysis of information propagation in the flickr social network. In *Proceedings of the 18th international conference on world wide web* (pp. 721–730). ACM.

Chung, C. K., & Pennebaker, J. W. (2014). Counting little words in big data: The psychology of communities, culture, and history. *Social Cognition and Communication*. (pp. 25–42). New York: Psychology Press.

Chung, J. E. (2013). Social interaction in online support groups: Preference for online social interaction over offline social interaction. *Computers in Human Behavior, 29*, 1408–1414.

Cohn, M. A., Mehl, M. R., & Pennebaker, J. W. (2004). Linguistic markers of psychological change surrounding September 11, 2001. *Psychological Science, 15*, 687–693.

Crabtree, J. W., Haslam, S. A., Postmes, T., & Haslam, C. (2010). Mental health support groups, stigma, and self esteem: Positive and negative implications of group identification. *Journal of Social Issues, 66*, 553–569.

Cutrona, C. E. & Russell, D. W. (1990). Type of social support and specific stress: Toward a theory of optimal matching. In B. R. Sarason, I. G. Sarason, & G. R. Pierce (Eds.). *Social support: An interactional view* (pp. 319–366). Oxford: John Wiley & Sons.

Cutrona, C. E. & Suhr, J. A. (1992). Controllability of stressful events and satisfaction with spouse support behaviors. *Communication Research, 19*, 154–174.

Darke, S., Hall, W., Wodak, A., Heather, N., & Ward, J. (1992). Development and validation of a multi-dimensional instrument for assessing outcome of treatment among opiate users: the Opiate Treatment Index. *British Journal of Addiction, 87*, 733–742.

Davison, K. P., Pennebaker, J. W., & Dickerson, S. S. (2000). Who talks? The social psychology of illness support groups. *The American Psychologist, 55*, 205–217.

De Choudhury, M., Counts, S., & Horvitz, E. (2013). Predicting postpartum changes in emotion and behavior via social media. In *Proceedings of the SIGCHI Conference on Human Factors in Computing Systems* (pp. 3267–3276). ACM.

De Choudhury, M., Gamon, M., Counts, S., & Horvitz, E. (2013). Predicting depression via social media. Retrieved from http://repository.cmu.edu/cgi/viewcontent.cgi?article=1272&context=hcii.

Dirkse, D., Hadjistavropoulos, H. D., Hesser, H., & Barak, A. (2015). Linguistic analysis of communication in therapist-assisted internet-delivered cognitive behavior therapy for Generalized Anxiety Disorder, *Cognitive Behaviour Therapy, 44*, 21–32.

Edwards, D. (1997). *Discourse and cognition*. London: Sage.

Eysenbach, G., Powell, J., Englesakis, M., Rizo, C., & Stern, A. (2004). Health related virtual communities and electronic support groups: systematic review of the effects of online peer to peer interactions. *British Medical Journal , 328*, 1166.

Finfgeld, D. L. (2000). Therapeutic groups online: The good, the bad, and the unknown. *Issues in Mental Health Nursing, 21*, 241–255.

Galston, W. A. (2000). Does the internet strengthen community? *National Civic Review, 89*, 193–202.

Gee, A. & McGarty, C. (2013). Aspirations for a cooperative community and support for mental health advocacy: A shared orientation through opinion-based group membership. *Journal of Applied Social Psychology, 43*, 426–441.

Giessner, S. R. & van Knippenberg, D. (2008). "License to fail": Goal definition, leader group prototypicality, and perceptions of leadership effectiveness after leader failure. *Organizational Behavior and Human Decision Processes, 105*, 14–35.

Goodwin, C. & Heritage, J. (1990). Conversation analysis. *Annual Review of Anthropology, 19*, 283–307.

Gordon, A. J. & Zrull, M. (1991). Social networks and recovery: One year after inpatient treatment. *Journal of Substance Abuse Treatment, 8*, 143–152.

Groshkova, T., Best, D., & White, W. (2013). The assessment of recovery capital: Properties and psychometrics of a measure of addiction recovery strengths. *Drug and Alcohol Review, 32*, 187–194.

Gustafson, D. H., Hawkins, R., Boberg, E., Pingree, S., Serlin, R. E., Graziano, F., & Chan, C. L. (1999). Impact of a patient-centered, computer-based health information/support system. *American Journal of Preventive Medicine, 16*, 1–9.

Haslam, S. A. (2014). Making good theory practical: Five lessons for an Applied Social Identity Approach to challenges of organizational, health, and clinical psychology. *British Journal of Social Psychology*, 53, 1–20.

Haslam, S. A., O'Brien, A., Jetten, J., Vormedal, K., & Penna, S. (2005). Taking the strain: Social identity, social support, and the experience of stress. *British Journal of Social Psychology, 44*, 355–370.

Hogg, M. A. (2001). A social identity theory of leadership. *Personality and Social Psychology Review, 5*, 184–200.

Jetten, J., Haslam, C., & Haslam, S. A. (Eds.). (2012). *The social cure: Identity, health and well-being*. New York: Psychology Press.

Jetten, J., Haslam, C., Haslam, S. A., Dingle, G., & Jones, J. M. (2014). How groups affect our health and well-being: the path from theory to policy. *Social Issues and Policy Review, 8*, 103–130.

Kaskutas, L. A. (2009). Alcoholics Anonymous effectiveness: Faith meets science. *Journal Addictive Diseases, 28*, 145–157.

Kaskutas, L. A., Bond, J., & Humphreys, K. (2002). Social networks as mediators of the effect of Alcoholics Anonymous. *Addiction, 97*, 891–900.

Kelly, J. F., Magill, M., & Stout, R. L. (2009). How do people recover from alcohol dependence? A systematic review of the research on mechanisms of behavior change in Alcoholics Anonymous. *Addiction Research & Theory, 17*, 236–259.

Livingston, J. D., Milne, T., Fang, M. L., & Amari, E. (2012). The effectiveness of interventions for reducing stigma related to substance use disorders: a systematic review. *Addiction, 107*, 39–50.

Lyons, E. J., Mehl, M. R., & Pennebaker, J. W. (2006). Pro-anorexics and recovering anorexics differ in their linguistic Internet self-presentation. *Journal of Psychosomatic Research, 60*, 253–256.

McKenna, K. Y. & Bargh, J. A. (1999). Causes and consequences of social interaction on the Internet: A conceptual framework. *Media Psychology, 1*, 249–269.

McLellan, A.T., Kushner, H., Metzger, D., Peters, R., Smith, I., Grisson, G., Pettinati, H., & Argeriou, M. (1992). The fifth edition of the addiction severity index, *Journal of Substance Abuse Treatment, 9*, 199–213.

Marsden, J., Gossop, M., Stewart, D., Best, D., Farrell, M., Lehmann, P., Edwards, C., & Strang, J. (1999). The Maudsley Addiction Profile (MAP): A brief instrument for assessing treatment outcome. *Addiction, 93*, 1857–1868.

Mislove, A., Marcon, M., Gummadi, K. P., Druschel, P., & Bhattacharjee, B. (2007, October). Measurement and analysis of online social networks. In *Proceedings of the 7th ACM SIGCOMM conference on Internet measurement* (pp. 29–42). ACM.

Mo, P. K. H., & Coulson, N. S. (2010). Living with HIV/AIDS and use of online support groups. *Journal of Health Psychology, 15*, 339–350.

Moorhead, S. A., Hazlett, D. E., Harrison, L., Carroll, J. K., Irwin, A., & Hoving, C. (2013). A new dimension of health care: systematic review of the uses, benefits, and limitations of social media for health communication. *Journal of Medical Internet Research, 15*, e85.

Pennebaker, J. W., Booth, R. J., & Francis, M.E. (2007). Linguistic Inquiry and Word Count: LIWC [Computer software]. Austin, TX: LIWC.net

Pennebaker, J. W., Boyd, R. L., Jordan, K., & Blackburn, K. (2015) The Development and Psychometric Properties of LIWC2015. Austin, TX: LIWC.net.

Philips, D., & Shaw, K. (Eds.). (2013). *The politics of literature and the literature of politics*. Basingstoke: Palgrave Macmillan UK.

Potter, J., & Wetherell, M. (1987). *Discourse and social psychology: Beyond attitudes and behaviour*. London: Sage.

Preece, J. (2001). Sociability and usability in online communities: Determining and measuring success. *Behaviour & Information Technology, 20*, 347–356.

Rafalovich, A. (1999). Keep coming back!: Narcotics Anonymous narrative and recovering addict identity. *Contemporary Drug Problems, 26*, 131–157.

Rappaport, R. A. (1993). Distinguished lecture in general anthropology: The anthropology of trouble. *American Anthropologist, 95*, 295–303.

Rodham, K., McCabe, C., & Blake, D. (2009). Seeking support: An interpretative phenomenological analysis of an internet message board for people with complex regional pain syndrome. *Psychology & Health, 24*, 619–634.

Savic, M., Best, D., Rodda, S., & Lubman, D. I. (2013). Exploring the focus and experiences of smartphone applications for addiction recovery. *Journal of Addictive Diseases, 32*, 310–319.

Shneiderman, B. (2008). Science 2.0. *Science, 319*, 1349–1350.

Shahab, L. & McEwen, A. (2009). Online support for smoking cessation: A systematic review of the literature. *Addiction, 104*, 1792–1804.

Slatcher, R. B., Chung, C. K., Pennebaker, J. W., & Stone, L. D. (2007). Winning words: Individual differences in linguistic style among US presidential and vice presidential candidates. *Journal of Research in Personality, 41*, 63–75.

Spears, R., Postmes, T., Lea, M., & Wolbert, A. (2002). When are net effects gross products? Communication. *Journal of Social Issues, 58*, 91–107.

Stewart Loane, S., & D'Alessandro, S. (2013) *Value in an Online Health Community: It's more than health information*. Paper presented at the Australian and New Zealand Marketing Academy Conference, Auckland, New Zealand. Retrieved from www.anzmac.org/conference_archive/2013/papers/anzmac2013-048.pdf.

Stewart Loane, S. & D'Alessandro, S. (2014) Empowered and knowledgeable health consumers: The impact of online support groups on the doctor–patient relationship. *Australasian Marketing Journal, 22*, 238–245.

Stewart Loane, S., Webster, C. M., & D'Alessandro, S. (2015) Identifying consumer value co-created through social support within online health communities. *Journal of Macromarketing, 35*, 353–367.

Substance Abuse and Mental Health Services Administration (SAMHSA). (2012). *Results from the 2012 national survey on drug use and health: Summary of national findings*. Retrieved from www.samhsa.gov/data/sites/default/files/NSDUHresults2012/NSDUHresults2012.pdf.

Tanis, M. (2007). Online social support groups. *The Oxford Handbook of Internet Psychology*, 139–154.

Tausczik, Y. R. & Pennebaker, J. W. (2010). The psychological meaning of words: LIWC and computerized text analysis methods. *Journal of Language and Social Psychology 29*, 24–54.
Van der Zanden, R., Curie, K., Van Londen, M., Kramer, J., Steen, G., & Cuijpers, P. (2014). Web-based depression treatment: Associations of clients' word use with adherence and outcome. *Journal of Affective Disorders, 160*, 10–13.
Vayreda, A. & Antaki, C. (2009). Social support and unsolicted advice in an online bipolar disorder forum. *Qualitative Health Research, 19*, 931–942.
Verkuyten, M. (2001). 'Abnormalization' of ethnic minorities in conversation. *The British Journal of Social Psychology, 40*, 257.
Wallwork, J. & Dixon, J. A. (2004). Foxes, green fields and Britishness: On the rhetorical construction of place and national identity. *British Journal of Social Psychology, 43*, 21–39.
Walther, J. B. & Boyd, S. (2002). Attraction to computer-mediated social support. In C. A. Lin & D. Atkin (Eds.), *Communication technology andsociety: Audience adoption and uses* (pp. 153–188). Cresskill, NJ: Hampton Press.
White, M. & Dorman, S. M. (2001). Receiving social support online: Implications for health education. *Health Education Research, 16*, 693–707.
White, W. L. (1998). *Slaying the dragon: The history of addiction treatment and recovery in America.* Bloomington, IL: Chestnut Health Systems/Lighthouse Institute.
White, W. L. (2009). The mobilization of community resources to support long-term addiction recovery. *Journal of Substance Abuse Treatment, 36*, 146–158.
Winzelberg, A. J., Classen, C., Alpers, G. W., Roberts, H., Koopman, C., Adams, R. E., & Taylor, C. B. (2003). Evaluation of an internet support group for women with primary breast cancer. *Cancer, 97*, 1164–1173.
Zinken, J., Zinken, K., Wilson, J. C., Butler, L., & Skinner, T. (2010). Analysis of syntax and word use to predict successful participation in guided self-help for anxiety and depression. *Psychiatry Research, 179*, 181–186.

10

SOCIAL IDENTITY MAPPING: MEASURING SOCIAL IDENTITY CHANGE IN RECOVERY FROM ADDICTION

Catherine Haslam, Genevieve A. Dingle, David Best, Jock Mackenzie and Melinda Beckwith

To exist is to change, to change is to mature,
and to mature is to go on creating oneself endlessly

(*Henri Bergson, 1911*)

Throughout our lives periods of change and transition are inevitable, whether it is starting school, taking up employment, moving house, having children, retiring, or moving into care. Some transitions are planned and some unexpected, but all are associated with varying degrees of uncertainty; even those that change our lives for the better. How we manage that uncertainty is key to protecting well-being and ensuring successful transition, and this, we argue, has its basis in the availability of strong supportive networks of relationships with others, particularly groups of others. It is from these relationships that we gain the support required to manage and adjust to change, and this is even more vital when that change is especially challenging, as in the case of recovery from addiction. As we will argue, the challenge in this life transition lies in engineering the process of social identity change – one that involves moving away from drug using networks to sustained engagement with networks supportive of recovery. Social identity theorizing provides a framework to understand the role that social identities play in this transition and a basis from which to map their influence. In this chapter, we outline a theoretical framework that explains adjustment to social identity change and introduce the Social Identity Mapping (SIM) tool to measure such change in the process of recovery.

Life change as social identity change

When life changes, so do our relationships. Clearly some endure, but there will also be those that become more or less important or even lost in the context of altered goals, needs, ambitions and motivations that emerge in response to life change. These relationship changes are far from trivial, given the major role that our social networks play in protecting, and sometimes threatening, health and well-being in the process of transition (Haslam, Jetten, Postmes, & Haslam, 2009; Jetten, Haslam, Haslam, Dingle, & Jones, 2014; Jetten, Haslam, Iyer, & Haslam, 2009). However, not all social relationships are equal in this regard. For, as the social identity approach highlights, social group relationships are particularly influential in adjusting to life change – even more so than our relationships with a significant other (for examples see Glei, Landau, Goldman, et al., 2005; Gleibs, Haslam, Haslam, & Jones, 2011; Haslam et al., 2010; Haslam, Cruwys, & Haslam, 2014). Moreover, such influence is only possible where there is a strong basis for shared identification, connectedness and belonging with those groups. So how do social groups influence our response to life change? It was in seeking an answer to this question that the Social Identity Model of Identity Change (SIMIC, Haslam et al., 2008; Jetten, Haslam, Iyer, & Haslam, 2009; Jetten, Haslam, Haslam, & Branscombe, 2009) was developed.

SIMIC draws on two related theories discussed in the previous chapters – *social identity theory* (e.g., Tajfel & Turner, 1979) and *self-categorization theory* (e.g., Turner, Hogg, Oakes, Reicher, & Wetherell, 1987) – that together form the basis of the social identity approach. Fundamental to both these theories is the idea that when they are internalized into a person's self-concept, social groups provide an important basis for self-understanding. The more one identifies with the group, the more influential that group becomes in informing a person's thinking, their behaviour and views of the world. Such connectedness can be extremely helpful when experiencing life transitions because shared group membership of this form provides access to psychological resources (e.g., social support) that people can draw on to cope with change. When we define ourselves as a member of a particular support group, such as Alcoholics Anonymous, this provides a basis to share in the positive experiences of its group members (e.g., staying sober), but also to share disappointment in relation to others (e.g., if a member relapses) and be ready to offer support. At the same time, though, these events are unlikely to have the same significance or meaning for outsiders (e.g., for members of a stroke support network) who have different group-based interests and goals.

Clearly though, there are both benefits and costs associated with such identification. In terms of benefit, strong group identification provides a basis for giving and receiving social support, which is vital when we are challenged by, or are trying to make, significant life changes (Haslam, Reicher, & Levine, 2012; Schmitt, Branscombe, Postmes, & Garcia, 2014). The downside of such identification is that, when we lose important group memberships, this reduces our sources of support and tends to diminish our sense of self (Haslam et al., 2009). Of course, the balance of these benefits and costs differ in the context of substance misuse and depend on the nature of the group and its influence. Strong identification with substance using groups is costly for someone in the transition to recovery, as those groups are unlikely to encourage behaviours that promote sustained recovery.

Breaking away from such groups, which Dingle and colleagues characterize as 'breaking good' (Dingle, Stark, Cruwys, & Best, 2015), provides a more effective strategy to begin the recovery journey and to sustain it (Best, Ghufran, Day, Ray, & Loaring, 2008). Yet strong identification with other groups unconnected with substance use (i.e., identification as a parent, family member, an employee), has been shown to have a positive influence on recovery (Dingle, Cruwys, & Frings, 2015). Clearly then, to understand the role that particular social groups play in a person's recovery journey, knowledge of the content and meaning of those identifications is critical. This is the primary purpose of SIM, to which we come shortly – to reveal the structure, nature and content of people's social identifications in a way that is simple and accessible.

The Social Identity Model of Identity Change (SIMIC) extends this theorizing to account for the role of social identity processes in the context of life change. As shown in Figure 10.1, multiple social identities are a key protective factor. The greater the number of positive and important group memberships one has, the more resources one can draw on when coping with a life change. This protection is enabled through two pathways. First, the more groups one belongs to, the more likely it will be that at least some of one's old networks remain intact, thereby providing a sense of *social identity continuity* after a life-changing event (Haslam et al., 2008). However, such continuity, in an AOD context may not be desirable in the case of all group memberships, particularly where group norms and behaviours revolve primarily around substance use. Here it might be better to distance oneself from these groups, in the process of losing or letting go of certain social identities, rather than maintain them (Dingle et al., 2015) to support sustainable life change.

To counter this loss and provide a basis for self re-definition, SIMIC points to the importance of developing new valued group memberships and associated *new social identities*. Multiple group membership contributes to this by providing an experiential platform to join new groups (see Cruwys et al., 2014). However, for these new groups to have the capacity to provide a strong basis for positive support, they must be compatible with other valued groups to which the person belongs (Iyer, Jetten, Tsivrikos, Postmes, & Haslam, 2009). This is because relationships are typically strained when new and existing identities are at odds with each other, and such tensions between past and present identities undermine the capacity for either to be a positive resource (Jetten, Haslam, Haslam, Dingle, & Jones, 2014). Such tension is not uncommon in the process of recovery from addiction, particularly when trying to simultaneously juggle social groups that encourage substance misuse alongside others that promote abstinence. When seen in this light, we gain a better understanding of the challenges people experience in staying on the path to recovery.

SIMIC, when originally conceived, drew on evidence from studies of students transitioning to university and older adults moving into care. Nevertheless, its relevance to substance misuse has been considered in previous research. Dingle and colleagues (Dingle et al., 2015b) have shown that social identity continuity

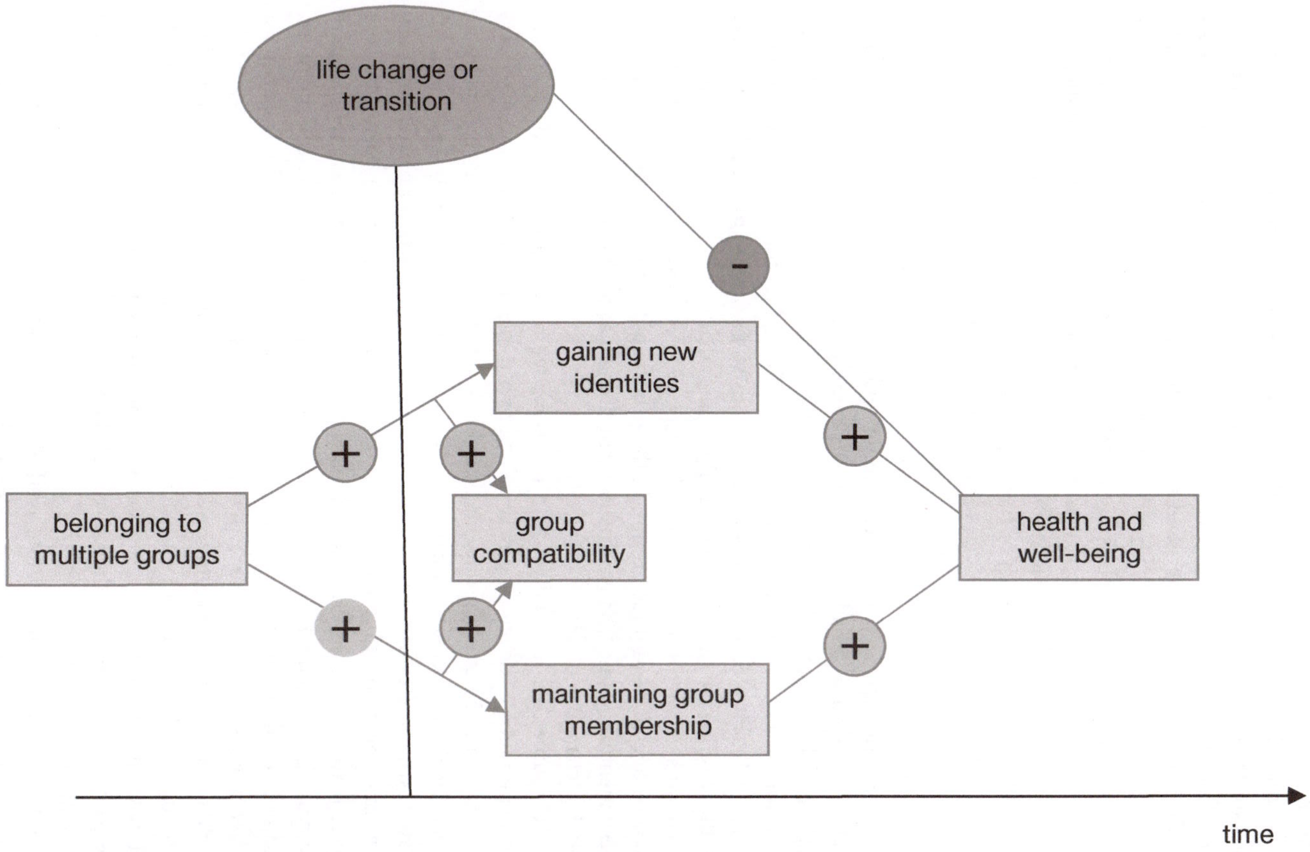

FIGURE 10.1 The Social Identity Model of Identity Change (adapted from Jetten et al., 2009).

is detrimental to the health of substance users to the extent that it involves the retention of the user identity. In this context, the development of a new, and relatively stronger, recovery identity predicted better outcomes from treatment in a Therapeutic Community (TC). Clearly then, the SIMIC pathway relevant to building new social identities held greater curative value for this population.

Taking this further, the Social Identity Model of Recovery (SIMOR; Best et al., 2016) considers the interplay between existing (e.g., using) and new (i.e., recovery) social identities in recovery from substance misuse. SIMOR argues that recovery involves a socially negotiated transition, in which the balance of social networks supportive of substance use and recovery undergo change. This involves a reduction in the importance of one's using groups, whose norms revolve around substance use, to enable the emergence and strengthening of a recovery identity, supported by groups who value and encourage abstinence. The argument here is that simply reducing the influence of groups harmful to health is not sufficient for sustained recovery. This is because any loss of group membership, even of groups that are bad for our health, essentially diminishes one's psychological resources and supports (see Jetten et al., 2014). Rather, and in line with SIMIC, social identity loss needs to be balanced with gains in identification with other group memberships to ensure the availability of support needed to transition to recovery (see John's social identity map for illustration). Drawing on this reasoning, SIMOR makes a clear prediction about the influence of social networks in recovery. Specifically, it argues that transitioning to recovery requires a specific form of social identity change, in which there is a shift from a network comprised predominantly of groups engaged in using to one comprised predominantly of multiple groups supportive of recovery.

Along these lines, Frings and Albery (2015) also highlight the importance of social identity processes to recovery in their Social Identity Model of Cessation Maintenance (SIMCM). This model focuses specifically on the contribution that group therapy, of the form offered by many specialist alcohol and drug treatment providers, makes in consolidating a recovery identity that provides the necessary strengthening of self-efficacy to help people maintain their recovery goals. The main difference between SIMCM and SIMOR lies in their contextual framing. SIMCM focuses on the role of specific recovery-focused social therapeutic groups, whereas SIMOR takes a broader approach to capture people's wider social reality, that accounts for the influence of all a person's using and recovery group networks in understanding recovery trajectories.

Having an understanding of the nature of people's social identities and the manner in which they might affect recovery is clearly vital to treatment, though it has been largely neglected to date. For this understanding to assist recovery, we need a method that gives those in the process of this transition knowledge about how their relationships can be optimally managed to support recovery goals. Social Identity Mapping provides such a tool, allowing a comprehensive assessment of a person's network of social group memberships. However, in the adaptation proposed here, we measure the normative behaviour of group members in relation to their substance use and practices to evaluate SIMOR's predictions about their influence on recovery trajectories. In the next section we discuss the origins of the tool, describe its application in the context of recovery from substance misuse, and provide some case studies that include maps created by individuals in treatment for problematic substance use to evaluate predictions about the nature of social identity change.

Social Identity Mapping

Social Identity Mapping (SIM) was originally developed for use in organizations. It is part of an applied intervention – the Actualizing Social Identity and Personal Identity Resources (ASPIRe) program – that aims to improve team and organizational identification (see Haslam, Eggins, & Reynolds, 2003; Eggins, O'Brien, Reynolds, Haslam, & Cocker, 2008; Reynolds, Eggins, & Haslam, 2010). Understanding, and working with, the social identities that influence the lives of employees in the organization is a critical part of this process and these are identified early in the program as part of the process of Ascertaining Identity Resources (AIRing). To achieve this, there was a need to devise a concrete means for people to identify the group memberships that were important to them and influenced their work behaviour. It was in addressing this objective that SIM was created.

SIM prioritizes respondents' social group relationships to understand those that are self-defining, and hence most likely to shape their thoughts and behaviour in a range of contexts. In the original version of SIM there are four distinct stages in map construction (see Cruwys et al., 2016). The first involves identifying and naming people's social group memberships, each of which are rated for their importance. Post-it notes of three different sizes are used to represent these groups, with the largest used to represent the most important group memberships and the smallest for the least important. Second, participants are asked to rate each group on a range of dimensions – including, but not restricted to, how positive they feel about the group, how representative they are of the group, and how much time in a typical month they spend with the group. These dimensions can be modified depending on what is considered to be theoretically important for the context in which the tool is being used (e.g., if group contact is a key factor in predicting outcomes, then this might be a dimension on which to focus). Third, respondents position the groups with those closer together more similar to each other and those further away more different. Finally, respondents are asked to indicate the compatibility between any two groups by drawing lines between the appropriate groups; with straight lines indicating highly compatible groups, wavy lines reflecting moderate compatibility, and jagged lines for highly incompatible groups. The resulting map provides a simple illustration of the number of groups in a person's social network (as an index of multiple group membership), their importance, and their compatibility – all of which have been identified in SIMIC as critical predictors of adjustment to life change.

This tool has since been used in several clinical contexts. Jetten et al. (2009) used SIM to illustrate the social group network of a 52-year old woman who had suffered a stroke. Her map illustrated the social groups to which she belonged in the period before and after the stroke, allowing her to see the changes in her support network, and how she might draw on her various groups as psychological resources to optimize her adjustment post-stroke. In substance using populations, SIM has been used to illustrate social group networks among a case series receiving treatment in a TC for problematic substance use. In the resulting paper, the focus was on the number of group memberships, their importance, and the strength in links between those groups to index compatibility (Best et al., 2014). Important in the substance misuse literature are networks supportive of recovery, typically indexed through the numbers of people in one's networks who are abstinent (Litt, Kadden, Kabela-Cormier, & Petry, 2009; Longabaugh, Wirtz, Zywiak, & O'Malley, 2010). To capture this aspect of social identity content, a slight modification to SIM was introduced in the Best et al. (2014) paper in which the using behaviour of the group's membership was recorded – specifically reflecting the number of active users, social users, non-users, and those in recovery. What this added for the cases reviewed was an understanding of the basis for incompatibility between groups, that appeared to be driven largely by the using behaviour of group members. The more 'user' groups (i.e., defined as being comprised primarily of people with problematic substance use) to which one belongs, the more challenging the recovery transition (Best et al., 2014). Importantly, in both papers, SIM provided a quantifiable means of documenting people's social groups that was readily understood by those completing the maps, but also by clinicians who could use this information to help clients meet therapeutic goals (whether in post-stroke adjustment or maintaining recovery).

In this chapter, we take the SIM approach used by Best and colleagues a step further to trial one final amendment; to include the respondent (as 'me') in the maps to capture inter-relationships between personal and social identities in the transition to recovery. We trialed this adaptation to SIM in the context of measuring the impact of treatment offered in therapeutic communities, using the tool to document people's social group networks over time alongside recognized predictors of recovery.

Case studies

Our case studies draw on data from five people, all male, identified by pseudonym. Clearly, a case series drawing on people with problematic substance use is not generalizable to all in recovery, though our focus on a single gender was an attempt to capture greater similarity in social experience, given this is likely to differ substantially between men and women. All participants were interviewed soon after entry to a Therapeutic Community (TC) for the treatment of problematic substance use (Time 1, T1), and six months later (T2). Participants were guided in producing their SIM, indicating the number of group memberships, their importance, using patterns within groups, and compatibility in terms of commonality and conflict. Individual groups are shown as circles, the size of which varies according to their importance (largest = very important, smallest = least important). The proportion of group members' using patterns are indicated via shading, with the heavy, casual and non-users differentiated from those in recovery and for whom using status was unknown. Generally speaking, the shading provides a basic indicator of using behaviour, with darker shading indicating heavier use and lighter shading indicating abstinence and recovery. Compatibility is indicated by lines between the respondent ('me') and their social groups, with thick lines indicating strong commonality, thin lines some commonality and jagged lines significant incompatibility or conflict.

To provide evidence of the value of SIM in capturing identity change processes, we differentiate between two types of map; those that illustrate (a) social identity change reflected in social group loss or gain (see Figures 10.2, 10.3 and 10.4), and (b) social identity continuity reflected in no change (see Figures 10.5 and 10.6), in people's networks over time. In an attempt to triangulate data, these maps are presented alongside quantitative data comprising responses to scales predictive of enhanced health and well-being following life change (as indicated in SIMIC) and of recovery from problematic substance use. Data from six scales are reported and presented together with relevant SIM data in Table 10.1.

1 *Multiple group membership* (Haslam et al., 2008): This four item scale measures the extent to which people felt they belonged to multiple social groups (e.g., I have strong ties with lots of different groups). Each item is rated on a 7-point scale (1 = strongly disagree, 7 = strongly agree) and an average of these ratings is reported.
2 *Social Support* (Haslam, O'Brien, Jetten, Vormedal, & Penna, 2005): This measure incorporates the four distinct sources of social support identified by House (1981) comprising emotional support, companionship, instrumental support, and informational support. The four items are rated on a 7-point scale (1 = not at all, 7 = completely), with the average of these ratings reported.
3 *User Identification*: This scale is an adapted version of the original measure of social identification, developed by Doojse, Ellemers, & Spears (1995). The measure indexes the extent to which people identify with a particular group, in this case with substance using groups. The four items are rated on a 7-point scale, (1 = do not agree at all, 7 = agree completely), and again the average rating is recorded.
4 *Recovery Identification*: This scale comprised four items indexing the extent to which people identified as being in recovery. These were also rated on a 7-point scale (1 = do not agree at all, 7 = agree completely) and the average rating was recorded. Both this and the user identification scale have been adapted for use in AOD populations (Buckingham et al., 2013).
5 *The Australian Treatment Outcomes Profile* (Ryan et al., 2014): The three items separately indexing physical health, mental health, and quality of life from this

scale were used. The items are provided in Table 10.1, and people are simply asked to rate each on a 10-point scale (0 = poor, 10 = good).

6 *Recovery Capital* (Groshkova et al., 2012): This was indexed using the Assessment of Recovery Capital scale. Respondents are asked to indicate their agreement to 50 statements about recovery (e.g., I engage in activities and events that support my recovery). The number of endorsed items is summed, with higher scores indicative of greater recovery capital.

For those whose maps indicate a shift in social identity, constituting a move away from defining oneself primarily as a 'substance user' to someone in recovery, we predict there should be parallel evidence of reduced identification with substance using groups, together with enhanced health, well-being, access to social support and recovery capital.

Evidence of social identity change in SIM

Three cases out of the five experienced significant changes in their social networks, characterized either by social identity loss (i.e., a reduction in the number of social groups between T1 and T2, see the map produced by John in Figure 10.2), or social identity gain (i.e., an increase in the number of social groups between T1 and T2, see the maps produced by David and Matt in Figures 10.3 and 10.4, respectively). This change in the nature of social groups was associated with increased recovery capital and enhanced health and well-being in two participants (David and Matt). Poorer health outcomes were observed in the participant John, who experienced a loss in groups defined primarily by substance use, which were not adequately replaced, leaving a network largely supportive of recovery but one that was nevertheless impoverished compared to that at T1.

John was 34 years of age when he completed his first map. At this time, he had a long history of treatment for problematic substance use that included counseling, pharmacotherapy, two previous admissions to a TC as well as inconsistent attendance at Alcoholics Anonymous (AA) and Narcotics Anonymous (NA) meetings. He has an extensive history of cannabis use (his primary drug) in addition to heroin and crystal methamphetamine (i.e., ice) used intravenously. John has been on long-term disability support with only occasional work as a labourer. At T1,

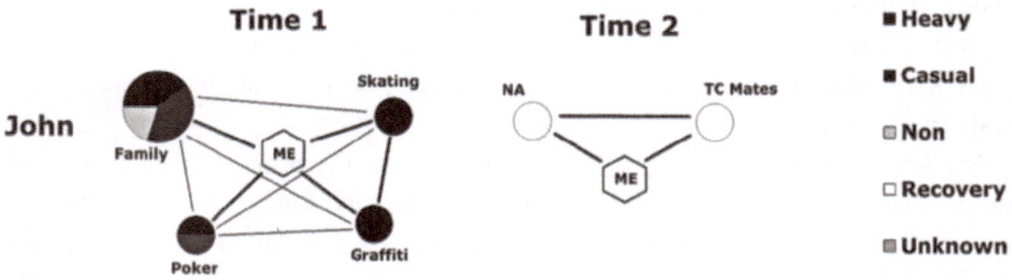

FIGURE 10.2 Social identity maps produced by John at Times 1 and 2.

his map was characterized by relationships with groups comprising drug users, including his family. Of the four groups he identified, only one (his family) included a member (his mother) who was a non-user. Consistent with predictions from SIMOR, John's predominant monoculture of drug use at this time presents significant challenges to recovery as further evidenced in low levels of perceived recovery capital and high identification as a substance user (see Table 10.1). By T2, there was a radical change in his social group networks, now a monoculture of groups supporting recovery; notably, the TC and NA. With using groups now essentially lost, one might predict on the basis of previous research that this would be associated with better health, well-being and recovery capital to support abstinence. There was certainly some support for this in his recovery capital and health ratings, which improved from T1 to T2, but not in the availability of social support and his well-being, both of which were largely unchanged. His identification as a 'user' was also unchanged. However, this may reflect his adherence to the 12-steps promoted through NA membership, where it is believed that addiction is not cured and that a person with problematic substance use will always need to be in recovery. Notable in John's case was the fact that the recovery networks gained to counter the loss of using networks were not sufficient to replace all networks lost and his social groups comprised not only moderately important groups from which to draw upon for support, but also one that may be more vulnerable upon leaving the TC. This is reflected in his lowered multiple group membership ratings. Thus, while John's map provides evidence of social identity change in a positive direction, the relative lack of important and multiple social group resources are likely to challenge sustained recovery.

This was not the case for David and Matt, who also had similar histories of extensive substance use and treatment in TCs, alongside admissions for detox and rehabilitation. Both began with relatively empty social maps at T1, and both improved by T2 with increases in their overall number of social groups and the number they deemed important. David was 31 years of age when he completed his T1 map. His primary drug of concern was alcohol, but he also used cannabis, as well as prescription and illicit drugs. His T1 network comprised two groups whose activities centered on drinking. By T2, the size of his network had changed to include three groups predominantly supportive of recovery and, particularly protective for this period of life change, a greater number of important group memberships. Associated with this was an increase in self-reported measures of health, well-being and recovery capital. Similar to John, David's T2 SIM was more recovery focused, but the difference lay in the number of available and important group networks, providing the social capital and support necessary to maintain gains made in recovery.

For Matt, his primary drug of concern was ice. At the time of his first map, he was 33 years of age, married with young children and working to pay off his house, but not living at home due to his substance use. As evident in his T1 map, he identified a single social group network that encompassed his social world – his immediate family, all non-users – though, he also identified several individuals he

TABLE 10.1 SIM, recovery, health and well-being data as a function of social identity status

Measure		SIM: No. of Groups	SIM: No. Important Groups	SIM: No. Groups with More Users	SIM: No. Groups with More Supporting Recovery	Multiple Group Membership	Social Support	User ID	Recovery ID	ATOP Physical Health	ATOP Mental Health	ATOP QoL	Assessment of Recovery Capital ARC
Example Item						I belong to lots of different groups.	Do you get the emotional support you need from other people?	I would describe myself as a drug user.	I would describe myself as being in recovery.	In the past four weeks, how would you rate your physical health?	In the past four weeks, how would you rate your psychological health?	In the past four weeks, how would you rate your quality of life?	Having a sense of purpose in life is important to my recovery journey.
Score Total						Mean	Mean	Mean	Mean	Single	Single	Single	Sum
Scale Range						1–7	1–7	1–7	1–7	0–10	0–10	0–10	0–50
Favourable Direction		higher	higher	lower	higher	higher	higher	lower	higher	higher	higher	higher	higher
a) Social Identity Change	Time												
John	T1	4	1	4	0	5.8	3.3	7.0	5.3	5	3	8	29
	T2	2	0	0	2	3.5	3.3	7.0	6.3	6	8	8	38
David	T1	2	0	2	0	4.5	3.8	6.5	6.0	5	5	6	37
	T2	5	3	1	3	4.8	4.3	5.0	5.6	7	7	7	48
Matt	T1	1	1	0	1	2.8	2.0	4.5	4.0	2	2	2	33
	T2	6	4	0	5	3.5	5.3	4.5	6.7	7	7	7	45
b) Social Identity Continuity	Time												
Brian	T1	4	2	2	2	1.8	3.5	6.3	2.6	9	9	2	19
	T2	4	1	4	0	4.0	3.5	6.0	5.0	5	5	3	23
Mike	T1	3	1	3	0	5.0	4.5	7.0	6.0	3	3	1	28
	T2	2	0	2	0	4.3	4.8	6.0	6.0	3	3	1	33

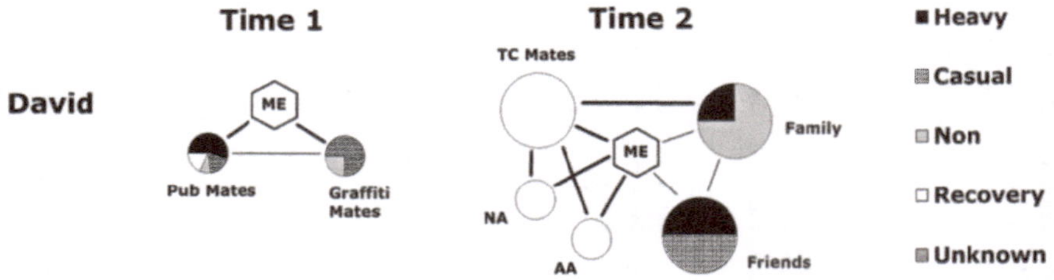

FIGURE 10.3 Social identity maps produced by David at Times 1 and 2.

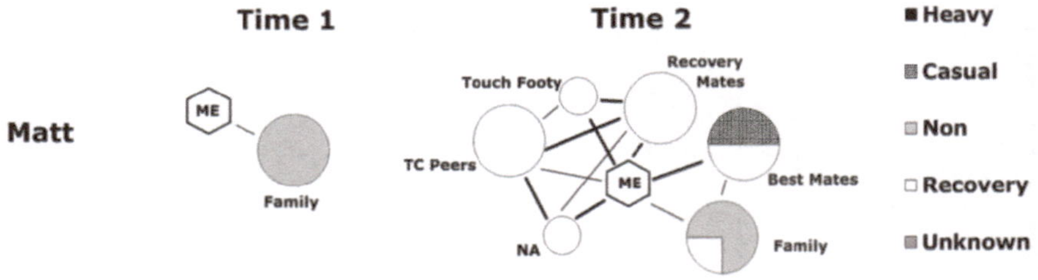

FIGURE 10.4 Social identity maps produced by Matt at Times 1 and 2.

knew who were moderate to heavy drug users from whom he had cut himself off. Like David, by T2 he had made significant gains in his social group memberships; now comprising six groups, four of whom were very important sources of support.

In line with SIMOR's prediction, for David and Matt, social identity change involving a gain in group memberships defined by their support for recovery, was associated with greater recovery capital, more perceived social support, and enhanced health and well-being outcomes. Interestingly, there was no evidence in any of the three cases of a marked change in self-definition, or identification, as a substance user, but this is still relatively early in the recovery journey of each participant. As alluded to earlier, this may have limited predictive value given the importance that NA, of which all were members, places on recognizing that you will always have a problem with substance use. Hence identification as a 'user' is likely to be retained for as long as membership of a 12-step program remains an important and salient basis for self-definition. Where there was evidence of some identity change, it was in terms of the degree to which people identified as being in recovery. Both John and Matt indicated an improvement in their identification as someone in recovery, whereas for David, there was a marginal reduction between T1 and T2.

Evidence of social identity continuity in SIM

Not everyone benefits immediately from treatment, and this is certainly the case with substance misuse. The two remaining cases provide examples of people who experienced no change in their social networks in response to seeking treatment.

The first of these, Brian, was 39 years of age at T1 and had an extensive history of IV drug and alcohol use. This was Brian's first TC experience, but he had many years of other treatment including detox, pharmacotherapy, and counseling. Two of Brian's T1 social groups were described primarily as using/drinking groups (drumming and users) but every group contained at least someone in recovery. At T2, those groups remained, one had become less important (the commune) and two had increases in the proportion of group members who were using or drinking (commune and pub groups). In Mike's case, T1 was his first experience of any form of treatment. He was 28 years of age at this time and ice was his primary drug of concern. His T1 map highlighted the predominantly heavy drug use in all of his group networks, and this monoculture of heavy drug use did not change at T2. Interestingly, both Brian and Mike indicated they had slightly higher recovery capital by T2, but this was not associated with any meaningful change in their identification as a 'user', and there was either an associated decline (in Brian's case) or a combination of no change together with very low ratings (in the case of Mike) on health and well-being indices. Interesting too, these were the only maps of the five showing considerable conflict in relationships and, as argued in SIMIC, such incompatibility undermines change. Neither case developed any sense of connection with others in the TC, which has also been noted as important in recovery (Dingle et al., 2015a). Consequently, in both cases, we have evidence of failure to negotiate social change to support recovery and, as SIMOR would predict, this is associated with poorer outcomes on the whole. Further feedback at T2 indicated that these clients had returned to the same substance use and social interactions, despite TC treatment.

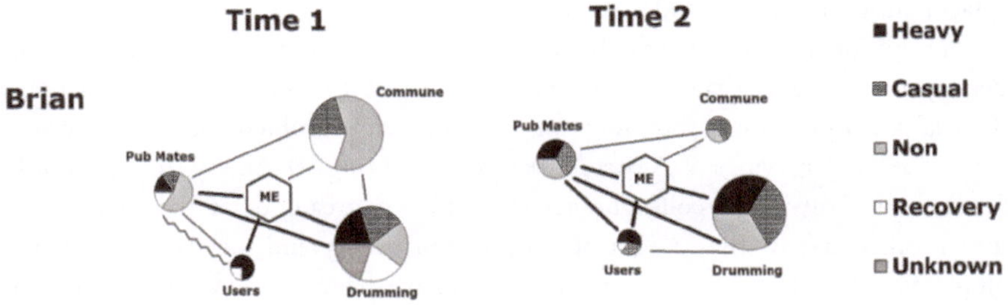

FIGURE 10.5 Social identity maps produced by Brian at Times 1 and 2.

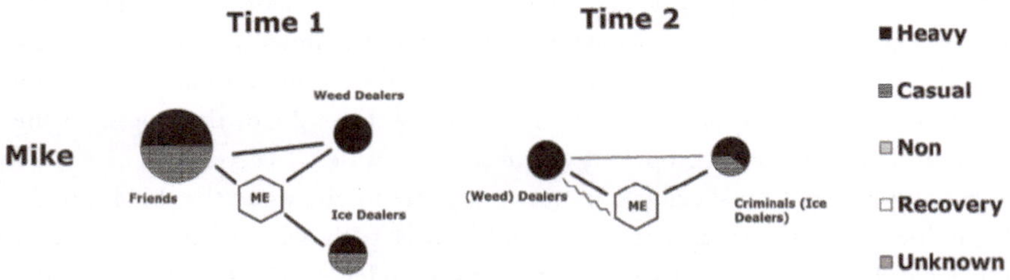

FIGURE 10.6 Social identity maps produced by Mike at Times 1 and 2.

As highlighted in previous research (Dingle et al., 2015a), social stability, reflected in social identity continuity, should not be the goal of treatment targeting substance misuse. While continuity in social identities has value in other contexts (e.g., in recovery from illness, brain injury, adjusting to moving, retiring), maintenance of one's connection to groups that are seen as important and that engage in predominantly heavy substance use supports continued engagement in problematic using behaviour, and has a detrimental effect on recovery and associated health and well-being outcomes. The maps created by Brian and Mike provide a clear illustration of these effects.

Added value in using SIM to capture social identity change

Application of social identity theorizing to the addictions field highlights the vital role that social relationships, and the identities that underpin them, play in facilitating recovery (Best et al., 2016; Frings & Albery, 2015). What SIM adds to this process is a capacity to account for differences in recovery trajectories, reduced recovery capital and poorer health outcomes, in a visual form that can readily be understood by researchers, clinicians and participants. When looking at the maps created by Mike, for example, we can easily account for his difficulties in persevering with recovery and his low life quality, particularly when we see the extent to which his social network is defined predominantly by groups engaged in heavy substance use. Indeed, these maps can become a useful therapeutic tool for clients to see how they might better engage with and/or change their existing social networks to meet their recovery goals. SIM is more accessible to clients than mean ratings on existing recovery measures, and so are likely to be more successful in facilitating meaningful and relevant change.

An additional benefit is that SIM can provide a quantifiable index of social identity components that are theoretically relevant to understanding processes of social identity change, that underpin recovery from problematic substance use (Best et al., 2016; Frings & Albery, 2015; see also Frings & Albery, this volume). To this end, Cruwys and colleagues (2016) outline in greater detail these particular dimensions and how they might be used to test theory and mechanisms underlying treatment effects. In the present chapter we have focused on concepts of group number (both overall and of important groups) to index multiple group membership, the proportion of group members engaged in substance use to index networks predominantly defined by their using or recovery status, and commonality to index group compatibility. There are certainly more dimensions that can easily be added to SIM (e.g., ratings of how positive people feel about their groups, how representative they are of the group, see Cruwys et al., 2016) that speak to the theoretical and practical complexity of substance misuse.

Having its focus on social group networks, one might argue that SIM ignores the influence of significant others or individuals with whom our respondents interacted. Interestingly though, three of our respondents indicated there was little change in these particular relationships. The only changes noted were by John and

David, who both cut their individual ties with people who were using, but retained other relationships. Cutting ties with using groups can certainly make a positive contribution to recovery trajectories, but the greatest change in both respondents' networks of social ties was to their social groups. The implication here is that group ties do the heavy lifting in buffering any negative consequences of life change, as supported by other research (Haslam et al., 2014; 2016). Clearly though, more data drawn from larger samples are required to make definitive statements about the contribution of individual and group-based relationships in supporting the transition to recovery.

Conclusion

As the cases illustrate, life change can be hard, particularly when it involves recovery from problematic substance use. In this context, the TC provides a window of opportunity to support the social identity change necessary for recovery to be maintained in the longer term. It does so through providing a space for people to develop new social relationships, particularly those that support recovery, at a time when there is reduced access to using networks that are likely to compromise recovery. What SIM offers is a means to oversee and understand these processes of social identity change. Not only does it provide a vehicle to test theories that speak to addiction recovery, but it has great potential for use as a therapeutic tool to promote social network change in strategic ways that assist clients to engineer the transition to recovery (see Best et al., 2014).

The inevitability of change, highlighted in our opening quote from the French philosopher Henri Bergson, opens the way for recovery. As we argue here, the challenge lies in creating the right balance in social networks to achieve sustained recovery, in the context of negotiating life's ongoing changes to social relationships. The beauty of SIM is that it offers a way to both conceptualize and direct that change.

References

Bergson, H. (1911). *Creative evolution*, translated by Arthur Mitchell, New York: Henry Holt and Company.

Best, D., Beckwith, M., Haslam, C., Haslam, S.A., Jetten, J., Mawson, E., & Lubman, D. I. (2016). Overcoming drug and alcohol addiction as a process of social identity transition: The Social Identity Model of Recovery (SIMOR). *Addiction, Research and Theory, 24*, 111–123.

Best, D., Ghufran, S., Day, E., Ray, R., & Loaring, J. (2008). Breaking the habit: A retrospective analysis of desistance factors among formerly problematic heroin users. *Drug and Alcohol Review, 27*, 619–24.

Best, D., Lubman, D., Savic, M., Wilson, A., Dingle, G., Haslam, S.A., Haslam, C., & Jetten, J. (2014). Social and transitional identity: Exploring social networks and their significant in a therapeutic community setting. *Therapeutic Communities: The International Journal of Therapeutic Communities, 35*, 10–20.

Buckingham, S.A., Frings, D., Albery, I.P. (2013). Group membership and social identity in addiction recovery. *Psychology of Addictive Behaviors, 27*, 1132–40.

Cruwys, T., Dingle, G.A., Hornsey, M.J., Jetten, J., Oei, T.P.S., & Walter, Z.C. (2014). Social isolation schema responds to positive social experiences: Longitudinal evidence from vulnerable populations. *The British Journal of Clinical Psychology*, *53*, 1–16.

Cruwys, T., Steffens, N.K., Haslam, C., Haslam, S.A., Jetten, J., & Dingle, G.A. (2016). The Social Identity Mapping (SIM) tool: An instrument for comprehensive assessment of subjective group memberships. *Journal of Affective Disorders*, *194*, 188–195.

Dingle, G.A., Cruwys, T.C., & Frings, D. (2015). Social identities as pathways into and out of addiction. *Frontiers in Psychology*, *6*, 1795.

Dingle, G.A., Stark, C., Cruwys, T., & Best, D.A. (2015). Breaking good: Breaking ties with social groups may be good for recovery from substance misuse. *British Journal of Social Psychology*, *54*, 236–254.

Doosje, B., Ellemers, N., & Spears, R. (1995). Perceived intragroup variability as a function of group status and identification. *Journal of Experimental Social Psychology*, *31*, 410–436.

Eggins, R.A., O'Brien, A.T., Reynolds, K.J., Haslam, S.A., & Cocker, A.S. (2008). Refocusing the focus group: AIRing as a basis for effective workplace planning. *British Journal of Management*, *19*, 277–293.

Frings, D., & Albery, I.P. (2015). The Social Identity Model of Cessation Maintenance: Formulation and initial evidence. *Addictive Behaviors*, *44*, 35–42.

Glei, D.A., Landau, D.A., Goldman, N., Chuang, Y-L., Rodrıguez G., et al. (2005). Participating in social activities helps to preserve cognitive function: An analysis of a longitudinal, population-based study of the elderly. *International Journal of Epidemiology*, *34*, 864–871.

Gleibs, I., Haslam, C., Haslam, S.A., & Jones, J. (2011). Water clubs in residential care: Is it the water or the club that enhances health and well-being? *Psychology and Health*, *26*, 1361–1378.

Groshkova, T., Best, D., & White, W. (2012). Assessment of recovery capital: Properties and psychometrics of a measure of addiction recovery strengths. *Drug and Alcohol Review*, *32*, 187–194.

Haslam, C., Cruwys, T., & Haslam, S.A. (2014). 'The we's have it': Evidence for the distinctive benefits of group engagement in enhancing cognitive health in ageing. *Social Science and Medicine*, *120*, 57–66.

Haslam, C., Cruwys, T., Milne, M., Kan, C-H, & Haslam, S.A. (2016). Group ties protect cognitive health by promoting social identification and social support. *Journal of Aging and Health*, *28*, 244–266.

Haslam, C., Haslam, S.A., Jetten, J., Bevins, A., Ravenscroft, S., & Tonks, J. (2010). The social treatment: Benefits of group reminiscence and group activity for the cognitive performance and well-being of older adults in residential care. *Psychology and Aging*, *25*, 157–167.

Haslam, C., Holme, A., Haslam, S.A., Iyer, A., Jetten, J., & Williams, W.H. (2008). Maintaining group membership: Identity continuity and well-being after stroke. *Neuropsychological Rehabilitation*, *18*, 671–691.

Haslam, S.A., Eggins, R.A., & Reynolds, K.A. (2003). The ASPIRe model: Actualizing Social and Personal Identity Resources to enhance organizational outcomes. *Journal of Occupational and Organizational Psychology*, *76*, 86–113.

Haslam, S.A., Jetten, J., Postmes, T., & Haslam, C. (2009). Social identity, health and well-being: An emerging agenda for applied psychology. *Applied Psychology: An International Review*, *58*, 1–23.

Haslam, S. A., O'Brien, A., Jetten, J., Vormedal, K., & Penna, S. (2005). Taking the strain: Social identity, social support and the experience of stress. *British Journal of Social Psychology*, *44*, 355–370.

Haslam, S.A., Reicher, S.D., & Levine, M. (2012). When other people are heaven, when other people are hell: How social identity determines the nature and impact of social support. In Jetten, J., Haslam, C., & Haslam, S. A. (Eds.), *The social cure: Identity, health, and well-being* (pp. 157–174). Hove, UK: Psychology Press.

Iyer, A., Jetten, J., Tsivrikos, D., Postmes, T., & Haslam, S.A. (2009). The more (and the more compatible) the merrier: Multiple group memberships and identity compatibility as predictors of adjustment after life transitions. *British Journal of Social Psychology, 48*, 707–733.

Jetten, J., Haslam, C., Haslam, S. A., & Branscombe, N. (2009). The social cure. *Scientific American Mind, 20*, 26–33.

Jetten, J., Haslam, C., Haslam, S. A., Dingle, G., & Jones, J.J. (2014). How groups affect our health and well-being: The path from theory to policy. *Social Issues and Policy Review, 8*, 103–130.

Jetten, J., Haslam, S.A., Iyer, A., & Haslam, C. (2009). Turning to others in times of change: Social identity and coping with stress. In S. Stürmer, & M. Snyder, M. (Eds.), *The psychology of prosocial behavior: Group processes, intergroup relations, and helping* (pp. 139–156). Oxford: Blackwell.

Litt, M.D., Kadden, R.M., Kabela-Cormier, E., & Petry, N.M. (2009). Changing network support for drinking: Network support project 2-year follow-up. *Journal of Consulting and Clinical Psychology, 77*, 229–242.

Longabaugh, R., Wirtz, P.W., Zywiak, W.H., & O'Malley, S.S. (2010). Network support as a prognostic indicator of drinking outcomes: The COMBINE study. *Journal of Studies on Alcohol and Drugs, 71*, 837–846.

Reynolds, K.J., Eggins, R.A., & Haslam, S.A. (2010). Uncovering diverse identities in organisations: AIRing versus auditing approaches to diversity management. *Asia Pacific Journal of Human Resources, 48*, 45–57.

Ryan, A., Holmes, J., Hunt, V., & Lintzeris, N. (2014). Validation and implementation of the Australian Treatment Outcomes Profile in specialist drug and alcohol settings. *Drug and Alcohol Review, 33*, 33–42.

Schmitt, M.T., Branscombe, N.R., Postmes, T., & Garcia, A. (2014). The consequences of perceived discrimination for psychological well-being: A meta-analytic review. *Psychological Bulletin, 140*, 921–948.

Tajfel, H. & Turner, J. C. (1979). An integrative theory of intergroup conflict. In W. G. Austin & S. Worchel (Eds.), *The social psychology of intergroup relations* (pp. 33–47). Monterey, CA: Brooks/Cole.

Turner, J.C., Hogg, M.A., Oakes, P.J., Reicher, S.D., & Wetherell, M.S. (1987). *Rediscovering the social group: A self-categorization theory*. Oxford: Blackwell.

11

BUILDING BRIDGES TO POSITIVE SOCIAL IDENTITIES

The Social Network Diagram and opiate substitution treatment

Edward Day

Addiction to a psychoactive substance such as alcohol or heroin is a complex biopsychosocial problem. Once an individual is dependent on a substance and seeking professional treatment, the natural history of the problem is likely to involve many years of struggle, with periods of abstinence quickly followed by lapse and relapse back to regular use (Hser, Longshore, & Anglin, 2007). Many people do reach the status of sustained abstinence and recovery, but mortality rates are high and the problem is often accompanied by high levels of morbidity in the individual and their family (Darke, 2011).

The Social Identity Model of Recovery (SIMOR) argues that the move away from dependent substance use and into recovery is a fundamentally social process, underpinned by transitions in the composition of the individual's social network (Best et al., 2016). When new recovery-oriented groups are perceived as attractive, beneficial and relevant there is a concurrent development of a new recovery-based social identity. This chapter explores this process through the eyes of a clinician working in professional treatment services, with a particular focus on heroin users and opiate substitution treatment (OST). With the SIMOR in mind, how can the clinician organise their treatment response to maximise social levers towards change? What techniques are available, and how effective are they?

The chapter will be divided into three sections. The first two sections will review two sources of positive social identity available to individuals receiving professional treatment – the individual's naturally occurring social network (i.e., family, friends and acquaintances) and communities of people in recovery. The first section will outline what is known about the composition of natural social networks, how they are established and how they influence treatment outcome, before briefly reviewing the evidence for treatment interventions to enhance social network support. In the second section, the potential benefits of the recovery community will be explored, alongside the evidence for assertive linkage techniques to connect clients receiving OST to them. Finally, section three will describe the Social Network Diagram (SND), a simple clinical technique that enables the clinician to help their clients harness the potential power of these two groups.

Section 1: Naturally occurring social networks and the support that they provide

The past three decades have seen a recognition by researchers of the important role that families and friends of drug users can play in influencing the course of the drug problem and in helping change problematic behaviours (Copello & Orford, 2002; Copello, Velleman, & Templeton, 2005). Social support, defined as 'resources provided by other people', has been linked to a wide range of health-related outcomes, including mortality, physical disease, and psychological symptoms (Holt-Lunstad, Smith, & Layton, 2010). It has been hypothesised to protect people from the harmful effects of stress and enhance overall subjective well-being. Possible mechanisms include reduction of negative affect, increase in positive affect and stress buffering (Cohen, Gottlieb, & Underwood, 2000). At the same time, it is recognised that heroin users spend increasing amounts of time with fellow users as their drug using career progresses (Best, Hernando, Gossop, Sidwell, & Strang, 2003; Gogineni, Stein, & Friedmann, 2001), and that drug use by members of the social network is a stronger predictor of injecting drug users' continued use than neighbourhood characteristics such as level of drug-related arrests (Schroeder et al., 2001).

If the clinician is to consider harnessing social support for change, he or she needs to understand how social networks develop over time, and what factors are likely to influence their size and composition. What does research tell us about how people meet new friends or an intimate partner? What is the average size of a network? How can we gauge its potential level of support?

How do social networks change over time?

Social networks are 'the set of people with whom an individual is directly involved' i.e., there is a repeated interaction between the individual and the network member and a mental representation of the relationship as social (Baumeister & Leary, 1995). The *personal* network is a sub-network of closer, personal relationships in the global network such as family members, friends and other close confidants, and this may be further sub-divided into a friendship network, a family network, or a work-related network. Two theories (socioemotional selectivity theory and social convoy theory) have been proposed to explain how an individual's social network changes over the life course (Carstensen, 1995; Kahn & Antonucci, 1980). Both predict a similar pattern of changes, with a rapid expansion in the number of diverse, informal social contacts in adolescence, followed by a steady pruning back to fewer closer relationships as life progresses. Relations in the inner circle (spouse/core family) are more stable throughout the life span, but those in the periphery of the network are less stable and are influenced by changes in external circumstances.

Life events have a considerable impact on the size and composition of the social network (Wrzus, Hänel, Wagner, & Neyer, 2013). 'Normative' life events are those that have a high probability at a certain age or stage in the life course, e.g., puberty, school or work entry, marriage, parenthood, retirement, widowhood, some of which increase network size and others decrease it. For example, puberty tends to lead to an expansion of the network due to an increasing number of relationships with peers and non-relatives. Marriage also extends the social network of both spouses, but doesn't usually produce a straightforward sum of the two networks. Starting work increases contact with people who may enter the network as co-workers or friends, although existing friendships may diminish due to decreased time or social comparison processes. In contrast, parenthood often reduces social networks for both structural and psychological reasons (less free time, different routines, less association with friends without children). However, the reductions tend to occur in peripheral relationships, and contact with family members may increase. The loss of a spouse also leads to a reduction in total network size due to a process of social withdrawal, but this gradually normalises over time.

'Non-normative' life events are experienced by only a few people, but are particularly relevant to the OST population. They are less predictable in terms of timing, but consistently lead to a reduction in size of social network (Wrzus et al., 2013). The death of a close relative has a similar effect to that of loss of a spouse, and like divorce tends to reduce social networks through loss of friends but also through focus on close, supportive relationships at the cost of more peripheral ones. Relocation strongly affects extra-familial relationships with people living in the same area, and social network size reduces. Peripheral, less close relationships are among the first to dissolve, whereas close, long-lasting relationships are less likely to be affected.

Current evidence suggests that the general quantity and quality of social relationships in industrialised countries are decreasing, and greater social mobility, delayed marriage, reduced intergenerational living, increased single residence households, and dual career families may have all contributed (Putnam, 2000). The onset and maintenance of drug use disorders has been shown to be associated with smaller personal social networks (Tracy & Biegel, 2006). However, qualitative research suggests that people who experience remission of a drug use problem have an increased social connection to others (McIntosh & McKeganey, 2000), increased reliance on the support of family and friends (Granfield & Cloud, 2001), and increased activities and time spent with non-drug using social network members (Best, Ghufran, Day, Ray, & Loaring, 2008; McIntosh & McKeganey, 2006). One large epidemiological study reports that personal networks of friends, neighbours and religious groups are first to change in remission, possibly because drug using network members are exchanged for non-users. However, personal networks including an individual's spouse, their children and volunteer groups were larger among individuals with no drug use disorder, compared to those who had ever experienced a drug use disorder (Mowbray & Scott, 2015).

The few studies that have attempted to quantify the social networks of people receiving OST show that a significant amount of support is available. In a recent study of UK OST clients, 118 participants identified a total of 820 network members with a mean network size of 6.9 people (Day et al., 2013). Two-thirds of the social network was made up of family members with the remaining third mostly friends, with a few self-help group members or professionals. Approximately a third of the sample had a drug-free partner, and the sample as a whole had regular contact with an average of nearly five valued network members from whom they received support.

How do people meet new friends or an int imate partner?

In OST samples approximately 40 per cent of participants report having a current sexual partner, of which 20 per cent are active heroin users (Day et al., 2013; Goehl, Nunes, Quitkin, & Hilton, 1993). Social scientists have surveyed people about where and how they met their intimate partner and close friends for more than a century (Rosenfeld & Thomas, 2012). Traditionally, family of origin and primary and secondary school were the most important institutions that brought heterosexual couples together. Later in the twentieth century friends and the workplace, two social institutions associated with later life stages, started to gain importance, and since the rise of the internet the percentage of people meeting their partners online has risen dramatically (Rosenfeld & Thomas, 2012). The importance of school as a source of potential friends is important even in adult life, as studies on Social Behaviour and Network Therapy (SBNT) suggest that (non-drug using) friends from an earlier period of a client's life can be willing and helpful participants in therapy (Copello, Williamson, Orford, & Day, 2006). Likewise, the importance of work as a source of positive social network support should encourage clinicians to explore interventions with the goal of achieving employment.

The relationship between social support and treatment outcome

The largest body of research into social networks and substance use comes from the study of alcohol use disorders (AUDs). Although alcohol has a large impact on the social environment of the individual, a first conclusion from this research is that there is plenty of available social support for this population. Mowbray and colleagues compared social network ties to friends, family, and communities among individuals with a past-year diagnosis of AUD to individuals with no lifetime diagnosis of AUD in a large national epidemiological study (Mowbray, Quinn, & Cranford, 2014). Both social network size and social network diversity was significantly smaller among individuals with alcohol dependence, compared to individuals with alcohol abuse or no AUD, but these differences disappeared when other social and clinical factors were controlled for. The authors concluded that individuals with AUD have social networks similar to those without AUD in the general population and that interventions focused on reducing alcohol use could benefit from harnessing these networks.

The UK Alcohol Treatment Trial (UKATT), the largest trial of psychosocial treatment for alcohol problems conducted in the UK (The UKATT Research Team, 2001), systematically collected data on social network composition of those entering the trial. Participants were asked to name a maximum of 12 'important' people they had spent most time with over the previous three months, and describe each of them using demographic and drinking-related characteristics. Overall, 4,677 'important people' were named by 740 participants entering routine alcohol treatment, and all participants could name at least one 'important person', with an average of 6.5 across the whole sample. The majority of people entering alcohol treatment named their partner as the most important person, although parents, adult children, siblings and other family members were also mentioned (Copello & Walsh, in press).

The second conclusion is that the size and nature of the social network has a considerable impact on the outcome of the AUD and its treatment (Hunter-Reel, McCrady, & Hildebrandt, 2009; McCrady, 2004). Researchers have divided the concept of social support into *structural* support (the quantity of social ties) and *functional* support (the availability of support functions such as affection). These categories can be further divided into *general* support and *abstinence-specific* support (i.e., support that is only provided contingent on the individual remaining abstinent). Support can also be both positive and negative, as network members may also provide dysfunctional role models, reinforce maladaptive behaviour, and provide 'environmental cues' associated with substance use. These categories are summarised in Table 11.1.

Structural factors such as a greater number of supportive relationships and number of non-drinking friends have been reported to be predictors of abstinence (Booth, Russell, Soucek, & Laughlin, 1992; Gordon & Zrull, 1991; Humphreys, Moos, & Finney, 1996; Mohr, Averna, Kenny, & Del Boca, 2001; Rosenberg, 1983; Zywiak, Longabaugh, & Wirtz, 2002). Likewise, higher levels of social support have been correlated with reductions in drinking after treatment (Beattie, 2001; Havassy, Hall, & Wasserman, 1991), and in particular the level of support provided by the most important person in the network (Barber & Crisp, 1995).

In terms of functional support, there is consistent evidence for the role of family support, with both general and abstinence-specific support associated with more abstinent days and less relapse (Booth et al., 1992; Gordon & Zrull, 1991; Humphreys et al., 1996; Rosenberg, 1983; Zywiak et al., 2002). Good family adjustment and functioning is associated with better drinking outcomes (McCrady, 2004), whereas negative family behaviours such as withdrawing, avoiding or tolerating drinking are associated with higher levels of drinking (McCrady, Hayaki, Epstein, & Hirsch, 2002). Intimate partner or spousal support is particularly significant, but is generally greater for men than women (McCrady, 2004). However, friends are also important, and an analysis of Project MATCH data showed that having more non-drinking friends was linked to more positive outcomes, and more drinking friends to worse outcomes (Mohr et al., 2001). The best outcomes occur when support for abstinence comes from all members of the network.

TABLE 11.1 Summary of terms used in describing social support

		POSITIVE *Enhances a person's physical or psychological well-being*	***NEGATIVE*** *Occurs if either the outcome of the support is negative, or if the recipient is not ready or willing to receive it*
GENERAL	Structural	Social connectedness or embeddedness in a social network e.g., number of close friends	Small social network or lack of connectedness in social network
	Functional	The availability of help from others that does not specifically address substance use e.g., affection, advice, financial support	Negative interactions with members of the social network e.g., emotional or physical abuse
ABSTINENCE-SPECIFIC	Structural	The number of non-drug users / people in recovery in the social network	The number of active drug users in the social network
	Functional	Encouragement from others to seek help for a drug use problem e.g., from treatment services or mutual aid groups	Offers of drugs or encouragement to use drugs

Overall, alcohol-specific support is a better predictor of outcomes than general support (Beattie, Longabaugh, & Fava, 1992). More support for abstinence from the most important people in the social network has been associated with lower relapse rates (Beattie & Longabough, 1999; Longabaugh, Wirtz, Beattie, Noel, & Stout, 1995), and increased support for drinking has been associated with poorer outcomes (Longabaugh, Wirtz, Zweben, & Stout, 1998; Mohr et al., 2001). The relationship between general support and outcomes is generally positive but is less clear. There may be an interaction between general and abstinence-specific support, as when abstinence-specific support occurs in the context of high levels of general support, there is a greater correlation with abstinence (Beattie & Longabough, 1999).

Complex interactions between the various types of support have been reported. In a series of studies, Longabaugh and colleagues proposed that the effect of alcohol-specific support on drinking outcomes (i.e., the balance between support for abstinence and support for continued drinking) is moderated by factors such as the size of the social network, the amount of contact that the individual has with it, and the subjective value of the network to the individual. They termed this concept 'social investment' (Longabaugh, Beattie, Noel, Stout, & Malloy, 1993). Social support for abstinence predicts better drinking outcomes in those with high social investment in their network (Beattie & Longabaugh, 1997), but is unrelated to abstinence in those with low investment in their network (Longabaugh et al., 1993; Longabaugh et al., 1995). Hunter-Reel et al. have reported that the relationship between alcohol-specific social support (for drinking and not drinking) and drinking outcomes is partially mediated by motivation (Hunter-Reel, McCrady, Hildebrandt, & Epstein, 2010). The relationship between the individual and social support factors is also likely to be bidirectional. The social support system influences an individual's functioning, but the individual's interpersonal skills and functioning are also likely to affect the social network (Hunter-Reel et al., 2009).

In contrast to the alcohol field, there has been relatively little research on the influence of social network support on illicit drug use. OST is an effective treatment for decreasing illicit opiate use, HIV risk behaviour, criminal activity and accidental overdose-related death (Connock et al., 2006). However, heroin and other illicit drug use persist in a proportion of OST recipients, even when treatment includes optimised psychosocial treatment strategies. It is clear that a range of extra-treatment factors maintain drug use, including intra-personal, inter-personal and environmental factors.

Social learning theories view drug use as a learned behaviour governed by reinforcement processes. These theories suggest that the social networks of drug users are similar to those of non-drug users in terms of structure and function but consist mainly of people who use and approve of illegal drugs. Emotional and functional attachments to other drug users may therefore reinforce drug use in the context of a larger society that discourages those activities (El-Bassel, Chen, & Cooper, 1998). Having even a single person in the social network who uses the same drug of abuse is predictive of poorer outcomes (Havassy et al., 1991), but treatment may have an impact on this. A study of 245 injecting drug users attending Baltimore Needle Exchange Program found that participants that entered OST had a 20 per cent decrease in the odds of having friends that used drugs (Lloyd et al., 2008). Higher levels of general structural support (i.e., number of people in the user's network) and greater abstinence-specific functional support (emotional support from a partner) have been shown to be related to reductions in risk of relapse, independent of the type of drug use (Havassy et al., 1991). Likewise, abstinence-specific support such as a reduction in the number of drug users in the network and less exposure to drug use by network members predicted abstinence from cocaine use in OST clients (Wasserman, Stewart, & Delucchi, 2001). In a sample of adult injecting drug users not receiving treatment, having fewer drug users in the social network was a predictor of cessation of drug use over a six-month period (Latkin, Knowlton, Hoover, & Mandell, 1999).

These results have led researchers to conclude that it is important to break ties with drug-using associates, and that further work is required to develop interventions that increase drug users' success in altering social network composition. Treatment research has pointed to a potential role for family and social network members in helping to initiate treatment, in influencing its course and outcome, and in both reducing the likelihood of relapse and supporting the long-term maintenance of change (Copello, Velleman, & Templeton, 2005). For example, Higgins et al. have shown that the involvement of a significant member of one's social network in behavioural treatment is a predictor of abstinence in cocaine-dependent individuals (Higgins, Budney, Bickel, & Badger, 1994). Likewise, patients enrolled in buprenorphine maintenance therapy randomly assigned to network therapy (involving one or multiple members of a patient's social network) had significantly more negative urine samples (65 per cent) across 18 weeks of treatment than those in a control group (Galanter et al., 2004).

Social network-orientated therapies

Accepting the role of social identity change in the process of recovery, how can clinicians work to support change in social networks and social group membership? Two theoretical strands run through the research literature on building social support, dividing the field of prospective supporters into two possible categories (Gottlieb, 1988).

First, interventions may target people in the client's existing natural network who are already significant sources of social influence, with the aim of enhancing both general and abstinence-specific support (Copello et al., 2006; Copello et al., 2005). The levels of contact with partner, family members and friends reported in the research described above suggest this is a feasible approach. Related to this activity are interventions that work with family members to promote the engagement of substance misusers into treatment, and those that support family members affected by the substance misuse of a relative (Copello et al., 2005). Several possible interventions have been reported, including the following.

Network therapy

Network therapy was developed by Galanter (1999), and has been tested with cocaine (Galanter, Dermatis, Keller, & Trujillo, 2002) and opiate users (Galanter et al., 2004). It aims to build skills by using a cognitive-behavioural approach to relapse prevention, incorporate the involvement of the participant's naturally occurring social network members to enhance outcomes, and reinforce skills learned in treatment sessions by completing activities outside of sessions. In the research evaluations, treatment sessions are delivered twice per week for 24 weeks, and almost 80 per cent of participants had a naturally occurring support network member who attended all sessions, evenly divided between friends and family members. The number of network sessions attended was significantly associated with reduced relapse.

Social behaviour and network therapy (SBNT)

This intervention was initially developed for use with a population seeking treatment for AUD, and can be used with both people who have an existing social support network and those that don't. The primary goal is to maximise the participant's positive social support for change in drinking behaviour, but a secondary aim is to reduce exposure to social network members that support alcohol misuse (Copello, Orford, Hodgson, & Tober, 2009). Feasibility and treatment outcomes have been reported for 24 individuals receiving OST receiving the intervention (Copello et al., 2006). Network members attended sessions in 80 per cent of cases, and were primarily (70 per cent) family members. Although there were no significant changes in network composition of heavy drug users for participants, there were significant increases in family cohesion and satisfaction as well as reductions in conflict between participants and their network members. SBNT has the added advantage of providing benefits to the network members too, with the potential to reduce the reported high levels of physical and psychological symptoms associated with living with drug or alcohol dependence (Copello et al., 2005; Ray, Mertens, & Weisner, 2009; Williamson, Smith, Orford, Copello, & Day, 2007).

Motivated stepped care (MSC)

The third phase of the MSC program (Brooner & Kidorf, 2002; Kidorf, Brooner, & King, 1997) includes a social network intervention designed to help participants meet other drug-free people, create or develop drug-free social support, and to help increase social reinforcement for drug abstinence. The goal is to identify a drug-free adult friend, family member or community volunteer to attend a minimum of six weekly group sessions, and meet with the participant once per week outside the session. The support person monitors and documents the participant's weekly participation in social and recreational activities with abstinent people, and helps them to identify and attend further drug-free social activities (Kidorf et al., 1997).

The community reinforcement approach (CRA)

The Community Reinforcement Approach (CRA) "is a broad-spectrum behavioural treatment approach for substance abuse problems . . . that utilises social, recreational, familial, and vocational reinforcers to aid clients in the recovery process" (Meyers & Smith, 1995 p. 1). It is a treatment based on social learning theory that arranges both personal and environmental abstinence reinforcers. Functional analysis is used for individuals to identify positive reinforcers of abstinence in their life and cues or triggers to drug use. Specific sessions focus on problem-solving skills, drug refusal training, communication skills, and social/recreational counselling (Azrin, Sisson, Meyers, & Godley, 1982; Meyers & Smith, 1995). A randomised trial comparing CRA with treatment as usual in a sample of 165 patients receiving OST found that the CRA group performed better than the standard counselling group in the likelihood of achieving eight, 12 or 16 consecutive weeks free from opioid use, and in overall reductions in drug use (Abbott, Weller, Delaney, & Moore, 1998). Patients treated with CRA in combination with methadone maintenance have shown reduction in opioid use as well as improvement in legal status, psychiatric symptoms and vocational and social functioning (Abbott, 2009).

A variant of CRA, Community Reinforcement and Family Training (CRAFT), uses the same principles of behavioural reinforcement to help concerned significant others (CSOs) to motivate treatment-refusing people with a substance use disorder to enter treatment. CRAFT has been modified to create a new manualised treatment, Community Reinforcement and Family Training for Treatment Retention (CRAFT-T), to work with the CSOs of people already in treatment to increase retention in treatment and recovery support. When tested in opioid-dependent individuals (Brigham et al., 2014), CRAFT-T resulted in a moderate but non-significant effect on treatment retention, and had a larger effect when the CSO was a close family member. It also had a significant positive effect on opioid and other drug use.

A second set of strategies focuses on 'grafting on' new social ties to the existing network, including linking the patient to mutual help groups and other communities of recovery. These will be explored in section 2.

Section 2: The recovery community and how to access it

Although recovery from a substance use disorder may be the rule rather than the exception (White, 2008), the prognosis for long-term recovery varies by type and degree of problem and by personal, family and community recovery capital (Granfield & Cloud, 1999, 2001; White & Cloud, 2008). Over 16 million people worldwide aged 15 or over used heroin or opium in 2013 (United Nations Office on Drugs and Crime, 2015), and it is estimated that nearly a quarter of these will develop opioid dependence (Anthony, Warner, & Kessler, 1994). Heroin dependence is one of the most problematic patterns of behaviour to change once established, presenting as a chronic and relapsing disorder (Hser, Evans, Grella, Ling, & Anglin, 2015). Dependence on opiates develops relatively quickly, and once established is incredibly persistent with high rates of morbidity and mortality. For example, a review of the Civil Addict Program in California reported that only 50 per cent of the surviving addicts (20 per cent of the original sample) had maintained heroin abstinence for more than five years when interviewed over 30 years later (Hser, 2007). When considering all treatment modalities for opioid dependence and combining the results of several long-term outcome studies, approximately 10–15 per cent of treatment seekers achieve abstinence from illicit drugs within one year, 25 per cent by five years and 66 per cent by 12 years (Best, Day, & Morgan, 2006). However, the OST populations studied had been using heroin for an average of 10 years before entering treatment, meaning a heroin-using career of between 10 and 20 years for the majority (Anglin, Hser, & Grella, 1997; Gossop et al., 1997; Joe, Chastain, & Simpson, 1990).

The process of ending a period of dependence and achieving recovery, i.e., establishing voluntary control over drug use, good physical and psychological health, and 'citizenship', is relatively poorly understood. Given the complexity of the situation, multiple factors are likely to interact to bring about the initiation of recovery, including both push (avoidance) factors and pull (approach) factors

(Best et al., 2010; Granfield & Cloud, 1999). Push factors include a general reduction in the positive effects of drugs over time combined with pressures from family or the courts, mental or physical health concerns, or financial problems. Pull factors may include unexpected shifts in lifestyle (e.g., a new relationship or job), exposure to positive recovery role models, family and social support, or emergence of new beliefs (e.g., religious conversion).

Key turning points in the drug-using career include entering treatment, imprisonment, or a range of unpredictable life events. An important task of OST services may be to keep people alive until one of these turning points arise. It is argued that exposure to the personal stories and lives of people in recovery can serve as a catalyst for this personal transformation, and peer-based recovery support can form the basis of social learning and reinforcement of recovery messages and values (Best et al., 2010). It is therefore important that the treatment clinician is constantly searching for ways to connect their clients with communities of people in recovery.

The evidence for assertive linkage

Treatment interventions may target people who, by virtue of their own life experiences (e.g., recovery from drug use) and personal characteristics, can become meaningful sources of support. This approach therefore makes an attempt to add new ties to the existing social network (Gottlieb, 1988). There is evidence from studies with AUDs that changing social networks to be more supportive of abstinence can be achieved by an intervention explicitly designed for that purpose, and this in turn is related to improved outcomes. Litt et al. (Litt, Kadden, Kabela-Cormier, & Petry, 2009) randomly assigned alcohol-dependent patients to three conditions (network support, network support with contingency management, and a control) and treatment outcomes were assessed at three-month intervals over 15 months. Increased support for abstinence in the network was only prominent in the network support conditions, and the addition of a single abstinent friend to the social network improved outcomes by 27 per cent.

Mutual self-help treatments have a powerful effect in sustaining abstinence and recovery, and many different mutual aid organisations have been described (see Humphreys, 2004 for a full description). The majority of research has been conducted with Alcoholics Anonymous and related 12-step treatment, and shows that they are at least as effective as other (professionally-led) interventions (Humphreys et al., 2004). A review of AA's mechanisms of action concluded that the positive effects of 12-step group involvement on abstinence for alcohol 12 months later is mediated by quality of friendships, network support for abstinence, and a larger social network and greater network support (Kelly, Magill, & Stout, 2009). Evidence suggests that active referral strategies by clinicians are better than passive ones. A brief intensive referral intervention was associated with improved 12-step group involvement and substance use outcomes even among patients with considerable previous 12-step group exposure and formal treatment (Timko, DeBenedetti, & Billow, 2006). In the UK, attendance at 12-step groups post-residential treatment was associated with greater rates of abstinence, and active referral by 12-step peers increased these attendance rates (Manning et al., 2012).

Professional treatment staff are an important source of referral for people attending 12-step groups, and yet many clinicians fail to 'refer' the majority of their clients, citing a range of reasons for not doing so (Day, Gaston, Furlong, Murali, & Copello, 2005; Day, Wall, Chohan, & Seddon, 2015; Wall, Sondhi, & Day, 2014). Referral rates have been associated with staff beliefs and knowledge about 12-step groups (Day et al., 2005; Vederhus, Kristensen, Laudet, & Clausen, 2009; Wall & Day, 2014), as well as the overall attitude of their employing organisation (Day et al., 2005; Laudet & White, 2005). In the case of Narcotics Anonymous (NA), there is also uncertainty about whether OST can be reconciled with 12-step group attendance. NA has not received the same degree of attention from the academic and professional communities (White, Budnick, & Pickard, 2011), and there is not yet a clear evidence base to support NA attendance as an effective strategy in helping people to move from OST to abstinent recovery. Opiate substitution programmes and 12-step programmes have been considered incompatible (Ronel, Gueta, Abramsohn, Caspi, & Adelson, 2010). As William White has described, a 12-step programme harnesses a process of spiritual awakening that

> . . . includes an acknowledgment that no future drug use of any kind is possible, and NA's philosophy of complete abstinence is rooted in the collective experience of its members that all past attempts that fell short of complete abstinence ended in pain and tragedy. Therefore the use of any medication to treat addiction is considered the antithesis of the first step i.e., a continued effort at control rather than surrender.
>
> (White, 2011 p. 13)

The level of acceptance of OST patients within TSGs is variable, and restrictions on OST clients may be applied in some cases (e.g., the right to claim 'clean time', speak at meetings, sponsor others or hold service positions) (White, 2011; White et al., 2013).

These reservations aside, the most pragmatic strategy is to utilise both approaches to building support simultaneously. Section 3 outlines a simple strategy for starting this process, and describes experience in using it in clinical practice.

Section 3: The Social Network Diagram

The Social Network Diagram (SND) is a simple technique for use in clinical practice that serves both as a method for introducing the concepts of social identity and building social support for change, and a valuable jumping off point for planning social network and assertive linkage interventions. Drug treatment services in the UK have traditionally had a focus on the individual rather than their wider social environment (Copello & Orford, 2002; Copello & Templeton, 2012). Potential reasons include issues of confidentiality and nervousness about revealing personal details to potential authority figures, combined with a lack of training and supervision in family- or systems-orientated treatment approaches. However, there is now a growing awareness that involving family and social network members in the treatment process can be beneficial to both the individual with the addiction and their concerned significant others (Copello, Templeton, & Powell, 2010; Copello et al., 2005). A narrow focus on drug use and its coexisting problems also tends to close down the therapeutic space, leading to a preoccupation with risk and problems. Clients of drug treatment services may expect to discuss negative issues in their life, missing an opportunity to explore strengths and abilities. By focussing on their social identity as a drug user, clinicians may fail to help their clients recognise and celebrate other social roles, e.g., father, brother, son, friend, employee. Working with a client to construct a visual representation of their social network helps broaden this viewpoint.

The construction of an SND usually takes a whole clinical session (45–60 minutes), and can be used as part of the initial assessment process or as a regular review of treatment. A good assessment is often a valuable tool in helping an individual make changes in their life, particularly if it is done in an empathic and constructive manner. The SND is a form of node-link map, and follows the same principles. Node-link mapping is a simple technique for presenting verbal information in the form of a diagram or 'map' made up of 'nodes' containing key information and 'links' showing how this information is connected. It has been shown to have positive benefits for counselling interactions with clients, irrespective of the style of counselling used (Dansereau & Simpson, 2009; Dansereau, Dees, Greener, & Simpson, 1995):

- greater client readiness and motivation for treatment
- improved therapeutic relationship between clinician and client, and greater client perception of treatment session quality
- enhanced client confidence and self-esteem
- reduced the number of missed counselling sessions and positive urinalyses (for illicit drugs) during and after treatment

Observations of mapping-enhanced counselling sessions and discussions with counsellors suggest that this technique helps to create a sense of collaboration by taking the direct focus off the client and putting it on a diagram or map summarising the therapeutic issues. For clients who are uncomfortable maintaining eye contact, node-link mapping provides a relevant, alternative visual stimulus and therefore can reduce anxiety. Maps 'worked on' during a session can be given to a client as a prompt or structure for homework between sessions. They may also be reintroduced by the counsellor to evaluate changes and progress. The benefits of mapping make them a natural fit with attempts to turn the medically led process of 'treatment planning' into the positive and aspirational process of 'recovery planning'. As described by Borkman (1998), clients are directly responsible for developing their own recovery plans, within a context of help from positive peer role models (Borkman, 1998). Recovery planning 'becomes a skill acquired by clients', and node-link mapping is a technique that facilitates this.

In the spirit of all node-link maps, 'a picture is worth a thousand words'. When returning to a SND several days after it has been constructed with a client, clinicians report that it is easy to pick up the details of even the most complex cases using the brief notes and summaries included in the nodes. Less than a minute reviewing a SND can bring a wealth of material covered in a previous session to mind. The technique is easy to learn and can be supported by a number of available manuals or toolkits developed in the UK (Day, 2010, 2013).

The technique

The process of constructing a SND begins with a statement such as the following:

> I am going to ask you to think about people who have been important to you both recently and in the past. These might be people you have seen face-to-face, people you have spoken to on the phone, or people you have had contact with via social media. They could be family members, friends, acquaintances, fellow users, people in recovery, or professionals. As we talk about them we are going to mark them on this "social network diagram" so that we can get an understanding of the support you have from people around you.

It is important to note the focus on people who have been important to the client, rather than those that have been supportive. This has the result of highlighting drug users and sellers in addition to non-using family or friends. Group memberships exert influence through the transmission of social norms, and a strong link to a group of heavy drug users is a barrier to potential recovery. Social Identity Theory proposes that people's sense of self is derived from their membership of various social groups. The resulting social identities serve to structure an individual's values, norms and goals, i.e., what they think, what they do, and what they want to achieve (Best et al., 2016; Haslam, 2014). If a goal of the therapist is to help the client make contact with positive alternatives to existing group memberships, it is useful to map out the balance between those supporting and encouraging continuing use and those modelling positive aspects of recovery. When this technique is used in research a fixed timeframe (usually the past three months) is put on the process. However, in clinical practice it is often useful to elicit the names of people the client was friendly with before they became a regular user of drugs, as this group can both model recovery-focused social norms and be a key source of practical support. Such individuals carry none of the 'baggage' of the drug-using identity, and are often able to adopt a positive, forward-thinking approach to goal setting and behaviour change.

The actual appearance of the SND can take many forms, but there are three basic rules that should be followed:

1 The network must be drawn out on paper, rather than just discussed. As described above, the process of reducing a large amount of information to a few key 'nodes' is therapeutic in itself, and drawing it out tends to reveal information about the relational aspects of people in the network. Some people prefer to use a blank piece of paper, but structured templates such as the one in the Routes to Recovery manual (www.nta.nhs.uk/uploads/phemapping manual.pdf, page 40) often help to consider different potential groups of network members systematically, e.g., family members, friends, people in recovery.
2 Use actual names to represent each person. It is possible to use social roles instead of names (i.e., 'father', 'friend 1'), but this tends to get confusing and limits the utility of the SND as treatment moves forward. Initials or even pseudonyms can be used if the client is concerned about confidentiality.
3 The client and the clinician shouldn't stop adding names to the SND until all possibilities have been exhausted. The aim is to build up as full a picture as possible of the client's social network, including groups that the client perceives to be 'drug-users' and those with a more recovery-orientated focus. Various techniques have found to be useful in clinical practice, including:
   - systematically asking about different groups of potential network members e.g., immediate family, extended family, friends, friends of friends, acquaintances, work colleagues, professionals, old school friends and so on
   - working through the past week day by day asking 'who have you seen or spoken to in the last week?'
   - asking 'if I was to ask you to scroll through the address book/recent contacts list in your mobile phone, who would be in there?' (the client will often bring out their phone and do just that!)
   - asking 'if I asked your mum/partner/brother', who would they add to the diagram?

The results: benefits of the Social Network Diagram

The author has extensive experience of using this technique in both clinical and research contexts, as well as providing both individual and group supervision in its use, either as a stand-alone intervention or as part of the initial stages of Social Behaviour and Network Therapy (Copello, Orford, Hodgson, Tober, & Barrett, 2002; Copello et al., 2006). An example of a SND (see Figure 11.1) drawn by a clinician in OST services is provided (all names and other details have been changed to protect anonymity).

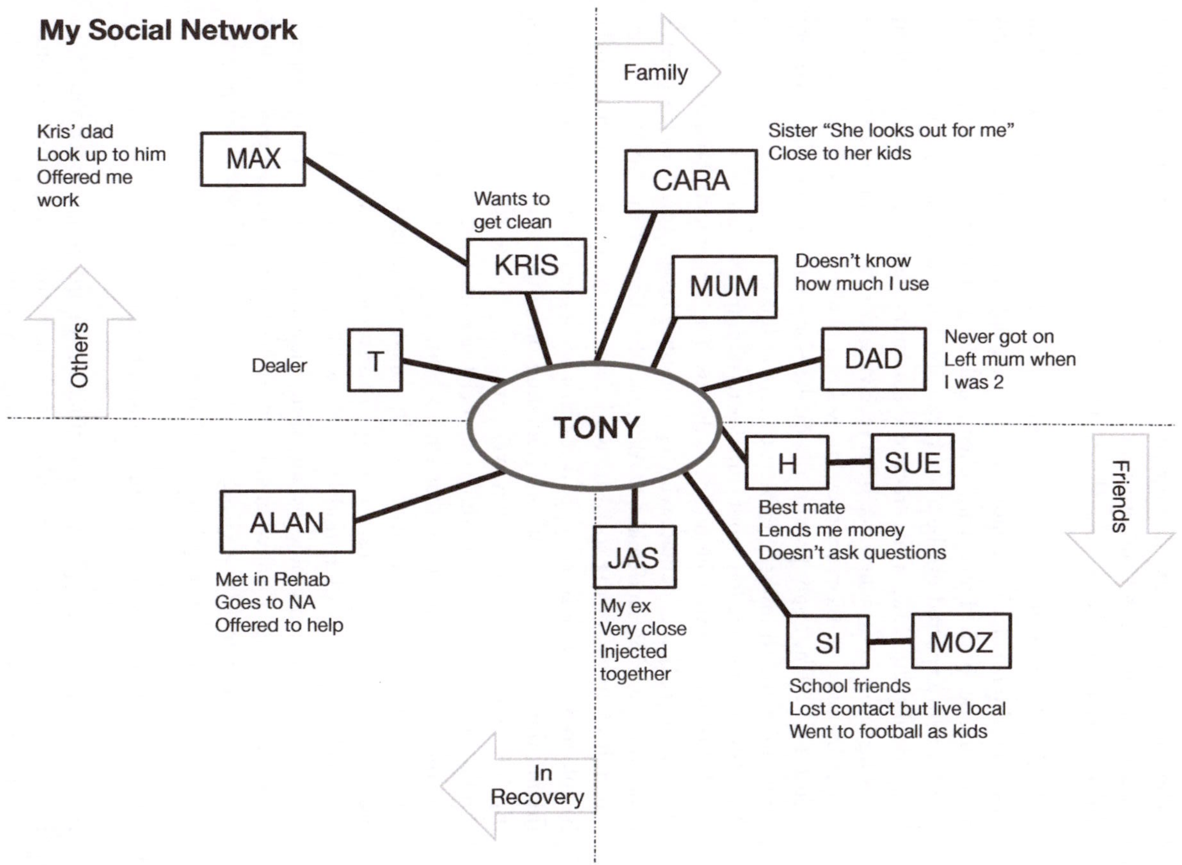

FIGURE 11.1 An example of a Social Network Diagram (SND).

Example

When asked to discuss their experience of producing a SND collaboratively with a client, most therapists comment that the process generated a lot of information that was new to them, even if they had been working with the client for some time. This may be due to the adoption of a completely new approach, or the use of a visual representation for the first time.

Clinicians have commented that the SND can:

1. Help the client to understand the make-up of their social network, and in particular the balance of supportive versus unsupportive people. The process often surprises both clinician and client, and the availability of more potential support than expected can be a boost to confidence and self-esteem.
2. Help to raise the issue of the 'recovery community'. It is noteworthy when working with clients who have been receiving OST for many years how few people in abstinent recovery they know (see the blank lower left quadrant in Figure 11.1). This might provide the catalyst for discussing the local recovery community and to instigate efforts at assertive linkage to it.
3. Provide more information about complex relationships within the family, which the client has previously felt unable to discuss. This might focus on their family of origin (e.g., lack of contact with a previously abusive father), or the client's own children and grandchildren. Although the focus of the SND is usually on adult members of the social network, and in particular those that might be able to provide positive support for change, some clinicians have reported finding the technique useful for elaborating on potential safeguarding issues involving children of which they were previously unaware.
4. Provide an insight into the different social identities that each person has. It is the author's experience that clients bring a particular identity to drug treatment services, influenced by the need to sustain benefits claims, prescriptions of medications, advocacy. This is not always a positive identity, and yet the process of considering the whole social network may bring to light very different sides to the same individual, e.g., a loving parent, a supportive sibling, a valued grandchild. If the SIMOR model predicts that recovery is sustained by a change in social identity, the SND can provide a valuable tool in clinical practice to start exploring this concept.

The SND is a direct route to two other forms of treatment.

1. Family members of people with substance use disorders have been shown to have very high rates of physical and mental health problems, and they are often an invisible population through a combination of stigma and ignorance. By identifying family members in the network who may benefit from support in their own right, the SND can help the clinician link people to effective therapies such as 5-Step treatment (Copello, Templeton, Orford, & Velleman, 2010a, 2010b), or to mutual self-help groups such as Al-Anon or Alateen.

2 Family or social network members can usually contribute to the treatment process. Formal, structured interventions such as Behavioural Couples Therapy or Social Behaviour and Network Therapy are recommended evidence-based treatments for both alcohol and drug problems in the UK (National Collaborating Centre for Mental Health, 2008; National Institute for Health and Clinical Excellence, 2010). However, even incorporating one positive network member into the treatment process can have beneficial outcomes (Litt et al., 2009), and incorporating positive role models into treatment is a key process in effective therapeutic strategies (Moos, 2007a, 2007b). The Routes to Recovery manual (Chapter 3) provides simple NLM tools for exploring and incorporating network members into relapse prevention plans and goals (Day, 2013).

Conclusions

The articulation of the SIMOR model has helped clinicians to focus on the social environment as a key mediator of behaviour change. Drug use is an activity that is subject to a wide variety of individual and environmental influences. Clinicians in OST clinics often focus on individual beliefs, attitudes and behaviours without considering the social environment in which they are constructed, tested and developed. One hour spent with a client every two to four weeks provides a narrow window into their world, and may fail to capture important influences that the client is subject to for the remainder of the time. If the process of recovery is underpinned by a change in social identity, it is important to assess the groups that an individual has regular contact with and with which they identify. A systematic attempt to help the client change their social identity is a valid therapeutic strategy, and constructing a SND is a useful first step. By understanding the people that are important to the client and with whom they spend most time, the clinician can adopt clinical strategies to connect the client to new forms of social support (e.g., by assertive linkage to communities of recovery community) or to better utilise the support that they already have.

A systematic process of training clinicians to use the SND in clinical practice is underway in Solihull in the English West Midlands. This process will explore the process from the perspective of both the clinicians and their clients, helping to map out the groups that are important to clients in OST. The second stage of the process will involve training clinicians to utilise information obtained from the SND to either invite members of the client's social network into treatment sessions, link them to support in their own right, or assertively link clients to mutual self-help groups such as NA or Self-Management and Recovery Training (SMART). It may then be possible to quantify the effect that such an approach has on treatment outcomes and the attitudes and beliefs of both clients and clinicians.

References

Abbott, P. J. (2009). A review of the Community Reinforcement Approach in the treatment of opioid dependence. *Journal of Psychoactive Drugs, 41*, 379–385.

Abbott, P. J., Weller, S. B., Delaney, H. D., & Moore, B. A. (1998). Community reinforcement approach in the treatment of opiate addicts. *American Journal of Drug and Alcohol Abuse, 24*, 17–30.

Anglin, M. D., Hser, Y-I., & Grella, C. E. (1997). Drug addiction and treatment careers among clients in the Drug Abuse Treatment Outcome Study (DATOS). *Psychology of Addictive Behaviours, 11*, 308–323.

Anthony, J. C., Warner, L. A., & Kessler, R. C. (1994). Comparative epidemiology of dependence on tobacco, alcohol, controlled substances, and inhalants: Basic findings from the National Comorbidity Survey. *Experimental and Clinical Psychopharmacology, 2*, 244–268.

Azrin, N. H., Sisson, R. W., Meyers, R. J., & Godley, M. D. (1982). Alcoholism treatment by disulfiram and community reinforcement therapy. *Journal of Behavioural Therapy and Experimental Psychiatry, 13*, 105–112.

Barber, J. G. & Crisp, B. R. (1995). Social support and prevention of relapse following treatment for alcohol abuse. *Research on Social Work Practice, 5*, 283–296.

Baumeister, R. F. & Leary, M. A. (1995). The need to belong: Desire for interpersonal attachments as a fundamental human motivation. *Psychological Bulletin, 117*, 497–529.

Beattie, M. C. (2001). Meta-analysis of social relationships and posttreatment drinking outcomes: Comparison of relationship structure, function and quality. *Journal of Studies on Alcohol, 62*, 518–527.

Beattie, M. C. & Longabaugh, R. (1997). Interpersonal factors and post-treatment drinking and subjective well-being. *Addiction, 92*, 1507–1521.

Beattie, M. C. & Longabough, R. L. (1999). General and alcohol-specific social support following treatment. *Addictive Behaviors, 24*, 593–606.

Beattie, M. C., Longabaugh, R., & Fava, J. (1992). Assessment of alcohol-related workplace activities: Development and testing of 'Your Workplace'. *Journal of Studies on Alcohol, 53*, 469–475.

Best, D., Beckwith, M., Haslam, C., Haslam, S. A., Jetten, J., Mawson, E., & Lubman, D. I. (2016). Overcoming alcohol and other drug addiction as a process of social identity transition: The social identity model of recovery (SIMOR). *Addiction Research & Theory, 24*, 111–123.

Best, D., Day, E., & Morgan, B. (2006). *Addiction careers and the natural history of change*. London: National Treatment Agency for Substance Misuse.

Best, D., Ghufran, S., Day, E., Ray, R., & Loaring, J. (2008). Breaking the habit: A retrospective analysis of desistance factors among formerly problematic heroin users. *Drug and Alcohol Review, 27*, 619–624.

Best, D., Hernando, R., Gossop, M., Sidwell, C., & Strang, J. (2003). Getting by with a little help from your friends: The impact of peer networks on criminality in a cohort of treatment-seeking drug users. *Addictive Behaviours, 28*, 597–603.

Best, D., Rome, A., Hanning, K. A., White, W., Gossop, M., Taylor, A., & Perkins, A. (2010). *Research for recovery: A review of the drugs evidence base*. Edinburgh, UK: Scottish Government Social Research.

Booth, B. M., Russell, D. W., Soucek, S., & Laughlin, P. R. (1992). Social support and outcome of alcoholism treatment: An exploratory analysis. *The American Journal of Drug and Alcohol Abuse, 18*, 87–101.

Borkman, T. J. (1998). Is recovery planning any different from treatment planning? *Journal of Substance Abuse Treatment, 15*, 37–42.

Brigham, G. S., Slesnick, N., Winhusen, T. M., Lewis, D. F., Guo, X., & Somoza, E. (2014). A randomized pilot clinical trial to evaluate the efficacy of Community Reinforcement and Family Training for Treatment Retention (CRAFT-T) for improving outcomes for patients completing opioid detoxification. *Drug and Alcohol Dependence, 138*, 240–243.

Brooner, R. K. & Kidorf, M. (2002). Using behavioral reinforcement to improve methadone treatment participation. *Science & Practice Perspectives, 1*, 38–48.

Carstensen, L. L. (1995). Evidence for a life-span theory of socioemotional selectivity. *Current Directions in Psychological Science, 4*, 151–156.

Cohen, S., Gottlieb, B. H., & Underwood, L. G. (2000). Social relationships and health. In S. Cohen, L. G. Underwood & B. H. Gottlieb (Eds.), *Social support measurement and intervention* (pp. 3-25). New York: Oxford University Press.

Connock, M., Juarez-Garcia, A., Jowett, S., Frew, E., Liu, Z., Fry-Smith, A., . . . & Taylor, R. (2006). Methadone and Buprenorphine for the management of opioid dependence: A systematic review and economic evaluation. *Health Technology Assessment, 11*, 1–171.

Copello, A., & Orford, J. (2002). Addiction and the family: Is it time for services to take notice of the evidence? *Addiction, 97*, 1361–1363.

Copello, A., Orford, J., Hodgson, R., & Tober, G. (2009). *Social behaviour and network therapy for alcohol problems*. London: Routledge.

Copello, A., Orford, J., Hodgson, R., Tober, G., & Barrett, C. (2002). Social behaviour and network therapy – basic principles and early experiences. *Addictive Behaviours, 27*, 345–366.

Copello, A. & Templeton, L. (2012). *Adult family members affected by a relative's substance misuse: A UK-wide survey of services for adult family members*. London: UK Drug Policy Commission.

Copello, A., Templeton, L., Orford, J., & Velleman, R. (2010a). The 5-Step Method: Evidence of gains for affected family members. *Drugs: Education, Prevention, and Policy, 17*, 100–112.

Copello, A., Templeton, L., Orford, J., & Velleman, R. (2010b). The 5-Step Method: principles and practice. *Drugs: Education, Prevention, and Policy, 17*, 86–99.

Copello, A., Templeton, L., & Powell, J. (2010). The impact of addiction on the family: Estimates of prevalence and costs. *Drugs: Education, Prevention and Policy, 17*, 63–74.

Copello, A. G., Templeton, L., & Velleman, R. (2006). Family interventions for drug and alcohol misuse: is there a best practice? *Current Opinion in Psychiatry, 19*, 271–276.

Copello, A., Velleman, R., & Templeton, L. (2005). Family interventions in the treatment of alcohol and drug problems. *Drug and Alcohol Review, 24*, 369–385.

Copello, A. & Walsh, K. (In press). Families, friends and addiction: Impacts, psychological models and interventions. In P. Davis, R. Patton & S. Jackson (Eds.), *Addiction psychology and treatment*. Oxford: Wiley Blackwell.

Copello, A., Williamson, E., Orford, J., & Day, E. (2006). Implementing and Evaluating social behaviour and network therapy in drug treatment practice in the UK: A feasibility study. *Addictive Behaviors, 31*, 802–810.

Dansereau, D. F., Dees, S. M., Greener, J. M., & Simpson, D. D. (1995). Node-link mapping and the evaluation of drug abuse counseling sessions. *Psychology of Addictive Behaviors, 9*, 195–203.

Dansereau, D. F. & Simpson, D. D. (2009). A picture is worth a thousand words: The case for graphic representations. *Professional Psychology: Research and Practice, 40*, 104–110.

Darke, S. (2011). *The life of the heroin user: Typical beginnings, trajectories and outcomes*. Cambridge: Cambridge University Press.

Day, E. (2010). *Routes to recovery via criminal justice: Mapping using manual*. London: National Treatment Agency for Substance Misuse.

Day, E. (2013). *Routes to recovery via the community*. London: Public Health England.

Day, E., Copello, A., Karia, M., Roche, J., Grewal, P., George, S., . . . & Chohan, G. (2013). Social network support for individuals receiving opiate substitution treatment and its association with treatment progress. *European Addiction Research, 19*, 211–221.

Day, E., Gaston, R. L., Furlong, E., Murali, V., & Copello, A. (2005). UK substance misuse treatment workers' attitudes to twelve-Step self-help groups. *Journal of Substance Abuse Treatment, 29*, 321–327.

Day, E., Wall, R., Chohan, G., & Seddon, J. (2015). Perceptions of professional drug treatment staff in England about client barriers to narcotics anonymous attendance. *Addiction Research & Theory, 23*, 223–230.

El-Bassel, N., Chen, D. R., & Cooper, D. (1998). Social support and social network profiles among women on methadone. *Social Service Review, 72*, 379–401.

Galanter, M. (1999). *Network therapy for alcohol and drug abuse*. New York: Guilford Press.

Galanter, M., Dermatis, H., Glickman, L., Maslansky, R., Sellers, M. B., Neumann, E., & Rahman-Dujarric, C. (2004). Network therapy: decreased secondary opioid use during buprenorphine maintenance. *Journal of Substance Abuse Treatment, 26*, 313–318.

Galanter, M., Dermatis, H., Keller, D., & Trujillo, M. (2002). Network therapy for cocaine abuse: Use of family and peer supports. *The American Journal on Addictions, 11*, 161–166.

Goehl, L., Nunes, E., Quitkin, F., & Hilton, I. (1993). Social networks and methadone treatment outcome: The costs and benefits of social ties. *American Journal of Drug and Alcohol Abuse, 19*, 251–262.

Gogineni, A., Stein, M., & Friedmann, P. D. (2001). Social relationships and intravenous drug use among methadone maintenance patients. *Drug and Alcohol Dependence, 64*, 47–53.

Gordon, A. J. & Zrull, M. (1991). Social networks and recovery: One year after inpatient treatment. *Journal of Substance Abuse Treatment, 8*, 143–152.

Gossop, M., Marsden, J., Stewart, D., Lehmann, C., Edwards, C., Wilson, A., & Segar, G. (1997). The National Treatment Outcome Research Study in the United Kingdom: six-month follow-up outcomes. *Psychology of Addictive Behaviors, 11*, 324–327.

Gottlieb, B. H. (1988). Marshaling social support: The state of the art in research and practice. In B. H. Gottlieb (Ed.), *Marshaling social support. Formats, processes and effects*. Newbury Park, CA: Sage.

Granfield, R. & Cloud, W. (1999). *Coming clean: Overcoming addiction without treatment*. New York: New York University Press.

Granfield, R. & Cloud, W. (2001). 'Social context and natural recovery': The role of social capital in the resolution of drug-associated problems. *Substance Use & Misuse, 36*, 1543–1570.

Haslam, S. A. (2014). Making good theory practical: Five lessons for an Applied Social Identity Approach to challenges of organizational, health and clinical psychology. *British Journal of Social Psychology, 53*, 1–20.

Havassy, B. E., Hall, S. M., & Wasserman, D. A. (1991). Social support and relapse: Commonalities among alcoholics, opiate users, and cigarette smokers. *Addictive Behaviors, 16*, 235–246.

Higgins, S. T., Budney, A. J., Bickel, W. K., & Badger, G. J. (1994). Participation of significant others in outpatient behavioural treatment predicts greater cocaine abstinence. *American Journal of Drug And Alcohol Abuse, 20*, 47–56.

Holt-Lunstad, J., Smith, T. B., & Layton, J. B. (2010). Social relationships and mortality risk: A meta-analytic review. *PLoS Medicine*, 7, e1000316.

Hser, Y-I. (2007). Predicting long-term stable recovery from heroin addiction: Findings from a 33-year follow-up study. *Journal of Addictive Diseases, 26*, 51–60.

Hser, Y-I., Evans, E., Grella, C., Ling, W., & Anglin, M. D. (2015). Long-term course of opioid addiction. *Harvard Review of Psychiatry, 23*, 76–89.

Hser, Y-I., Longshore, D., & Anglin, M. D. (2007). The life course perspective on drug use: A conceptual framework for understanding drug use trajectories. *Evaluation Review, 31*, 515–546.

Humphreys, K. (2004). *Circles of recovery: Self-help organizations for addiction*. Cambridge: Cambridge University Press.

Humphreys, K., Moos, R. H., & Finney, J. W. (1996). Life domains. Alcoholics Anonymous and role incumbency in the 3-year course of problem drinking. *Journal of Nervous and Mental Disease, 184*, 475–481.

Humphreys, K., Wing, S., McCarty, D., Chappel, J., Gallant, L., Haberle, B., . . . & Weiss, R. (2004). Self-help organizations for alcohol and drug problems: Toward evidence-based practice and policy. *Journal of Substance Abuse Treatment, 26*, 151–158.

Hunter-Reel, D., McCrady, B., & Hildebrandt, T. (2009). Emphasizing interpersonal factors: an extension of the Witkiewitz and Marlatt relapse model. *Addiction, 104*, 1281–1290.

Hunter-Reel, D., McCrady, B. S., Hildebrandt, T., & Epstein, E. E. (2010). Indirect effect of social support for drinking on drinking outcomes: The role of motivation. *Journal of Studies on Alcohol and Drugs, 71*, 930–937.

Joe, G. W., Chastain, R. L., & Simpson, D. D. (1990). Length of careers. In D. D. Simpson & S. B. Sells (Eds.), *Opioid addiction and treatment: A 12-year follow-up*. Malabar, FL: Keiger.

Kahn, R. L., & Antonucci, T. C. (1980). Convoys over the life course: Attachment, roles and social support. In P. B. Baltes & O. G. Brim Jr. (Eds.), *Life-span development and behavior* (Vol. 3) (pp. 253–286). New York, NY: Academic Press.

Kelly, J. F., Magill, M., & Stout, R. L. (2009). How do people recover from alcohol dependence? A systematic review on mechanisms of behaviour change in Alcoholics Anonymous. *Addiction Research and Theory, 17*, 236–259.

Kidorf, M., Brooner, R. K., & King, V. L. (1997). Motivating methadone patients to include drug-free significant others in treatment: A behavioral intervention. *Journal of Substance Abuse Treatment, 14*, 23–28.

Latkin, C. A., Knowlton, A. R., Hoover, D., & Mandell, W. (1999). Drug Network Characteristics as a Predictor of Drug Use Among Adult Injection Drug Users: A Prospective Study. *The American Journal of Drug and Alcohol Abuse, 25*, 463–473.

Laudet, A. B. & White, W. L. (2005). An exploratory investigation of the association between clinicians' attitudes toward twelve-step groups and referral rates. *Alcoholism Treatment Quarterly, 23*, 31–45.

Litt, M. D., Kadden, R. M., Kabela-Cormier, E., & Petry, N. (2009). Changing network support for drinking: network support project 2-year follow-up. *Journal Of Consulting and Clinical Psychology, 77*, 229–242.

Lloyd, J. J., Strathdee, S. A., Pu, M., Havens, J. R., Cornelius, L. J., Huettner, S., & Latkin, C. A. (2008). The impact of opiate agonist maintenance therapy on drug use within social networks of injecting drug users. *The American Journal on Addictions, 17*, 414–421.

Longabaugh, R., Beattie, M. C., Noel, N., Stout, R., & Malloy, P. (1993). The effect of social investment on treatment outcome. *Journal of Studies on Alcohol, 54*, 465–478.

Longabaugh, R., Wirtz, P. W., Beattie, M. C., Noel, N., & Stout, R. (1995). Matching treatment focus to patient social investment and support. 18-month follow-up results. *Journal of Consulting and Clinical Psychology, 63*, 296–307.

Longabaugh, R., Wirtz, P. W., Zweben, A., & Stout, R. L. (1998). Network support for drinking, Alcoholics Anonymous and long-term matching effects. *Addiction, 93*, 1313–1333.

McCrady, B. S. (2004). To have but one true friend: Implications for practice of research on alcohol use disorders and social networks. *Psychology of Addictive Behaviors, 18*, 113–121.

McCrady, B. S., Hayaki, J., Epstein, E. E., & Hirsch, L. S. (2002). Testing hypothesized predictors of change in conjoint behavioral alcoholism treatment for men. *Alcoholism: Clinical and Experimental Research, 26*, 463–470.

McIntosh, J. & McKeganey, N. (2000). Addicts' narratives of recovery from drug use: constructing a non-addict identity. *Social Science & Medicine, 50*, 1501–1510.

McIntosh, J. & McKeganey, N. (2006). The recovery from dependent drug use: Addicts' strategies for reducing the risk of relapse. *Drugs: Education, Prevention and Policy*, 7, 179–192.

Manning, V., Best, D., Faulkner, N., Titherington, E., Morinana, A., Keaney, F., . . . & Strang, J. (2012). Does active referral by a doctor or 12-Step peer improve 12-Step meeting attendance? Results from a pilot randomised control trial. *Drug and Alcohol Dependence, 126*, 131–137.

Meyers, R. J. & Smith, J. E. (1995). *Clinical guide to alcohol treatment: The community reinforcement approach*. New York: The Guilford Press.

Mohr, C. D., Averna, S., Kenny, D. A., & Del Boca, F. K. (2001). 'Getting by (or getting high) with a little help from my friends': An examination of adult alcoholics' friendships. *Journal of Studies on Alcohol, 62*, 637–645.

Moos, R. H. (2007a). Theory-based active ingredients of effective treatments for substance use disorders. *Drug and Alcohol Dependence, 88*, 109–121.

Moos, R. H. (2007b). Theory-based processes that promote the remission of substance use disorders. *Clinical Psychology Review, 27*, 537–551.

Mowbray, O., Quinn, A., & Cranford, J. A. (2014). Social networks and alcohol use disorders: Findings from a nationally representative sample. *The American Journal of Drug and Alcohol Abuse, 40*, 181–186.

Mowbray, O., & Scott, J. A. (2015). The effect of drug use disorder onset, remission or persistence on an individual's personal social network. *The American Journal on Addictions, 24*, 427–434.

National Collaborating Centre for Mental Health. (2008). *Drug misuse: Psychosocial interventions*. London: British Psychological Society & The Royal College of Psychiatrists.

National Institute for Health and Clinical Excellence. (2010). *Alcohol-use disorders: Diagnosis and clinical management of alcohol-related physical complications*. Clinical guideline 100. London: NICE.

Putnam, R. D. (2000). *Bowling alone: The collapse and revival of American community*. New York: Simon & Schuster.

Ray, G. T., Mertens, J. R., & Weisner, C. (2009). Family members of people with alcohol or drug dependence: health problems and medical cost compared to family members of people with diabetes and asthma. *Addiction, 104*, 203–214.

Ronel, N., Gueta, K., Abramsohn, Y., Caspi, N., & Adelson, M. (2010). Can a 12-step program work in methadone maintenance treatment? *International Journal of Offender Therapy and Comparative Criminology, 55*, 1135–1153.

Rosenberg, H. (1983). Relapsed versus non-relapsed alcohol abusers: Coping skills, life events, and social support. *Addictive Behaviors, 8*, 183–186.

Rosenfeld, M. J. & Thomas, R. J. (2012). Searching for a mate: The rise of the internet as a social intermediary. *American Sociological Review*, 77, 523–547.

Schroeder, J. R., Latkin, C. A., Hoover, D. R., Curry, A. D., Knowlton, A. R., & Celentano, D. D. (2001). Illicit drug use in one's social network and in one's neighbourhood predicts individual heroin and cocaine use. *Annals of Epidemiology, 11*, 389–394.

The UKATT Research Team. (2001). United Kingdom Alcohol Treatment Trial (UKATT): hypothesis, design and methods. *Alcohol & Alcoholism, 36*, 11–21.

Timko, C., DeBenedetti, A., & Billow, R. (2006). Intensive referral to 12-step self-help groups and 6-month substance use disorder outcomes. *Addiction, 101*, 678–688.

Tracy, E. M. & Biegel, D. E. (2006). Regular social networks and dual disorders: A literature review and implications for practice and future research. *Journal of Dual Diagnosis, 2*, 59–88.

United Nations Office on Drugs and Crime. (2015). *World drug report 2015*. United Nations publication, Sales No. E.15.XI.6.

Vederhus, J.-K., Kristensen, O., Laudet, A., & Clausen, T. (2009). Attitudes towards 12-step groups and referral practices in a 12-step naive treatment culture; a survey of addiction professionals in Norway. *BMC Health Services Research, 9*, 147.

Wall, R. S. A. & Day, E. (2014). What influences referral to 12-Step mutual self-help groups by treatment professionals. *European Addiction Research, 20*, 241–247.

Wasserman, D. A., Stewart, A. L., & Delucchi, K. L. (2001). Social support and abstinence from opiates and cocaine during opioid maintenance treatment. *Drug and Alcohol Dependence, 65*, 65–75.

White, W., Budnick, C., & Pickard, B. (2011). Narcotics Anonymous: A chronology of the scientific and professional literature. Retrieved from: www.williamwhitepapers.com.

White, W., & Cloud, W. (2008). Recovery capital: A primer for addictions professionals. *Counselor, 9*, 22–27.

White, W. L. (2008). *Recovery management and recovery-oriented systems of care: Scientific rationale and promising practices*. Chicago, IL: Northeast Addiction Technology Transfer Center, the Great Lakes Addiction Technology Transfer Center, and the Philadelphia Department of Behavioral Health/Mental Retardation Services.

White, W. L. (2011). *Narcotics anonymous and the pharmacotherapeutic treatment of opioid addiction in the United States*. Chicago, IL: Philadelphia Department of Behavioral Health and Intellectual Disability Services & Great Lakes Addiction Technology Transfer Center.

White, W. L., Campbell, M. D., Shea, C., Hoffman, H. A., Crissman, B., & DuPont, R. L. (2013). Coparticipation in 12-Step mutual aid groups and methadone maintenance treatment: A survey of 322 patients. *Journal of Groups in Addiction & Recovery, 8*, 294–308.

Williamson, E., Smith, M., Orford, J., Copello, A., & Day, E. (2007). Social behaviour and network therapy for drug problems: Evidence of benefits and challenges. *Addictive Disorders and Their Treatment, 6*, 167–179.

Wrzus, C., Hänel, M., Wagner, J., & Neyer, F. J. (2013). Social network changes and life events across the life span: A meta-analysis. *Psychological Bulletin, 139*, 53–80.

Zywiak, W. H., Longabaugh, R., & Wirtz, P. W. (2002). Decomposing the relationships between pretreatment social network characteristics and alcohol treatment outcome. *Journal of Studies on Alcohol, 63*, 114–121.

12

ADDICTION, BEHAVIOURAL CHANGE AND SOCIAL IDENTITY

Overview and concluding comments

David Best and Sarah A. Buckingham

Editing this book has been a genuine pleasure that is a result of the commitment of the contributors and the wealth of materials that we have been presented with. While the primary objective of the volume was to bring together innovations in social identity theory and summarise the contribution that they have made to understanding the complex and contentious subject of recovery from substance addiction, much broader conceptual and methodological issues and innovations have been presented in the course of the book.

The challenge

Following our overview in Chapter 1, where the basic definitions and conceptual origins of both recovery and social identity theory are laid out, Haslam in Chapter 2 offers a broad context for the development of social identity approaches in applied contexts, but challenges those who attempt to do so to be aware of and engage with the "political" in their endeavours. What Haslam argues is that the power of social identities is embedded within groups and so to mobilise the huge potential of social identity approaches requires applied social identity practitioners to work with and not against the groups they engage. This is an enormous challenge to those from positivistic research backgrounds and to clinicians and practitioners who have spent years developing specialisms and expertise that allows them to assert their primacy in clinical and applied decision-making.

The challenge is, however, entirely consistent with a recovery philosophy that promotes peer engagement (White, 2009) and an underling principle of empowerment (Leamy et al., 2011). For this reason, the recovery research area – and the equivalent "positive" approaches to mental health recovery, restorative justice and positive psychology – are all predicated on a model of transparency, engagement and empowerment and this should provide a philosophical foundation for this process of inclusion. However, it is also a methodological concern, especially for those who are using quantitative methods predicated on positivistic assumptions (such as the use of implicit associations or the secondary analysis of social media posts) to ensure that the application of their work at the very least engages and empowers the groups they study and work with.

The second key point that Haslam argues, in relation to politics, is that "applied research . . . puts researchers on the spot by requiring them to make choices about the social identities they want to promote". While at one level this may seem straight-forward in the context of recovery – most researchers would say that recovery is a good thing – and so is not like studying the social identities of Jihadists or Nazis, it does provoke challenging questions about moving from 'bad' social groups and identities to 'good' ones. Much of the work on social network mapping has been around the idea that recovery is associated with moving from using to pro-social networks and we have to be aware that it is the meaning and value that group members ascribe to the groups that we need to work with and that we need to avoid simplistic categorisations and value judgement on groups that are associated with complex social identities. The next section will turn to addressing how our contributors have approached Haslam's final challenge – of how application can develop theory and how theory can be applied and deployed to improve practice.

Applying social identity theory around recovery activities

The contributions to this book have addressed the issues raised by Haslam in three key ways, each of which will be addressed in turn:

1 by improving the conceptualisation and framing of recovery from addiction
2 by introducing novel methods and techniques for the study of recovery processes and activities
3 by extending the scope of the recovery model to address other areas where a recovery and social identity perspective can improve our understanding

Contributing innovation in the understanding of recovery

Kelly, Bergman and Vilsaint's chapter provides an overview of the evidence around mutual help organisations (MHOs) and recovery and in particular the evidence for the role of Alcoholics Anonymous in recovery. The chapter summarises the research evidence showing the impact of MHO involvement not only on substance use but also on mental health problems and on quality of life. The key link in this review is around the importance of network support for sobriety and the evidence that transitions in peer groups (from those supportive of drinking to those supportive of recovery) play an important role in the recovery process. Critically, the paper reviews the evidence for the mechanisms underpinning behaviour change concluding that "those who help others also help themselves by reinforcing their own desire to change, increasing their self-esteem through the perception of helpfulness to others, and enhancing their self-efficacy and sense of autonomy". The authors conclude that the sense of belonging and identification generated in such groups increases commitment to group values and norms and so leads to a commitment to the resultant behaviours, and so suggesting that the evidence for the effectiveness of mutual help organisations is entirely consistent with a social identity approach.

Malton combines social influence theory with a social identity model in an analysis of original data drawn from a study of a drug and alcohol rehabilitation programme in UK prisons. Using Fiske's (2004) model of social influence, Malton argues that behaviour change can be propelled through a small number of social motives that are manifest in group treatment programmes that draw on the kind of mutual help organisations overviewed by Kelly and colleagues. The author argues that not only can such motives explain the onset of offending and substance use (and the link between the two) but that this model has a critical role to play in desistance and recovery. Malton's emphasis on belonging as a key component in shaping values and beliefs is entirely consistent with the theme of social identity transition critical to the recovery process outlined in this volume.

Buckingham's work on social identity with a group of smokers who have all attempted to quit introduces the Associative Reflective Model of Social Identification (ARMS) to explore the link between conscious (reflective) and implicit (associative) identification processes and goes on, through empirical testing, to demonstrate the importance of non-reflective processing in predicting the likelihood of relapse or indeed sustaining effective behavioural change. This not only addresses potential concerns about self-presentational biases in research respondents who have desires about the social desirability of their group memberships, it may also help to uncover entrenched commitments to identities that the individual themselves is not aware of. From a science perspective, the implicit approach may also increase the variance in behaviour that social identity approaches can offer and may provide the foundations for an enhanced and comprehensive model of social identity.

A second contribution from South Bank University is presented in Frings and Albery's chapter reviewing the evidence in favour of the Social Identity Model of Cessation Maintenance (SIMCM). SIMCM also integrates the ideas of implicit and explicit identity and is based on the impact of salience of a recovery identity on self-categorisation and efficacy. The authors also argue that membership of a group that promotes substance use cessation will generate a positive differentiation between the self-as-a-group member and members of other groups, which in turn helps to build self-esteem. Frings and Albury go on to assert the importance of the interpretation of context in the assessment of options and opportunities in a given situation. Basing this work on the group therapy context, they argue that listening to narratives of successful change help to generate both a set of social pay-offs and supports that they can change the cost-benefit assessment of high-risk situations for substance misuse relapse.

However, Frings and Albery also argue that such processes are not exclusively conscious, arguing "that in all likelihood the initial cognitive activity associated with a perceived stimulus is likely to be that characterised by implicit processes" that they assert increases the predictive power of social identity models. Furthermore, such approaches also extend the methodologies available to social identity researchers from the questionnaire (with associated issues of self-presentational bias) to more experimental approaches characterised by the Implicit Association Test. They suggest that not only may such identities not be accessible to conscious process, but that when motivation or cognitive resources are limited, implicit identities may be particularly important for the process of self-categorisation and so decision-making. The authors conclude by suggesting that, when recovery-oriented identities are activated, their effects are mediated not only by conscious processes such as contextualisation and social support but also by implicit processes such as selective attention.

Innovative methodologies in social identity research

The use, by both Buckingham and by Frings and Albery, of Implicit Association tests to tap into pre-conscious identities, is one example of how research questions in the area of social identity has extended the research methods available and used in recovery research. In this section we will explore three more such approaches – the Social Identity Mapping model outlined by Haslam et al., a second clinical visualisation technique reported by Day, and the social network analysis of social media posts deployed by Bliuc and colleagues.

Social Identity Mapping (SIM), was originally developed in the context of organisational psychology (e.g., Reynolds, Eggins, & Haslam, 2010), but has been adapted for a range of clinical contexts (Cruwys, Steffens, Haslam, Haslam, Jetten, & Dingle, 2016). This model was then adapted to the context of addiction recovery by Best et al. (2014) to map each group in terms of the number of active users, social users, non-users, and those in recovery. This creates a visualisation method that has both research and clinical implications, mapping group membership and identity against the use profiles of groups, identifying those social identities consistent with and inimical to recovery aspirations.

The method actively engages the participant and gives them a greater sense of feedback and ownership than is achieved by completing multiple questionnaires and provides a richness and diversity of data that can be explored and built upon over time using the same or repeat maps. This approach provides a method of collecting social identity data that could be developed electronically in the form of an app or an online self-help package, and the evolution of social identity maps over time and across recovery journeys provides a convenient and accessible way to gather large amounts of data on issues as diverse as group membership, internal cohesion and inter-group conflict which can be used to predict changes in recovery status over time.

Linked to this, and also embedded within a clinical tradition, is the contribution by Day, which involves the use of node link mapping around social networks. The Social Network Diagram (SND) comes from a strong UK and US heritage of using visual 'maps' to support the therapeutic engagement based on a strong and consistent evidence base (Dansereau & Simpson, 2009; Dansereau, Dees, Greener, & Simpson, 1995). As Day argues, the SND can help to clarify issues around social networks with clients but can also provide a mechanism for raising issues about recovery communities and groups, and to address questions of existing and emerging social identities. Compared to the SIM technique outlined above, the focus is more closely on individual relationships but both techniques create visual ways of engaging research participants (or clients) in a creative task that brings issues of networks and identity to the forefront and by doing so provides a vehicle for linking networks, and the meaning they have for people, to the recovery process.

The third method that has been explored in the mapping of recovery and identity is based on social network analysis using data from social media. Bliuc et al. have used information available through open access social media (in this case posts and comments on a Facebook page) to construct a social network map and generate a series of hypotheses about movements and transitions within the network as markers of social identification and belonging. While the chapter primarily outlines methodological options and new opportunities that arise both from a new type of data and from a set of technologies that allow its capture and analysis, data are also presented about the evolution of online social media activity in a recovery community linked to housing and employment. This analysis demonstrates not only the pattern of growth of a social network but also how its development is linked to both bonding and bridging capital – in other words the incorporation of new group members and the management of their relationships with those outside the active membership of the group.

What the Facebook analysis offers is a low-cost, replicable and convenient method of tracking both the group and the individual within the group through not only social network analysis but also through linguistic analysis of content. Thus, there is an accessible documentary source that allows the measurement of changes in both the content of activity and its linguistic consistency with other members of the network (a strong marker of social identification). This data is incredibly rich in terms of the capacity for assessing linguistic markers of identity, of tracking the emotional tone and belonging (identification) in posts and the extent of social acceptance to posts by other members of the network. This creates a new 'lexicon' for social identity research that can be linked to more traditional research methods – mapping retention in services and interviews assessing social functioning and wellbeing.

In all three of these examples, new research methods (social identity mapping and online social network analysis) provide novel methods for capturing aspects of social networks and social identities that can both stand alone and be merged into wider programmes of mixed methods research. Two of the methods create bridges between research and clinical practice (and in doing so generate opportunities for reflection on the importance of social networks not only to identity but also to esteem and wellbeing), and all three increase the scope and potential for research in this area. However, as the social media analysis demonstrates, in doing so, they provide ways of testing new questions and generating insights into the process of social identification that would be impossible to obtain in other ways. Thus, using the online network, we are able to test how language shifts as people move within the network and what impact reinforcement of communication has in binding individuals to groups and the values and goals of the group.

Extending the social networks and recovery model to other areas of investigation

There are two key contributions in this area – one relating to the extension of the work to young people and the second to the management and treatment of obesity. Miller, Wakefield and Sani discuss group identification issues for young people with substance misuse problems, in the context of the identity transitions (personal and social) that characterise the transitions through adolescence. The authors argue for the importance of group factors in a range of health behaviours suggesting that "the quality of [such] relationships (e.g., having a sense of connectedness, good communication, support, involvement, and belonging within the group) can help protect against risky health behaviours and mental health problems". Thus, the authors report on previous research showing that high peer engagement and group commitment has been linked to smoking behaviour in adolescents, and they make the point that commitment to the peer group can be either beneficial or harmful, depending on the norms of the group. However, the authors report on their own previous research suggesting that multiple group involvement may be protective against the harmful norms of any one group, and conclude that the key health implication is the need to provide means to link young people engaged in risky or harmful behaviours to groups with healthy norms. There are two issues – one around interventions and a second around multiple group memberships that will be returned to in the concluding section below.

The final chapter for consideration in this section takes a public health perspective to addressing the issue of obesity using a social identity model. Farrow, Tarrant and Khan start from the assumption that "there is now a large body of evidence demonstrating that connections to and within social groups are important determinants of people's cognitions about what are healthy and acceptable behaviours, as well as their motivation and engagement with those behaviours". While the authors discuss naturally occurring groups, the authors also consider the clinical implications of social identity and group effects on obesity and touch on similar territory to Bliuc and colleagues by considering the implications of online support groups and the potential they offer for studying social networks through a virtual platform. The authors report on their own research on group weight loss programmes and find that there is a strong social identification component to the engagement and effectiveness of these groups. What is particularly notable about their findings is the association reported between the level of social identification with the group and the perception of support from participating in it.

Overall conclusions – addressing the Haslam challenge

The key question that we started this concluding chapter with was around the 'political' in social identity theorising and practice. Haslam argued that we should prioritise the social in identity and the importance that SIT places on personal and subjective definitions of groups and identities. The most obvious way this challenge is addressed in the current work is through the clinical research techniques of Day and Haslam and colleagues who have developed clinical research methods that attempt to unpick and make sense of the subjective experience of social identity and the complexity that surrounds it. The attempts at visualisation in both of these models creates a framework not only for subjectivity but for participant involvement in the interpretation of the resulting data and so can fulfil the reflexive demands of an 'empowering' recovery model.

However, the political is also addressed in the voices given to excluded and stigmatised groups including those suffering from obesity, alcohol and drug users in prison, smokers and alcoholics, adolescent substance users and ex-offenders and ex-users attempting to reintegrate into communities on release from prison. The volume is a celebration of the centrality of social identity to all of our lives but also of the potential that group transitions can have in transforming lives and enabling excluded and marginalised populations to achieve meaning, connections and hope (Leamy et al., 2011).

Much of this work is based on the concept of group transitions as a key process in recovery where the assumption is that a key process is moving from using groups to recovery groups (or at least from groups supportive of use to groups supportive of recovery). However, the findings from Miller and colleagues with young people suggests that this might not be necessary if there are enough other groups and identities available to the individual within their existing social networks. This also raises questions about the coherence or conflict between groups and within groups and the underlying issues for social identity complexity and also for motives and identities that may not be accessible to consciousness. The notion of changes in groups and from one group to another is an area that requires considerably more research attention, particularly as it is becoming increasingly prominent as the basis for clinical interventions.

Future research directions

The area of implicit identity and the development of the underlying measurement techniques, as outlined in the chapters by Buckingham, and by Frings and Albury, is an extremely exciting opportunity to supplement and to test self-report methods and this could also be extended for use in intervention studies around social identity change (of the kind reported by Buckingham (this volume and by Dingle et al., 2015). Further, the area of developing interventions to support identity transition from excluded and stigmatised groups to positive and pro-social groups that can harbour and nurture self-esteem and wellbeing, remains a process that has not been well enough understood in terms of readiness for this transition, motivations and issues around the speed and trajectory of change and the durability of any changes made.

This also introduces the question of 'torn identity' where there is tension between the aspirational and the existing identities and pulls from multiple and inconsistent groups as is often the case in recovery. There is also the wider agenda of embedding social identity theorising into a much wider range of addiction and other social science areas of exploration to challenge the often unquestioned primacy of the individual agent as the cause of behaviour. The current collection provides a compelling case for the centrality of groups processes (and underlying identity issues) to changing complex behaviour, while reminding us politically that we should not scapegoat individuals for their inability to change and that we all have a role in the reintegration of those struggling to achieve lasting recovery and a positive life quality embedded in groups that provide meaning and hope. The final point is a political one – for populations striving for recovery, the journey is fundamentally a social one and all of us are potential members of the groups that include or exclude and so shift the odds of effective and enduring change.

References

Best, D., Lubman, D., Savic, M., Wilson, A., Dingle, G., Haslam, A., Haslam, C., & Jetten, J. (2014). Social identity and transitional identity: Exploring social networks and their significance in a Therapeutic Community setting. *Therapeutic Community Journal, 35*, 10–20.

Cruwys, T., Steffens, N., Haslam, S. A., Haslam, C., Jetten, J., & Dingle, G. (2016). *Social Identity Mapping (SIM): A procedure for visual representation and assessment of subjective group memberships*. Unpublished manuscript: University of Queensland.

Dansereau, D. F., Dees, S. M., Greener, J. M., & Simpson, D. D. (1995). Node-link mapping and the evaluation of drug abuse counseling sessions, *Psychology of Addictive Behaviors, 9*, 195–203.

Dansereau, D. F. & Simpson, D. D. (2009). A picture is worth a thousand words: The case for graphic representations. *Professional Psychology: Research and Practice, 40*, 104–110.

Dingle, G. A., Stark, C., Cruwys, T., & Best, D. (2015). Breaking good: Breaking ties with social groups may be good for recovery from substance misuse. *British Journal of Social Psychology, 54*, 236–254.

Fiske, S. T. (2004). *Social beings: Core motives in social psychology* (2nd ed.). Hoboken, NJ: John Wiley & Sons.

Leamy, M., Bird, V., Le Boutillier, C., Williams, J., & Slade, M. (2011). Conceptual framework for personal recovery in mental health: Systematic review and narrative synthesis. *British Journal of Psychiatry, 199*, 445–452.

Reynolds, K. J., Eggins, R. A., & Haslam, S. A. (2010). Uncovering diverse identities in organisations: AIRing versus auditing approaches to diversity management. *Asia Pacific Journal of Human Resources, 48*, 45–57.

White, W. (2009). *Peer-based addiction recovery support: History, theory, practice, and scientific evaluation*. Chicago, IL: Great Lakes Addiction Technology Transfer Center and Philadelphia Department of Behavioral Health and Mental Retardation Services.

INDEX